British LIFE and INSTITUTIONS

MARK FARRELL

Ernst Klett Verlag
Stuttgart Düsseldorf Leipzig

British Life and Institutions

British Life and Institutions Book   ISBN: 3-12-513380-7
British Life and Institutions Cassette   ISBN: 3 12 513381-5
British Life and Institutions CD   ISBN: 3-12-513382-3

Published by: Ernst Klett Verlag
Rotebühlstraße 77
70178 Stuttgart

Telephone: 0049 (0)711 6672-1333
Fax: 0049 (0)711 6672-2037
E-mail: klett-kundenservice@klett-mail.de

PN   6 5 4 3 2 1 / 05 04 03 02 01 00

Chancerel International Publishers Ltd
120 Long Acre
London WC2E 9PA

Printed in Italy

The publishers would like to thank the following for permission to reproduce images and copyright material:
Jean Aitchison p14; Allsport p125; St George Alphonse p89; Art Directors & TRIP p121; BBC p90; Big Issue p72; www.John Birdsall.co.uk p7, p11; The Anthony Blake Photo Library p115; Betty Boothroyd p37; BP Amoco p.l.c.(2000) p50tr; Bradford City Council Regeneration Marketing p114; The Bridgeman Art Library p10, p30, p52bl, p94, p95, p99bl, tr, p100tl, p104; John Bugeja LMPA p48; Burberry p9; Cartier p9; Jan Chipps Photography p23tl, p71, p87, p96, p123; Chiswick Community School p63; City of Liverpool p19tl; Countryside Alliance p22bmr; Department of the Environment, Transport and the Region, crown copyright p84; Derbyshire Family Health Services p69br; East of England Tourist Board Collection p19br; Empics Ltd/Michael Steele p122tr, John Marsh p124; Environmental Images/David Sims p24, David Dennis p25l, Vanessa Miles p25r; European Communities. Map source Eurostat. Reproduced by permission of the Publishers, the Office of Official Publications of the European Communities p54; Eurostar p86; Mary Evans Picture Library p16, p38, p118tr, p122bl; Cassi Farrell p115; David Farrell p102, p105tl; Mark Farrell p21bmr, p23bmr, p26, p55, p58, p62, p68, p70, p75, p81, p83, p91br, p98br, p109br, p110tl, br, p119bl; Friends of the Earth p28; Glasgow City Council p18bl; Glaxo Wellcome plc p53tl; Mavis Grant p67; the Green Party p39; Mike Gunnill p78; the Guy's, King's College and St Thomas' Hospital Medical and Dental School p69tl; Hammersmith & Fulham Council p34; Robert Harding p98tl; HarperCollins Publishers Ltd/Arundhati Roy/*The God of Small Things* p93; Veena Holkar p108tr, p121tl; House of Lords p33; Hulton Getty p49, p60, p83, p105br; The Hutchinson Library p74; Kensington & Chelsea Health Authority p69br; Kirwin Millard/Disney/Photographer Catherine Ashmore p106; Jeremy Lee p117; Life File Photographic Library Ltd p85, p112, p113, p115; Magnum Photos/Peter Marlow p82; Manchester City Council Marketing p18br; Mirror Syndication International p108bl; Mooney Photo p51bl; NSPCC p41br; Christine Osborne Pictures/MEP p12, p61, p76, p77br; Penhaligon p9; People for the Ethical Treatment of Animals p110; Popperfoto p17, p35, p40, p41tl, p45, p46, p47, p48, p49, p56, p59, p109tl; QA Photos Ltd p85; Rex Features Ltd p91tl, p92bl, tl; Shri Swaminarayan Mandir, Neasden, inspired by his Holiness Pramukh Swami Maharaj p77tl; Robin Smythe p126; Frank Spooner Pictures Ltd p120tl; Barbara Stock p13; Tony Stone p64, p65, p97br, p120br; The Guardian/David Sillitoe p101br; The Sun/News International Newspapers Ltd, 18th March 1997 p81; Telegraph Colour Library p86, p118bl, p119tr; Tesco p27l; Topham Picturepoint p20, p31, p32, p44, p95, p103, p107; The Welsh Language Board p11; UPPA p 100br; Welsh Slate Museum p11; West Country Tourist Board p97tl; Westminster Health Authority p69br; Dafydd Wigley p42; Yorkshire Tourist Board p21bml, p55tl.

Every effort has been made to trace the copyright holders of material in this book. The publishers apologise for any omissions and will be pleased to make the necessary arrangements when *British Life and Institutions* is reprinted.

Contents

Melting pot

The USA is often called a melting pot – a total mix of races and nationalities. In fact, the same could be said of Britain, except that the process took far longer. The British of today are the result of wave after wave of conquest, displacement, migration and mixing.

The builders of Stonehenge are lost in the mists of time, but it is known that from about 2000 BC, people called the Beaker Folk came to Britain from the European mainland. They in turn were replaced by the Celts, who also came from Europe. This is a pattern which repeats itself time and again: there was a drift to the west, or an expansion from the middle of Europe, and Britain was the end of the line. Julius Caesar brought an army here in 54 BC; later the Romans set up a colony and stayed until AD 410. It was then the turn of various Germanic peoples: the Angles, the Saxons and the Jutes. They were followed by the Danes and the Vikings, who repeatedly attacked the east coast of England. The Normans (Norsemen who had already settled in France) invaded successfully in 1066 (the one date in British history known to every schoolchild), and subjugated but did not expel the Anglo-Saxons and the Scandinavians. From Roman times on, the Celts moved or were pushed out to the edges of the British Isles, the so-called Celtic Fringe of Scotland, Wales and Ireland. All these peoples have left traces of themselves – not only archaeological fragments but also place names, parts of the language, and physical features such as hair colour and height.

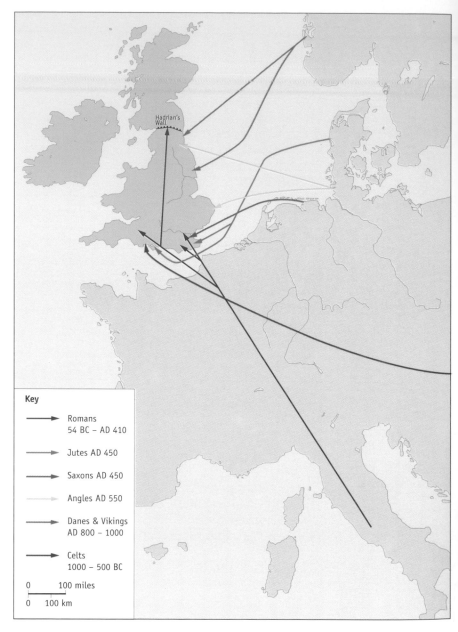

Key

→ Romans
54 BC – AD 410

→ Jutes AD 450

→ Saxons AD 450

→ Angles AD 550

→ Danes & Vikings
AD 800 – 1000

→ Celts
1000 – 500 BC

0   100 miles

0   100 km

By the time the Normans invaded Britain in 1066, the British people were already a mixture of many different peoples.

- **Have populations moved and changed in your part of the world, as they have in Britain?**
- **Does the study of history make you feel different about your country?**

After the Norman invasion, there was never again such a comprehensive takeover of the country. But many more people from all over the world ended up in Britain for one reason or another. One reason was persecution: Jews came from Spain at the end of the 15th century, and the Protestant Huguenots came from France in the 1680s, both in flight from hostile Roman Catholic regimes. In the 19th century, Britain was a haven for Italian political exiles such as the revolutionary Mazzini. In the first half of the 20th century, Jews again fled to Britain, this time from Eastern and Central Europe.

The next major stage of immigration was driven not by escape but by attraction – to a British labour market that was short of workers and an economy that offered lots of opportunity for business. In the 1950s, 60s and 70s, people from the Caribbean, Africa, the Indian sub-continent, Hong Kong and Cyprus all came to Britain to work. The National Health Service, London Transport and British Railways all sent teams abroad to recruit workers directly, as they could not find enough staff in Britain. Other industries were keen to take on immigrants as soon as they arrived. There was also a big niche in the market for ethnic restaurants – the British were ready to try some good foreign food.

What these countries of origin had in common, of course, was that they had been part of the old British Empire and they still belonged to the British Commonwealth. There was a special relationship with these countries, and until 1962, all Commonwealth citizens had the right of free entry and settlement in the UK. From that year on, immigration was progressively restricted, and today people from Commonwealth countries can only enter if their families are already living in Britain.

The most recent arrivals in Britain have not been from the Commonwealth but from countries with wars or other serious problems. The conflicts in the Horn of Africa in the late 1980s sent out refugees from Ethiopia, Somalia and Eritrea. Then Croatians, Serbs, Bosnians and Kosovars fled from the violent break-up of Yugoslavia. The late 1990s saw the arrival of gypsies escaping from some Eastern European countries such as Romania.

Racism

Every stage of immigration in Britain's history has given rise to opposition and hostility from those who consider themselves indigenous (but are in fact only earlier immigrants). The most recent arrivals are no exception: in 1998, Romanian families who arrived at the port of Dover had to be protected in secret locations after openly racist reports in the press inflamed public opinion against them.

As new groups of people settle in, establish themselves and integrate into the economy of the country, so feelings of resentment and hostility subside. It becomes clear that they are not competing for slices of a finite cake, but are becoming customers, co-workers, friends and family. Today, there is feeling against the Bosnians, but very little against the Jews and absolutely none at all against the Vikings!

At the present time, most racism in Britain is in the context of the black and Asian people. There is still a problem of discrimination in many areas of life, but particularly in employment. It is harder for them to get good jobs. Just look at the business or financial pages of any British newspaper; they are full of photos of middle-aged white men who make up the highly-paid managerial class.

It might be assumed that the fault lies with the education system. In fact, there are problems;

This carnival costume is decorated with NHS and London Underground signs to show why many African-Caribbeans first came to Britain.

• **What are the pleasures and pains of going to live in a different country?**
• **How do you think a country like Britain has benefitted from welcoming newcomers?**

for example, African-Caribbean boys are five times more likely to be suspended or expelled from school than white boys. But the correlation of poor education/poor employment is not straightforward. Asian children do particularly well at school and, as the chart below on the left shows, black women do better in higher education than white women. The disturbing trend illustrated by the chart below on the right is that African-Caribbeans do not get the jobs which, according to their qualifications, they deserve.

The Race Relations Acts of 1965, 1968 and 1976 made it illegal to discriminate against ethnic groups in employment, housing and education. But few cases come before the courts – discrimination is very hard to prove. In some fields the situation is worse than in others. A Law Society survey in 1994 found that white law students had a 47 per cent chance of getting a job compared with 7 per cent for black law students.

There has been, and there is, racism in Britain. It is clear that all is not well if you look at attitudes to the national flag. Whereas black Americans are perfectly happy with the Stars and Stripes, black Britons are uncomfortable with the Union Jack. The reason is that the racist parties of the far right, the National Front and the British National Party, have adopted the flag as their own, along with a vicious slogan: "There ain't no black in the Union Jack."

Since the arrival of black and Asian people in Britain, society has gone through three stages: the first openly racist, the second trying to be colour-blind, and the third accepting diversity and being active about integration. A few years ago, colour-blindness was a common claim; people and institutions said that they did not take any notice of colour, that they treated everyone alike. But this often meant that they did not really address the issue. Some people are still embarrassed to mention race – they will identify a black colleague with a description such as, "the tall guy with glasses who usually wears a red tie".

The recent, more open approach has involved training sessions for employees where equal opportunities issues of gender and race were discussed. Importantly, it has involved ethnic monitoring – the publication of clear statistics about the numbers of black and Asian people in the organisation, and the positions they occupy. This has made it possible to see exactly where ethnic groups were under-represented, and to start to rectify the situation.

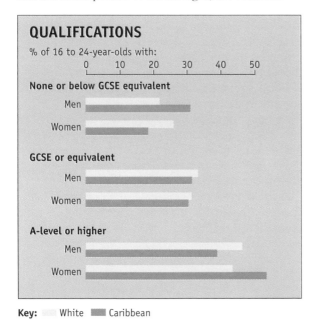

QUALIFICATIONS

% of 16 to 24-year-olds with:

Key: White ▰ Caribbean

Source: Policy Studies Institute

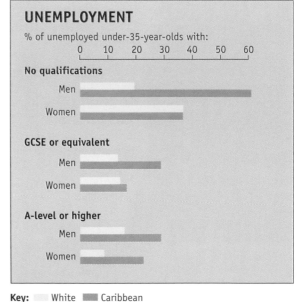

UNEMPLOYMENT

% of unemployed under-35-year-olds with:

Key: White ▰ Caribbean

Source: Policy Studies Institute

- **Is racism a problem in your country? If so, is it increasing or disappearing?**
- **Is it possible to combat racism with laws?**

Mixed-race families are becoming more common.

In social terms, one of the most significant developments has been the increase in mixed-race marriages: this is, after all, the ultimate breakdown of barriers. Another comparison with the USA is interesting: some 40 per cent of African-Caribbeans now marry whites in Britain, which is more than 12 times the rate in the United States. Not all the problems have been resolved, but it looks as though Britain is on the way to becoming a well-integrated multi-racial society.

The class system

"We are, by our occupations, education, and habits of life, divided into different species, which regard one another, for the most part, with scorn and malignity," wrote the 18th-century man of letters, Dr Johnson.

Every country in the world has a class system. But in some way, for some reason, the question of class seems to have a special meaning for the British. This is reflected in their image abroad. Hollywood films have featured lots of upper-class Englishmen, always snobbish and usually cruel or stupid. The whole world knows the stereotype of the English gentleman or lord, often with a monocle and tweed jacket, sipping whisky and reading *The Times*. Our class-ridden reputation goes back a long way: in 1755, a French traveller named Jean Rouquet wrote: "The Englishman always has in his hands an accurate pair of scales in which he scrupulously weighs up the birth and rank and wealth of the people he meets."

The British themselves are obsessed with the issue: it is at the centre of countless novels, plays and films, and the topic comes up again and again in the news media. A vast proportion of British humour

- **How might mixed-race marriages affect social attitudes to race?**
- **Do you think it is true that "every country in the world has a class system"?**

is based on the interaction between upper and working classes. Public figures occasionally state that the class system is at the root of the country's problems, or alternatively that the class system is dead.

The strangest feature of class in Britain is that it is not entirely dependent on money. It seems that you can in certain circumstances be high class and poor, or low class and rich. This is an important clue to the conundrum: the system must be based on something historical which does not exactly match present conditions. And that is precisely what Britain has: the royal family and all the dukes, earls and barons are a relic of feudalism. Although these vestiges of the old aristocracy add up to very small numbers of the population, they set the tone for the rest of the class structure. At least 200 years ago, the commercial middle class triumphed over the old land-owning nobles (and Napoleon called the British, "a nation of shopkeepers"), but in terms of style and attitude the victory has been the other way round.

A note of caution here: official statistics, of course, treat class as a strictly economic distinction. Government figures have mostly been based on a six-point scale of employment-types, very similar to the one below, which is used by market-researchers and advertisers.

Horse racing at Royal Ascot is a highlight of the upper classes' social calendar.

$\mathcal{A}$	Upper middle class (e.g. top managers, doctors and lawyers)
$\mathcal{B}$	Middle class (e.g. middle managers, teachers)
$\mathcal{C}1$	Lower middle class (e.g. office workers)
$\mathcal{C}2$	Skilled working class (e.g. electricians, car mechanics)
$\mathcal{D}$	Unskilled working class (e.g. farm or building labourers)
$\mathcal{E}$	Residual (e.g. unemployed)

Marketing people are the ultimate experts in questions of class – they have to make sure that advertisements for Mercedes cars and Rolex watches go in newspapers read by the As and Bs, and advertisements for cut-price cigarettes and car batteries appear where they will be seen by the C2s, Ds and Es.

However, unlike government statisticians, but in common with the rest of the British public, marketing people know that there are many other indicators of social class. Upper-class people cook French food for an evening meal which they call dinner or supper, and they drink wine with it; they watch tennis and rugby; they read *The Times* or *The Daily Telegraph*; they name their sons Piers or Edward, and their daughters Rebecca or Sophie; they listen to classical music; and they buy stocks and shares. Working-class people microwave ready-made supermarket meals for an evening meal which they call tea, and they drink tea with it; they watch snooker and football; they read *The Sun* or *The Daily Mirror*; they name their sons Darren or Paul, and their daughters Ashley or Lizzie; they listen to pop music; and they buy lottery tickets.

These are stereotypes, of course, which are humorous and only half-true. More seriously,

- **In your country, how wide is the division between rich and poor?**
- **In your country, is social class reflected in food, clothes, names and so on?**

the two really important indicators of class are education and accent. George Bernard Shaw wrote a satire on the linguistic aspects of class in his play *Pygmalion*, in which a professor takes a poor cockney flower-girl, Eliza Doolittle, and turns her into an upper-class lady by training her to speak with the right accent. In the preface to *Pygmalion*, Shaw writes: "It is impossible for an Englishman to open his mouth without making some other Englishman despise him." In simple terms, the higher the class, the more the accent resembles that of the royal family. Whereas most ordinary people have regional accents, the upper classes speak in exactly the same way from the south-east of England to the north-west of Scotland. This would seem a remarkable achievement, considering that children normally take on the accent

of their surrounding community rather than that of their parents. The explanation is the schools they go to. The most central unifying feature of the upper class is that its members go to private, fee-paying schools. Just 7 per cent of pupils in Britain are at private schools, which are quite expensive: the top ones such as Eton (for boys) and Roedean (for girls) cost £15,000 per year. So it is actually quite difficult to maintain your position in the upper class without a lot of money.

The British class system could be dismissed as just a piece of folklore, which makes a visit to the country all the more fun. But unfortunately it seems to get in the way of economic progress because important jobs do not always go to the most able people. While the rest of the world long ago decided that meritocracy was the way to develop successfully, relics of the feudal system still hold Britain back.

These advertisements appear in magazines that are read by social classes A and B.

- **Is there any connection between language and social class in your country?**
- **Karl Marx wanted a revolution to produce a classless society. Do you?**

The origins of English

English is basically a Germanic language with a lot of Latin words in it. In simple terms, that means that the grammar and many of the most frequent words are Germanic, and the more formal or technical vocabulary is Latinate. There is so much of this Latinate vocabulary that English is sometimes called a semi-Romance language.

This linguistic mixture is a result of historical events. But the simple historical facts appear not to explain everything about the development of the language. One interesting question is why did the British not learn Latin from the Romans? After all, France, Spain, Portugal and Romania all kept the imperial language after the end of the Roman Empire. The answer may be the distance from Rome; the province of Britannia was on the wild and uncooperative margins of Europe. Although the Romans were here for 400 years, they did not leave very much behind them. It is hard to know how much the Celtic language of the Britons took on a Latin flavour. Actually its living descendant, Welsh, has a lot of Latin roots in it, so perhaps in the 3rd and 4th centuries AD, they were on their way to creating another great Romance language. But it was not to be. The Anglo-Saxons who took over from the Romans in Britain were relatively untouched by Latin influences, so Celtic was replaced by Germanic, and the British romance with Romance was, temporarily, over.

In 1066, the French-speaking Normans invaded England. Over the next 300 years, their French merged with Anglo-Saxon to create a new language: the writing of Chaucer (1343–1400) is not very far from modern English. As in the rest of Europe, Latin, especially in its written form, remained for a long time the language of science, philosophy and the Church. But English was growing stronger; it was soon not only the language of everyday life but also that of a flowering literature. Caxton introduced printing into the country in 1476, and that did much to standardise forms – spelling was very inconsistent at that time. Latin and Greek classics and the Bible

The friar from Chaucer's Canterbury Tales, *written in the late 14th century.*

were translated into English. By the time of Shakespeare (1564–1616), the language was highly developed and very healthy indeed.

Britain's other languages

The Celtic peoples who gave way to the Anglo-Saxons did not disappear – they moved north and west, and their descendants live today in Scotland, Ireland, Wales, the Isle of Man and Cornwall. They went on speaking their Celtic languages, but of course shared the islands with a very dominant majority culture. From the 17th century onwards, the English imposed their language on huge areas of the world, from the north of Canada to the south of New Zealand, so the chances of the Celtic language surviving in Wales were pretty slim.

In fact, it is the Welsh who have preserved their linguistic identity more than any of the other Celtic peoples. The last native speaker of Cornish died in 1777 and of Manx (the language of the Isle of Man) in 1974. Gaelic in Scotland is spoken by no more than 80,000 people, mostly in the islands off the north-west coast; the only monolingual speakers are young children who have not yet been exposed to English. Irish Gaelic has about 100,000 speakers confined to small areas on the west coast. The Welsh language, by contrast, has a solid heartland in the

- **Which historical events have been important in the development of your language?**
- **Languages change over time; do you think this is a good or bad thing?**

north-west of the country and is spoken by half a million people: there is a TV channel and a lot of radio in Welsh, it is taught in schools and used by the nationalist political party, *Plaid Cymru.*

It is hard to find evidence that the English actually tried to kill off the Celtic languages in a systematic way – to commit linguicide. Their decline has been more a result of indifference from London, and a lack of will to preserve them on the part of the Celtic speakers themselves. But there have been abuses. In the 19th century, the English education system was imposed, and children were not allowed to speak Welsh at school: if they did, they were forced to wear a wooden board across their shoulders. Echoing this, a Welsh nationalist wrote: *"Dy iaith ar ein hysgwyddau megis pwn"* ("Your language is like a burden on our shoulders").

All official publications in Wales are produced in two languages.

Another language that has suffered from official neglect and prejudice is the language of the deaf: British Sign Language (BSL). As with Welsh, there was a period of history when it was educational policy to suppress signing, and to enforce lip-reading and speech. More recently, it has taken a political campaign by deaf activists to change this approach, and now deaf schools use and encourage signing. It is important to understand that real sign language is very different from the everyday body language and gestures used by the hearing community. The sign language of deaf people is a complex and highly developed form of expression with linguistic rules – not at all a vague international code. Users of BSL, for example, cannot understand American Sign Language.

Deaf people using British Sign Language.

It came as a surprise to many people when in 1987, a census showed that 172 languages were spoken by children in London schools: Chinese, Turkish, Italian, Ga, Yoruba, Thai, Spanish, Gujarati, Punjabi and 163 others. Some of these, like the West African language Ga, only have a couple of hundred speakers. But others, like Punjabi, are quite significant linguistic communities, with their own radio programmes, newspapers and videos, and classes for children – to ensure that they do not forget the language of their parents and grandparents.

Attitudes to the ancestral language differ a lot within immigrant communities. Among the Sikhs in west London, for example, it is only the older people who find it impossible to learn English, and who carry on speaking exclusively Punjabi. Everyone else is bilingual, some feeling more at home in Punjabi, and others, especially children who were born in Britain, preferring English. Many are perfectly at ease in either language, and switch between them effortlessly; it is common to hear a sentence begin in Punjabi and end in English.

After the English, the biggest language communities in Britain are the Welsh and then Asian languages such as Urdu, Punjabi, Gujarati

• **How many different languages are spoken in your country?**
• **What rights should minority language speakers have?**

and Bengali; Chinese, Greek, Arabic, Polish and Turkish are also quite well represented, as are West African languages such as Yoruba.

Arabic newspapers on sale in London

Dialects of English

A nasty shock awaits many visitors to Britain. Imagine you have learnt English for years, you can read newspapers and you have no problem following the television, but when you go into a fish and chip shop in Newcastle, you can not understand a word they are saying. The language has been standardised for a very long time, and regional dialects in Britain have largely died out – far more so than in Italy or Germany, for example. That is to say, the vocabulary of the dialects has died out, but the accents and a few bits of distinctive grammar remain. It is the accent which gives the visitor a problem in the fish and chip shop. Some accents are so strong that they present problems for British people, too. Variations within Britain are so great that accents from New York or Texas are often easier to follow than ones from Liverpool or Glasgow.

It is mostly the vowels which differ from one dialect to another. In Manchester, shut rhymes with put, and in the south it rhymes with but. Intonation patterns also differ between regions.

There is a kind of standard British English pronunciation, based in a confusing way on class and geography. It is the accent of the south-east, but not that of London itself. It could be said that the upper classes have a dialect of their own, with a pronunciation known as RP (Received Pronunciation). The majority of middle-class people speak a sort of classless, democratic version of RP, with a slight admixture of the local regional accent.

People's attitudes to the various regional accents depend on a whole range of historical and social factors. The Birmingham accent is considered ugly, cockney is associated with criminals, Scottish is thought of as serious and sensible, Irish as poetic. An interesting case is that of the so-called Westcountry accent. This comes from the south and west, which is the least industrial region; consequently the accent is identified with farm-workers, sometimes considered stupid by city folk. While all other varieties of English have been increasingly accepted on mainstream television and radio, Westcountry remains the Cinderella among accents, confined to comedy and gardening programmes.

To see the likely direction of change for the future, we need to look at the speech of young people. Here we find several interesting developments. One is a spread of a light London accent over much of the country – especially in areas like the West Country where it replaces the low-prestige local accent. Another is an openness, through the media, to American and Australian influences. The Australian effect is quite recent, and results from the huge popularity of Australian TV soap operas *Neighbours* and *Home and Away*. Strangely enough, this does not usually mean the adoption of vocabulary: nobody says *sidewalk* instead of pavement, or *gas* instead of petrol, however many American films they watch. It is rather the phrases, idioms and grammatical forms which are contagious. *No way* has caught on, as in the form: "No way am I going to go out with him." The use of the word *like* as a sentence-filler has become very common: "She was like really upset, and she just like walked out".

Americans and Australians sometimes use a rising, question-type intonation on statements, often in the

---

- **Dialects are disappearing in many languages around the world. Does it matter?**
- **In your country, do older people criticise the language of young people?**

middle or at the end of sentences: "I spoke with my teacher (rising intonation), and he said I had to redo the test." This is used to engage the attention of the listener; it means "Do you remember my teacher?" or "Are you listening?" To the great dismay of the older generation, this intonation is becoming very popular in Britain.

Sexism and language

Most language change is unconscious. Speakers do not make decisions to use certain forms; they just pick them up from the linguistic environment. But there is one important exception which has affected English along with many other languages: women are breaking out of their second-class role in society, and are trying to make the language reflect that fact. There is a problem of old-fashioned vocabulary, which is fairly easy to deal with: policeman, fireman and chairman can be changed to police officer, fire-fighter and chairperson or chair. But grammar presents greater difficulties. A book about baby-care in 1965 said things like: "When your baby gets his first tooth, you should give him something safe to chew." A new edition in 1973 changed that to "... his/her first tooth, you should give him/her ...". A new book on the subject in 1981

A Calcutta street sign in Bengali and English

used *she* in one chapter and *he* in the next. Even if you do not talk about babies very much, you cannot avoid the issue. After someone, anyone, nobody, everybody, a person, an employee and so on, it used to be common to use the masculine form.
For example, "If somebody wants to do this job himself, he can buy the tools at his nearest electrical shop." Actually this is a problem only for more formal language, as informal speech uses the plural they, them and their in these contexts: "If somebody wants to do this job themselves, they can."

The rule book

Something which has helped the language in its adaptations has been a tradition of pragmatism – a non-authoritarian attitude which has meant that there is no English Academy to legislate on questions of correctness. There is no big grammar book which lays down the law. There is the *Comprehensive Grammar of the English Language* by Quirk, Greenbaum, Leech and Svartvik, but this describes how the language is used, not how it should be used. Software makers such as Microsoft include style and grammar checkers in their word-processing packages. These are still fairly primitive, and most people quite rightly ignore them. But as they become more sophisticated, there is a danger that they will take on the role of the grammar police.

A world language

A billion people speak English, two-thirds of the world's scientists write in English, and 80 per cent of the world's electronic information is stored in English. One result is that the British are terribly lazy about learning other languages. The most important factor in language learning is motivation, and the British just do not have it.

Even so, the British are not really smug and self-satisfied about the world status of their language. Most British people are quite well aware that today it is out of their hands: the reasons for the popularity of English are either lost in history, or something to do with the superpower on the other side of the Atlantic.

• **Does the problem of sexism arise in your language? If so, how do you deal with it?**
• **How do you feel about the spread of English? Is it a threat or an opportunity?**

An interview with ...
Professor Jean Aitchison

Jean Aitchison is the Rupert Murdoch Professor of Language and Communication at the University of Oxford and has written and spoken extensively about English, the living language. Many foreign words have entered English, and English is spoken in many different ways in different parts of the world. She says that far from this causing a decline in the standards of English, the language has been positively strengthened.

About a billion people worldwide speak the English language today. Is that something to celebrate or is it a cause for concern?

I don't think it's a cause for either celebration or concern: it's just something that's happened. England and then America became very powerful politically and whenever anybody's powerful politically – as happened with Latin originally – then their language spreads. So I don't think we need to get either upset about it or cheer about it.

You mention the way English has been pulling in words constantly from other languages. Now, is it appropriate for a language to be quite so much of a mish-mash? How pure is English and do we need linguistic purity?

Linguistic purity is a myth. Every language always has sucked in words. Agreed, some more than others. But just sucking in words makes a language strong and it's natural. I mean, you can't stop it. And, I think, you'll find that lots of other languages suck in words. I mean French sucks in English words, it tries to stop them sometimes.

I don't think one needs to worry about this, I actually find it rather interesting the way we all borrow each other's words like that and the interesting thing is that it is words that are very easy to borrow; it's rather rare for constructions to be borrowed.

When we talk about linguistic standardisation with the growth of English as a global language, isn't it true that it's not really anything of the sort because people of different countries and cultures they speak English in a different way? And so it's really almost a different language wherever it's spoken?

I don't think it's necessarily a different language, because in many cases there is inter-communication. It is true that there are varieties of English which people start talking in far-flung

• **Do you feel that language change is a cause for concern?**
• **Which foreign words have entered your language?**

corners of the globe and lose contact with anyone else. In that case, yes, it does change and become rather different, but mostly when you find that people are making a huge fuss about something, it's not really very different.

Is there a need for minimum rules to govern the use of English and if there is a need for rules, who would actually police them? Who owns English today?

Well, first of all, everybody who speaks English owns English and I don't think although we're in England, England-English, I don't think we actually rule English in any way. There's no way in which anyone could police a language.

And Samuel Johnson, originally when he wrote his dictionary, he wanted to legislate for English and to set up a dictionary which would in a sense regulate the language, but he realised at the end that it was absolutely impossible and he suggested it would be like lashing the wind to try and stop language from changing.

Do we need English grammar, or is it just communication that is important and one doesn't need to worry about whether one's saying something correctly?

Well, there are two usages of the word grammar. One usage is of the natural patterns that are in anyone's mind. And if you didn't have a grammar in your head, you wouldn't be able to talk at all. On the other hand, there is a second type of usage of grammar, which is prescriptive grammars, where from the 18th century onwards, people started saying what they thought people ought to say, which actually had relatively little to do with what people actually said.

You have spoken about the "tadpole" model of language change as opposed to the "cuckoo" model – that is a gradual change in contrast with the sudden disappearance of words in the way that one cuckoo pushes the other out of the nest.

Is it true that the "cuckoo" model is a product of the information society?

No, I think it's just that people didn't understand how language changed. In the olden days, they thought that words, that languages gradually changed and they got very upset about it, and you'll often find that people who are trying to argue against modern language have this notion that somehow, we all ought to take a stand against our tadpole changing into a frog.

As I said in my cuckoo model, the newer often gets bigger and bigger and pushes the old one out of the nest, like a young cuckoo. And this is just a normal way of change and the two actually exist together for a time.

I think I've said somewhere that nobody gets upset that rivers erode their banks or that mountains kind of collapse over the years. Why do they get upset about language which is a natural phenomenon?

What are the biggest influences for change on the English language today?

Well, I think probably globalisation is the biggest influence. I think everything builds into it, but I don't think it's doing anything except push it along perhaps a bit faster in the direction it would have gone anyway. I don't think that sort of artificial human inventions such as Hollywood or Bollywood, or wherever, are actually going to change the language very much by themselves. They might make types of language available to people which they hadn't heard before.

To what extent do major companies that deal in information-technology influence the change of the English language?

I think they influence them rather less than anyone might think. I think the main problem I see is not so much that the English language is being altered by IT or anything like this, but that fewer languages are actually used on, say, the Internet.

• **Is there a correct form of a language?**
• **Is your language under threat? Or does it threaten other languages?**

Views of the city

"To one who has been long in cities pent;
'Tis very sweet to look into the fair
And open face of Heaven." Keats

One hundred and fifty years ago, the founder
of evolutionary theory, Charles Darwin,
predicted that the unpleasantness of life in
crowded cities would not change, but humans
would learn to love it. As far as the British
are concerned, he was almost right. Many city
dwellers today have cut all ties with the land
and live in happy ignorance of what goes on in
the country. The circuit of school or office,
supermarket and nightlife has become
a natural habitat.

This state of affairs is, however, comparatively
new. There is a much longer tradition of hostility to
the city. English literature is full of anti-urban
sentiment – the idea that God made the country and
man made the town. Britain's favourite poets are the
Romantics, who came from the country and loved it.
The most quoted poem in the English language is
Wordsworth's *Daffodils*, which evokes an idyllic
rural scene. Shelley wrote: "Hell is a city much like
London – a populous and smoky city." Novelist Jane
Austen did not think much of the capital city, either:
"Nobody is healthy in London, nobody can be."
And even the names of industrial cities upset her:
"One has no great hopes from Birmingham: I always
think there is something direful in the sound."

Charles Dickens, in a sense, broke the spell of the
rural myth. His novels are generally celebrations of
city life, and the background of London streets is as
important as the characters themselves. But even he
sees the negative side. In *Hard Times*, Manchester is
given the ugly name Coketown, and Dickens does
not paint a pretty picture of it: "It was a town of
machinery and tall chimneys, out of which
interminable serpents of smoke trailed themselves
for ever and ever, and never got uncoiled. It had a
black canal in it, and a river that ran purple with
ill-smelling dye ... inhabited by people to whom

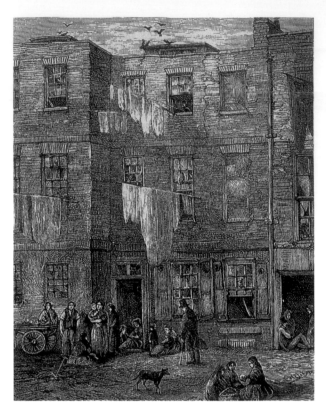

*In many of his novels Charles Dickens described slums
like these.*

every day was the same as yesterday and
tomorrow." His London is often foggy, muddy, cold,
wet and unfriendly: just read the opening page
of *Bleak House*.

The most famous exception to this negative
consensus is the great wit, literary critic and
dictionary writer Dr Johnson. He loved life
in London in the 18th century, hated going out of
the city, and said: "When a man is tired of London
he is tired of life; for there is in London all that life
can afford."

Mega-cities

In recent decades, people have been moving out of
city centres into suburbs, new towns, smaller towns
and the country. Villages and isolated farms and
cottages, which used to be full of agricultural
workers, are now the homes of people who drive to
their offices in town. Even so, Britain remains one of

- **In your country, is the traditional view of cities positive or negative?**
- **From your point of view, what are the best and worst things about city life?**

the most urbanised countries in the world, with nine in ten of the population living in towns or cities.

Britain's cities, at one time big by international standards, have long since been overtaken by giants like New York, Tokyo, Mexico City and São Paolo. But that does not mean that they are small. London has a population of almost seven million, and is the second biggest European city after Paris. Then there are a number of major conurbations: urban areas that started as collections of neighbouring towns, but have grown together and fused into massive single units. Birmingham is the main component of what is called the West Midlands, a mega-city about 57 kilometres across and with a population of more than 2.5 million. Manchester is grouped together with a ring of old industrial towns such as Stockport, Oldham and Bolton to make up Greater Manchester, again with just over 2.5 million people. Then there are the conurbations of West Yorkshire, Merseyside, Tyneside and Clydeside in Scotland.

The inner cities

The term inner city has come to have a specific meaning. not just the central area, but the older, densely populated parts of big cities with problems of decay and poverty. There has been a tendency for richer people to move away from the centre to suburbs where they can have gardens and bigger houses. This has left the historic centres to poorer residents who have not had the resources to maintain or improve their homes.

Big cities are by their nature anonymous places, and crime thrives on anonymity. For obvious reasons, crime also goes with unemployment. So inner-city areas in Glasgow, Birmingham, Manchester and many other cities found themselves in a vicious circle of deprivation. Drug-dealing, prostitution and crime were widespread. Services, including education, declined as people tried to move away rather than improve the situation. Many black and Asian people had the

misfortune to be living, and in a sense trapped, in these areas.

The attention of the whole country was finally drawn to these problems when, in 1981, riots broke out in inner cities. They started in Toxteth, Liverpool, and spread to Brixton, London, and Moss Side, Manchester. Buildings were burnt down, cars were turned over, and there were running battles between the police and young people in the streets. The riots were sparked off by arguments with the police, but the involvement of so many people showed clearly that there were more deep-seated causes.

Firefighters deal with a burning car after riots in Tottenham, north London, in 1985

There was trouble again in 1985, but more recently both government and private investment has brought about huge improvements in many of the inner city areas. Most have not, as was feared, continued to sink into decay and despair. Today there is a more positive attitude to the potential of city life. Living close together has great environmental benefits, and with good planning opens up possibilities of rich, convivial social life.

- **The growth of mega-cities seems to be natural. Is there any reason to limit their size?**
- **What are inner cities like in your country? Do they have the same problems as in Britain?**

Glasgow

If you join the two million tourists per year who visit Glasgow, you will be struck by the pride that Glaswegians have in their city. It's more beautiful and more interesting (they say) than the capital of Scotland, Edinburgh. It was the UK City of Architecture and Design in 1999 and, going back to 1990, it was chosen as European City of Culture. It looks good, there is a lot to do and see, and there is a positive buzz about the place. This is all very different from the atmosphere 30 years ago. Glasgow's slums, especially the infamous Gorbals, were known around the world as a case-study in urban decay: houses falling apart, poverty, crime and violence. There was conflict between Catholic and Protestant groups (allied to Celtic and Rangers football clubs respectively). The city had lost its industrial heart with the decline of shipbuilding. As a port, it was facing the wrong way – away from Europe. But Glaswegians are tough people; they had lost their business more than once in the past – first the tobacco trade in the 18th century and then the cotton trade in the 19th. Their

Prince's Square shopping centre, Glasgow

fortunes turned around as the slums were cleared; in the 1970s and 1980s massive investment went into new housing. They lost the Peugeot car factory, but new industries came in. The people themselves decided to transform the city.

Liverpool

Liverpool is a city waiting for a change of image. Parts of the centre, in particular the rebuilt Albert Dock, have already achieved that change, but most of the city is still suffering from the effects of long-term economic decline. Its former prosperity was built on the docks and international trade: initially, that was the triangular trade of slaves to America, sugar and cotton to England, and manufactured goods to Africa. Later, it was the leading British port for goods and people to and from America, but fell victim to the change in direction of British trade: ports facing Europe, like Dover and Felixstowe, expanded, and Liverpool lost business. The city has never fully recovered. Unemployment is very high; at one time in the Everton area of the city it reached a staggering 44 per cent. Liverpool receives regional funds from the EU as one of the poorest parts of Europe. All the evidence of past glory is there: St George's Hall, one of the finest neo-classical buildings in England, was constructed in 1840 with not only central heating but also an air-conditioning system – the air cooled by fountains and circulated by steam fans! But look around the city today and its problems are all too apparent.

Manchester has a thriving club and dance scene.

Manchester

Mancunians have long had a high opinion of themselves; until Birmingham overtook them, theirs was the second city in Britain. In common with all other industrial areas of the country, they have had hard times: the failure of declining businesses and unemployment. But today the city is busy and hard-working again.

Manchester United is by a wide margin the richest

- **Which of these cities would you most like to visit? Why?**
- **Have any of the cities in your country transformed themselves like Glasgow?**

Liverpool's waterfront and Pier Head

In spite of all this, there is something very powerful and attractive about the culture of the city; Liverpudlians have a tremendous charm and creativity. Actors, comedians, writers, musicians and sports stars – the British media would be lost without Liverpool's contribution. The Beatles were one in a long list of big Merseyside bands – in the 60s there was a whole rock style known as the Mersey Beat; *Brookside* the popular TV soap opera is set in Liverpool; Cilla Black, the nation's favourite TV presenter, has a Scouse accent and, of course, Liverpool is home to one of the world's great football teams.

football club in the world (number two is Barcelona); they make around £90 million per year. In the 1998–99 season, Manchester United won the Treble – the English league and cup competitions and the European Cup. The university is the biggest in Europe, and students are an important part of the city's life. One result of this is that there is a big club and dance scene, and a lot of rock musicians have started life in Manchester: members of Oasis and Simply Red are Mancunians.

Students are also important customers for the many hundreds of restaurants in the city – mostly Indian and Chinese. The Asian area of Rusholm offers a massive eating-out experience in the Curry Mile. There is the biggest Chinatown in Europe, with not only dozens of restaurants but also Chinese supermarkets; there is a Chinese food factory which makes two tons of noodles per hour; and every year the city has a Dragon-Boat Festival on the Manchester Ship Canal. There is also a lively area of pubs, cafés and clubs known as Gay Village.

Cambridge

Cambridge has no heavy industrial past to give it problems. On the contrary, its past is its fortune – the ancient university provides the basis for a vibrant modern economy. The first Cambridge college, Peterhouse, was founded in 1284, but there was a centre of learning in the town long before that. Today, the centre is a fascinating collection of beautiful old college buildings; you can take a boat down the River Cam and see some of the most impressive – Queens', King's, Trinity and St John's. Until 30 years ago, the university was the only big employer, and the economy of the town was depressed. But since then, there has been rapid growth in high-tech industry – computing, communications, biotechnology and so on. It started with a science park, a dense group of small research and development companies, which became the most successful of its kind in Europe. In a way, Cambridge is the victim of its own success: the old town is just not big enough to accommodate all the new activity; there is too much traffic and not enough housing. To solve the problems, there is now talk of creating a new town nearby, a sort of Cambridge number two out in the green fields.

King's College and the River Cam, Cambridge

- **Does it make any difference to a city to have a great football team, like Manchester?**
- **Which cities in your country would you recommend to a visitor? Which would you not?**

The landscape

Britain is one of the most densely populated countries in the world. But even so it is not all under concrete. Some parts of these islands are very beautiful and, in spite of their small size, there is a surprising variety of landscape.

The variety is the result of geology. Successive ice ages brought polar ice down to cover most of the British Isles. The south of England escaped altogether; the middle of the country was covered by ice 300,000 years ago; the north and west, including Scotland and Wales, were affected just 18,000 years ago – only yesterday in geological time!

The characteristic landscape of North Wales, the Lake District and the Highlands of Scotland is mountainous, but without the sharp peaks of the Alps, and with broad, rounded valleys. It was carved out of the hard rock by gigantic flows of ice, in some places 1,750 metres thick. The south and east of England are much tamer, with flat plains or gently rolling hills.

The position of the islands shapes the landscape in other ways. At the edge of the great expanse of the Atlantic Ocean, the weather is wet and temperate. The rivers are not record-breaking in length, of course, but there are lots of them; in fact, 1,500 major river systems. All this water is good for agriculture, as is the temperate climate.

Left untouched, Britain would be almost entirely covered by forest. At one time it was possible for a squirrel to leap branch to branch from Land's End in Cornwall to John O'Groats in the north-east of Scotland without ever touching the ground. But deforestation has been going on for a long time. Five thousand years ago, humans started to cut down trees to make room for farms just as people in the tropical rain forests do today. They also used wood for heating and cooking, often in the form of charcoal. Over the last millennium, other uses of wood have increased, especially house and ship building. From the 16th century, the huge British navy required lots of oak. Today, less than 10 per cent of the land is forested, a lower figure than in any other European country except Ireland.

The Norfolk Broads – a wetland paradise in East Anglia.

Almost all of Britain's countryside is, in fact, shaped by humans. The moors and heaths (open country covered with small plants such as heather) only exist because the trees were cut down. Britain's favourite boating lakes, the Norfolk Broads, were thought for hundreds of years to be natural, but it has now been discovered that in fact they are the result of medieval peat-digging.

A pattern of small fields separated by hedges or walls, is typical of the English countryside. These were first created in the Middle Ages and the process continued into the 19th century, mostly for the benefit of rich landowners, who wanted to keep the poor off their property. Common land, which used to be free for everyone to graze their sheep and cattle on, was made private by a long series of new laws – the Enclosure Acts. By 1860, half of the land in England was enclosed. In Scotland, landlords burned the homes of the peasants to make room for sheep; the Scottish landlord George Granville Sutherland-Leveson-Gower, the third Duke of Sutherland, owned more than 5,000 square kilometres.

- **How does the landscape in your country compare with that in Britain?**
- **Human activity has transformed Britain. Is this a good or a bad thing?**

All over the country, peasant farmers were pushed off the land and made their way to the new industrial cities, where they could sell their labour to the factory owners. Many emigrated to America and Australia. In modern times, mechanisation on farms has continued this trend, and now only 2 per cent of British workers are in agriculture.

The farmer – hero or villain?

The government often boasts that British farmers are among the most efficient in the world. This is quite true in the sense that large quantities of food are produced cheaply by a small workforce. But the cost in other ways is very high. Intensive methods increase health risks: about 30 per cent of chicken and eggs in Britain are infected with salmonella. Unnatural feeding practices brought about the disastrous outbreak of BSE, or mad cow disease. A huge amount of pollution is caused by the over-use of fertilisers and pesticides. To increase yields of wheat or oilseed rape, farmers remove hedges and kill off weeds; food chains are broken,

A patchwork of small fields, typical of the English countryside

and in the end most wildlife disappears. The loss of typical farmland birds in the last 30 years has been dramatic – and, some would say, tragic; familiar species like the song-thrush and yellowhammer have declined by more than 50 per cent. Huge areas of land are covered by single crops, and the visitor from the city is disappointed as the countryside begins to look like a gigantic open-air food factory.

Apart from farming methods, landowners come into conflict with city people in other ways, too. On a sunny Sunday afternoon, about 20 million British people will leave the towns and cities and visit the countryside. And the most popular activity in the countryside is simply walking through it. But where can they walk? After hundreds of years of enclosures, there is hardly any common land left.

Rapeseed oil production: this sort of monoculture excludes wildlife.

The wonderful voice of the song-thrush is heard less and less in Britain today.

- **How can farming and wildlife live together?**
- **What do you like or dislike most about the countryside?**

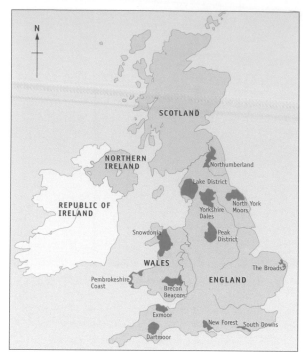

Britain's National Parks including the proposed New Forest and South Downs.

Every field, every moor, every river and every forest is owned by someone. In 1949, the Labour Government tried to change things radically with the National Parks and Access to the Countryside Act. As a result, ten lovely, but quite small, National Parks were created, including Snowdonia in Wales, Dartmoor in Devon, and the Lake District. Even in these parks, however, there is limited access for walkers, with a large number of fences and Keep Out signs. The government's original plan to open up the rest of the countryside failed completely in the face of opposition from the great landowners. No-one today owns as much as the Duke of Sutherland did in the 19th century, but there are still some very big estates, and a few thousand families still own 95 per cent of the land in the country.

For the last 50 years, there has been a cold war between the Ramblers Association (rambling means country walking) on the one side and the Country Landowners' Association on the other. The ramblers want the legal right to walk everywhere, as long as they do no damage, as, for example, in Sweden.

The landowners say that all these townspeople will destroy crops and frighten animals. Far from compromising, landowners are actually trying to reduce the limited access which currently exists: there are many thousands of kilometres of ancient paths, legal rights-of way across properties, but more than 50 per cent of these have been hidden or obstructed by landowners.

The countryside fights back

There seems to have been a breakdown of communication and understanding between the town and the country. In 1998, there was an extraordinary demonstration in London, when 250,000 people marched through the streets protesting about all sorts of problems faced by the countryside: low prices for farmers, bad public transport, too many houses being built on farm land, and the government's plans to ban foxhunting.

The foxhunting question may seem rather unimportant, but it is an issue which always excites a great deal of passion, both for and against. The countryside demonstrators said that hunting provides jobs for the people who look after the dogs and horses; that foxes are pests which must be killed; that townspeople are anti-hunting because they are soft and sentimental, and have forgotten the harsh realities of country life.

The Countryside March was a protest against government neglect and the insensitivity of people in towns and cities.

- Can you walk across private land in your country? Do people argue about access?
- In your country, is there any conflict between city and country people?

The Cotswolds

The Cotswolds are gentle green hills in the farming country to the west of England, near the ancient market town of Gloucester. A patchwork of small fields separated by old dry-stone walls and lines of trees make this a perfect example of traditional English countryside. Arable farming is balanced with cattle and sheep, and small patches of woodland. It has been a rich agricultural area since the Middle Ages, with the result that there are many examples of fine old architecture. Many farms, houses and churches, like the walls dividing the fields, are built of the

Cottages in the Cotswolds

local honey-coloured stone; others are half-timbered. Villages like Painswick, Bibury, Minchinhampton and Bourton-on-the-Water are small and beautifully kept. There are climbing roses around the doors of the cottages, and no satellite dishes. In fact, for many people it is a little bit too precious – a sort of museum that is fascinating to look at, but too claustrophobic to live in.

Scotland

There are 240 people per square kilometre in the UK. But most of these people live in England, and the figure for the Highlands of Scotland is less than 50 per square kilometre; the region is a beautiful, peaceful wilderness.

Scotland takes its special character from mountains and water: water in the form of lochs, rivers, streams, the sea and, (it has to be said) rain. The lochs come in two varieties: fresh water lochs such as the home of the monster, Loch Ness; and sea lochs, which are like Norwegian fjords, all the way down the west coast. Both kinds of loch are great for fishing and boating – or just looking at.

The mountains are not very high by world standards – the highest, Ben Nevis, is only 1,343 metres. But they have a special haunting beauty, with their rounded forms and their brown and purple colours. Large areas are spoilt by dull, lifeless tree plantations, but here and there are remnants of the magnificent original Caledonian forest. The wildlife is not easy to find, but is worth the effort: herds of red and fallow deer, wildcat, hare, otter and mountain birds such as grouse, short-eared owl and golden eagle.

The Scilly Isles are surprisingly different from the mainland, and exceptionally beautiful.

The Isles of Scilly

These are a magical collection of tiny, rocky islands out in the Atlantic Ocean off the south-west coast of England. They are almost always kept above freezing point by the warm waters of the Gulf Stream, so there is a whole range of plants – yuccas and exotic flowers – which cannot grow on the mainland. In the right weather the place looks semi-tropical. The islands are a mecca for bird-watchers.

- **Which of these parts of Britain attracts you most? Why?**
- **Which areas of your country would you recommend for tourists to visit?**

Green and pleasant land

The poet William Blake wrote 200 years ago of "England's green and pleasant land". In spite of their mainly urban lives, this image is still strong in British people's imagination. They love the countryside, cultivate gardens and watch hours of wildlife programmes on TV every week. Some of the first environmental organisations in the world started in Britain. The Royal Society for the Prevention of Cruelty to Animals (RSPCA) dates from 1824. The Royal Society for the Protection of Birds (RSPB) began life in 1889, and now, with over one million members, it is the largest voluntary wildlife-conservation body in Europe.

Recently the British have started to worry about losing their green and pleasant land under tarmac. In the mid-90s, a by pass was built around the pretty country town of Newbury in Berkshire: this was a motorway which cut straight through some of the most beautiful countryside in the south-east of England, and 10,000 trees had to be chopped down in the process. There were constant demonstrations by thousands of protesters during the building, and police had to protect the workers. There has been tremendous public opposition to major road-building projects ever since.

The government has sometimes acted to protect the environment. School geography books often have a section about the defeat of the London smog.

With coal fires in home and industry, terrible photo-chemical smogs were common events 60 years ago. In fact, there had been attempts to ban coal-burning in the city as far back as the 13th century. In 1952, a particularly thick smog covered London for four days and killed about 2,000 people. Four years later, Parliament passed the Clean Air Act; coal was replaced by oil and gas, and the problem was solved. The British are rather proud of this achievement.

Behind the image

Sadly, Britain's overall environmental record does not fit the rather flattering self-image. Actually, the British have been so careless about pollution that the country has been called the dirty man of Europe. On issue after issue Britain has fallen below the standards set by its neighbours – acid rain, climate change, toxic waste, recycling and sewage management.

Acid rain was one of the first cases of Britain exporting pollution and upsetting the neighbours. Acid rain is produced when sulphur dioxide (SO_2) and nitrogen oxides (N_2O) from factories or cars mix with water. British industry and power generation, much of it old-fashioned and coal-burning, produced massive quantities of these pollutants which, because of

Protesters at the site of the Newbury by pass

- Are you proud or ashamed of your country's environmental record?
- Would you protest against a new road or other building development?

the prevailing wind direction, were then carried over Scandinavia. Just one huge old power station, at the village of Drax in Yorkshire, gave off more sulphur dioxide than Sweden and Norway put together, and those countries suffered serious damage to their lakes and forests as a result.

Not surprisingly, acid rain also falls on parts of Britain. A recent study found Manchester to be the worst affected city in Europe – its buildings are being eaten away at an alarming rate. And 67 per cent of British forests have been damaged – the highest figure in Europe.

Drax is the largest coal-fired power station in Europe.

Climate change

Another problem related to power stations is the emission of carbon dioxide (CO_2). This is the principal gas responsible for the greenhouse effect. While it is not immediately harmful to humans (we produce it ourselves as we breathe), it may have disastrous effects on our habitat in the long term. Carbon dioxide is given off whenever fossil fuels like coal, oil and gas are burnt. Britain has a particularly high level of dependence on fossil fuels for electricity generation. This is partly because Britain uses less nuclear energy, but also because it gets so little energy from renewable sources such as hydroelectric and wind power.

Unfortunately, the main fossil fuel used in Britain is coal, which is especially dirty in terms of emissions.

The British government went along to the United Nations Earth Summit in Rio de Janeiro in 1992, and supported the resolutions. But subsequently Britain opposed the one practical measure that might have reduced CO_2 emissions – a green tax on fossil fuel use. Actually, the British record on emissions has improved considerably since then, but in a sense by accident: for economic reasons there has been a big switch from coal to natural gas from the North Sea, resulting in a 6 per cent drop in CO_2.

In the last 20 years, industry and the power stations have become more efficient, and CO_2 emissions have been going down as a result. But sadly these improvements are more than counter-balanced by another factor: road transport has grown enormously, and taken over the role as the top producer of pollutants including CO_2.

Traffic congestion and pollution are major problems.

Going nuclear

When the problems of acid rain and global warming became widely understood, those in the nuclear industry were delighted. Nuclear power is the clean alternative, they said. Of course, it is true that in many ways it is clean, with none of the emissions of fossil fuel burning. If only it did not have two little drawbacks – the risk (better appreciated since Chernobyl) of catastrophic accidents, and the insoluble problem of lethally dangerous radioactive waste.

- **Which do you think are the most serious environmental problems today?**
- **Is there anything that an individual person can do about these problems?**

The British experts were smug after Chernobyl: it could not happen here, they said, as management is so much better. But in reality there have been lots of problems in British nuclear power stations. In 1956, for example, there was a serious accident at what is now known as Sellafield, the centre of the UK nuclear industry. Then it was revealed that records at Dounreay power station in Scotland had been lost, so that no-one knew where all the nuclear waste was stored. In fact, the situation was so bad at Dounreay that in 1998 the government decided to close it down.

Quite apart from accidents, the normal process of waste disposal leads to all sorts of problems. High-level, very radioactive waste is stored in holes underground, but of course no-one wants it anywhere near them, so it is almost impossible to find sites for it. Low-level waste used regularly to be thrown or pumped into the sea. In 1986, a parliamentary committee wrote: "Sellafield is the largest recorded source of radioactive discharge in the world and as a result the Irish Sea is the most radioactive sea in the world." Understandably, the Irish were not too happy about this and complained many times. It was not until 1997 that the government joined other countries in banning this system.

There now seems to be little future for nuclear power in Britain. A defining moment came when, in the 1980s, the government privatised the electricity generators. It had always been said that nuclear power was cheaper than its competitors. But when plans were made to sell the industry and real economic calculations had to be made, the truth was revealed. Taking into account the gigantic costs of closing down power stations safely at the end of their lives, nuclear power was too expensive. No-one would buy the industry because it could not be run as a business.

Waste

Radioactive waste is not, of course, the only type of dangerous waste which is produced by Britain's consumer society. There are solvents, asbestos, heavy metals such as mercury and cadmium, and hundreds of other substances. Most developed countries try to separate these things from harmless rubbish, and to dispose of them carefully or recycle them. The British system has always been to throw everything into land fill sites and hope for the best. Of course, sooner or later these toxic materials leak out of the land fill and into the surrounding environment. The network of almost 5,000 toxic sites has been described by experts as a time bomb.

Britain's record on recycling waste is poor. They recycle about 7 per cent, compared with 30 per cent in Germany and nearer 80 per cent in some parts of Canada. No batteries and hardly any plastic are recycled here. Paper and glass are the only things commonly collected; even on paper recycling Britain is only 11th in the European league table.

Down on the farm

British farmers are highly efficient. Unfortunately, that means that they use massive quantities of chemical pesticides and fertilisers. It seems perverse to say so, but some of the blame for the situation in Britain belongs to the European Union (EU). The Common Agricultural Policy (CAP), which accounts for half of the EU's budget, encourages some very bad farming practices. Subsidies are given for increased mechanisation and more intensive methods. Prices for crops are guaranteed, so farmers know that they will get those prices however much they produce. This has several effects. One is simply

A paper and bottle recycling centre

- **How much does your country depend on nuclear power? Does it worry you?**
- **What sort of waste do you recycle? Could you do more?**

over-production, but another is more complicated. Farmers used to have a variety of crops and animals, so as to reduce risk if the price of one fell. Without that risk, they now tend to concentrate on just one crop; for example, wheat or sugar beet. This monoculture has a number of damaging effects; with no change of crop, the soil becomes exhausted and needs lots of chemicals to keep it productive.

Under EU rules, individual governments can encourage organic farmers with subsidies. All EU governments do that except France, Ireland and Britain. The demand for organic food in Britain is high, but most of it has to be imported from countries like Denmark.

Organic food is increasingly popular.

Green politics

Given the situation in Britain, there is clearly a role for an environmentalist political party. There is a Green Party but it has so far remained a minority middle-class party, without broad popular support, and the voting system in parliamentary elections has prevented them from winning any seats.

Of the major parties, the Liberal Democrats have for a long time been the greenest, but they are always the third party, with no realistic hope of power. The Conservatives have been very much the party of big business, and resolutely anti-green. The main reason for Britain's poor environmental record in modern times is that from 1979 to 1997

there was a Conservative government which simply did not believe in ecology. Mrs Thatcher had started her working life as a scientist, and she thought that this gave her the authority to argue with environmental experts about everything from BSE (a disease affecting cattle) to climate change. The Labour Government promised a very different approach, but since coming to power has disappointed environmentalists.

At grass-roots level, however, the situation is far more positive. The international organisation Greenpeace has over 200,000 members in Britain. Its policy is for high-profile publicity campaigns, and it won a historic victory against Shell in 1995, when it prevented the dumping in the North Sea of an old oil platform, the *Brent Spar*. Friends of the Earth is based on small local groups of activists; its membership in Britain is over 100,000 and growing steadily.

British attitudes have changed radically over the last few decades. Twenty years ago, it was quite normal to make fun of Prince Charles for his views on organic gardening and farming, and he was portrayed as an eccentric who talked to his flowers. Today, people are sick of food scandals such as BSE in beef and dioxins in poultry, and organic food is now big business. When the Prince recently spoke out against genetically modified (GM) foods, he received lots of public support. Renewable energy such as wind power is becoming ever more popular. People are crying out for solutions to traffic jams and air pollution. Now almost everyone has woken up to the environmental crisis that has been created. It is surely only a matter of time before these feelings are translated into political action.

- **Is organic food just a fashion, or will it be the food of the future?**
- **Would you ever join an environmental group like Greenpeace, or vote for a green party?**

An interview with ... Paul de Zylva

Paul de Zylva has been a campaigner for the protection of the environment for nearly 15 years – almost half his life. He has been involved in anti-road and airport campaigns. He says that he is always hoping, against all odds, that he will ultimately lose his job as an activist with the environmental pressure group, Friends of the Earth.

What were the original aims of Friends of the Earth, when it was set up in 1971?

Well, in this country – in England, Wales and Northern Ireland and Scotland as it was at that time, because at the moment Scotland is a separate organisation in the Friends of the Earth family, it had a very broad aim of trying to encourage governments and people of the world to look at the way they used resources and to protect the natural resources of the world and do things that would be with conservation in mind. I think at that particular time – we'd come out of the 1960s – when there was a very big worldwide movement and growing awareness that things weren't necessarily right. Pollution was starting to impact on people's lives and certainly the food that they ate and this was happening in ways that couldn't necessarily be known, it wasn't predicted. And people also started living a life realising that the industrial rush of life wasn't necessarily all good – it wasn't necessarily all bad but there are other ways of looking at things. So, I think Friends of the Earth in this country, in 1971, was responding to a number of huge problems but not being absolutely clear about how it was going to deal with them.

Have the group's aims stayed the same over the years?

I think the group's broad aims are obviously pretty much the same in that we're looking at the best use of natural resources in a way that isn't wasteful, in a way that doesn't create unnecessary pollution. But, what they've done as the movement has changed and we've looked at a broader range of issues. We have changed as a movement. We've started to become more involved in politics, not necessarily party politics, but what we have done is recognise that you can't be an environmental campaigner and ignore the decisions that are made in politics. Neither can you ignore the decisions based in business; so our ways of working have changed. And I think increasingly they've become more mainstream and accepted.

- **Do environmental organisations have to be politically active?**
- **What do you think about voluntary work?**

When did you join and why?
Well, I joined in 1985. I joined as a local group volunteer. Friends of the Earth in England, Wales and Northern Ireland has a network of 240 local groups made up of ordinary citizens, who feel that they need to come together and work on issues in their local community. And before I knew it, I was very much involved with the running of the group and starting to learn about issues that before I never thought had an impact on my life.

Would you say that Friends of the Earth and other large environmental awareness groups have become a bit like bureaucracies – they are more interested in their own survival than the actual issues that they are campaigning for?
No, I wouldn't agree with that at all and I wouldn't have agreed with that even if I were still a volunteer with Friends of the Earth. Amnesty International always says that we will go out of business when the last political prisoner is free. There is no need for Friends of the Earth to exist, if society has changed. Not just in this country but globally. So I think we're perfectly happy to be put out of business, if you like, and to go off and do other things.

What campaigns have you participated in?
Well, my actual role in Friends of the Earth is to co-ordinate campaigns in London, so effectively it means I become involved in any issues. Some of the key campaigns I've been involved with, let's say in the past year, have been, the whole proposal to expand Heathrow Airport. Already the world's busiest airport and the owners; British Airports Authority and British Airways, who are the main operator at Heathrow – they want to take a huge amount of land twice the size of Wembley Stadium. It's a vast place and they want to build a terminal, which would just mean more pollution for London, more land taken for development which will attract more traffic.

We're also doing some work on the transporting of nuclear waste through London from some of the nuclear power stations that are on the south coast of England. I'm also involved in trying to protect one of London's best wildlife sites, over in the east of London.

Have you had a lot of success in your campaigns over the years, rather than just in the last year?
Yes, I think we have since Friends of the Earth formed and certainly in the past 15 years. The successes have either been very short campaigns which have been won very quickly – when I say win a campaign it doesn't necessarily mean you win outright and you get exactly what you want. It can mean that you change the position of the government slightly, or yes, you do stop something entirely, or you get a new idea into society, into people's brains and into the way they think. But yes, over the years, we've been involved in campaigns that have stopped this government, the British government rather, throwing money down the drain by investing in wasteful technology, such as investing more in nuclear power. We've run successful campaigns, not on our own, but with coalitions with other people and other organisations, on the massive road-building programme in this country, which was destroying some of our best countryside and also not actually dealing with the transport problem.

What is the future of environmental issues?
I think the future of environmental issues is that it's going to become more mainstream. It's going to be seen less as some fringe sideline, some activity carried out by people who have nothing better to do, and they're just trouble-makers. And it may well be that some key leaders in the environmental movement actually end up becoming part of government – it's happened in Germany, for example, and if that's the way that it goes, then that's fine.

- **Do you think that environmental organisations have become like bureaucracies?**
- **Have you ever participated in a campaign of any sort?**

What's in a name?

Extraordinary though it seems, people in this country are genuinely confused about its name. Some say Britain or occasionally, if they are feeling patriotic, Great Britain. Customs officers and economists call it the UK. This presents a linguistic problem, as there is no adjective form (what could it be – UKish?) English people quite often forget all about their important neighbours and call it England. "This royal throne of kings, this sceptred isle ... This other Eden, demi-paradise ... This precious stone set in the silver sea ... This blessed plot, this earth, this realm, this England," says John of Gaunt in Shakespeare's play *Richard II*; if England was an island, where were Scotland and Wales at the time – under water? Then there is the nice general term which TV weather presenters like to use, the British Isles. But this one worries the Irish: does it include them as one of the "isles"?

The full name of the country is, of course, the United Kingdom of Great Britain and Northern Ireland. Very briefly indeed, the history is as follows. Wales was merged with England by King Henry VIII in 1543. Scotland followed with the Act of Union in 1707, after which the country was known as the United Kingdom of Great Britain. The Act of Ireland in 1801 united Britain and Ireland, but that unhappy union finally broke up in 1921, with only six mainly Protestant counties in the north of Ireland remaining in the UK. This remains the situation today.

King Henry VIII was as tough as he looked.

An unwritten constitution

While the shape of the country changed, the system of government also developed and transformed itself. Henry VIII was an autocratic medieval-style monarch, with very few limits on his power. Today, Britain has a monarch but within a parliamentary democracy. The transformation is (almost) complete. But, in contrast with almost every other country in the world, no dramatic event in British history has resulted in a written constitution.

In 1649, after a long and terrible civil war against Parliament, King Charles I was beheaded. There was then a period of republican government known as the Commonwealth. Surprisingly, the monarchy later re-established itself, although things would never be quite the same again. The Habeas Corpus Act of 1679 guaranteed certain basic freedoms for the citizen. In 1689, a Bill of Rights established Parliament as the central body of government. In the 19th century a number of Reform Acts gave the vote to more and more of the male population; in 1928, this was finally extended to all women over 21. Other laws were passed to limit the length of parliaments and the power of the House of Lords.

- **Do the names of countries cause any problems in your part of the world?**
- **Has your country got a written constitution? If so, is it a good one?**

These laws, however, have never been brought together into a single document. In fact, some aspects of the system are not even covered by laws, but rather by custom and practice. So it is often said that Britain has an unwritten constitution. It exists; but not as a document, but rather as a subject to be studied.

The monarchy

By far the strangest feature of the system is the role of the monarch. The Queen appears on paper to have tremendous power, but in fact has hardly any at all. The country is a kingdom, the government is Her Majesty's Government, laws are made by the Queen in Parliament, criminals are tried in the name of the Queen, and the Queen is the head of state. She dissolves Parliament before an election and she appoints the new Prime Minister (PM); she has a business meeting with the PM once a week, usually on Tuesdays; at the annual State Opening of Parliament she makes the Queen's Speech, which outlines the government's plans. She is the head of the Commonwealth (which includes 51 countries and a quarter of the world's population), and she is actually Head of State in 16 countries including Canada, Papua New Guinea and Jamaica. All this seems to add up to a dominant role within the system. But it does not: the key word here is *symbolic*.

The American President is both head of the government and head of state. This is also the case in France and in Russia, while in most countries around the world these two roles are separate. The all-but-powerless, ceremonial head of state is most commonly a president, but in a few places such as Denmark, the Netherlands, Norway and the UK, the job is done by a king or queen. Queen Elizabeth signs all the new laws that are presented to her; she cannot pick and choose. She appoints the leader of the majority party as Prime Minister, automatically. The Queen's Speech is in fact written for her by the government. Any power she may have is strictly personal: if PMs respect her opinion on something (such as the Commonwealth, on which

The Lord Chamberlain delivers the Queen's Speech at the State Opening of Parliament.

she is an expert), they will take her advice. Constitutionally, she has the right only, "to be consulted, to encourage, and to warn".

The separation of powers

In the USA the constitution enforces a strict separation between the executive, the legislature and the judiciary. Britain has some separation but not very much. The legal system is independent to a large degree: although the government of the day appoints judges, it cannot interfere with their work and it cannot get rid of those appointed by the previous government. But the executive and the legislature are not separate at all: in fact, the former is part of the latter. The law-making body is Parliament – the House of Commons and the House of Lords. The Commons is made up of all the Members of Parliament (MPs) chosen by election – about 650 of them. Within that there is the majority party, and within the majority party there is a group of ministers who are the government. The leader of the majority party is the head of the government, the Prime Minister.

• **Would you like to have a monarch and a royal family in your country?**
• **Why do some countries have a strict separation of powers? Is it a good thing?**

The Cabinet

The top ministers form an élite group of about 20, known as the Cabinet. These are the people who sit round a table with the PM and decide on the policies of the government. They have a rule of collective responsibility: in public they all have to agree with the decisions of the whole Cabinet.

The role of the PM is extremely important: he or she appoints all the members of the government, so every one of them owes their job to the PM. It is very hard to be independent, still less rebellious, in such circumstances. But much depends on the personal style of the PM. As with managers in business, or sports captains, some leaders are more authoritarian than others.

In recent times John Major was a PM who preferred co-operation and consensus. Tony Blair does not appear to tolerate opposition within his own party. Mrs Thatcher, the Iron Lady, was so tough that her Cabinet colleagues were all terrified of her. She once wrote: "I don't mind how much my ministers talk – as long as they do what I say". There is always a danger that the PM can take on a more presidential role, and in Mrs Thatcher's time people started to talk about the system becoming an "elected dictatorship".

Mrs Thatcher may have shown how dictatorial a PM can be. But, unwillingly, she also showed the limits of the post. When she became unpopular in the country, the Conservative Party saw that it was going to lose the next election because of her, and so it sacked her. Remember that the PM is the leader of the majority party; and that party can always change its leader if it is unhappy.

The two-party system

The voting arrangements in Britain have always tended to produce two major parties. In the 18th century, it was Tory versus Whig, then Tory versus Liberal, and in modern times, Conservative versus Labour. This fact is reflected in the constitution itself. The second biggest party in the House of Commons becomes the Official Opposition: its leader is paid a salary from the public purse and given an office.

The new Scottish Parliament opens for the first time, Edinburgh, in 1999.

As in the legal system, the parties confront each other and argue. The House of Commons is built for confrontation: two sets of seats face each other across a neutral no-man's land. In fact, the space between the two sides is two swords' lengths and one foot, to prevent fights! This theatrical way of doing things has some advantages. For one, it is easy for the public to understand. Also, it means that the government is always being publicly challenged, which is good for democracy.

It is significant, however, that the new Scottish parliament Chamber is built on a different model – a horse-shoe shape around a central Speaker's platform. This reflects the new voting system for Scotland, a form of proportional representation. If the rest of the UK moves away from the current first-past-the-post system, there will be more parties in Westminster, and there is likely to be a profound change in the way politics is done.

The House of Lords

There may be other constitutional monarchs around the world, but nowhere is there anything quite like the upper Chamber of the British Parliament, the House of Lords. In fact, it is difficult to talk about it in the present tense, as it is in the process of being radically changed. In the 1997 election, part of

- **If you were a prime minister, would you be dictatorial?**
- **Do you have two dominant parties in your country, or a number of smaller ones?**

Labour's manifesto was a promise to reform it – hardly surprising if you look at the extraordinary nature of the House of Lords before these reforms began.

The function of the upper Chamber is to act as a brake on the government of the day. Its members take a long, cool look at new legislation prepared by the Commons. They discuss it, revise it and sometimes send it back to be reconsidered. Their power has for a long time been very limited. Even before the 20th century it was accepted that the Commons was the real seat of power; but from time to time the Lords tried to take control.

The House of Lords in session

The problem was that the permanent Conservative majority in the Lords opposed the Commons when it was in the hands of its enemies, the Liberals. In 1909, the Liberals tried to introduce a radical People's Budget increasing taxes and benefits. The House of Lords did its best to stop the budget going through, and the Commons lost its patience. A law was passed to limit the powers of the upper Chamber: the Parliament Act of 1911. From then on, it could only delay new laws for a fixed period, and it could not alter budgets (normally the most important of government measures).

The problem of the Conservative majority did not, however, go away. It was still the main reason for

Tony Blair's promise to reform the Lords in 1997. The origin of this built-in, permanent Conservative majority was the bizarre and medieval composition of the House of Lords. Most members were from the ancient aristocracy: dukes, marquises, earls, viscounts and barons. These are hereditary titles, like the monarchy, passed on from father to son through the generations.

In recent years, it has been the practice to create new lords, known as life peers. Senior politicians such as ex-Prime Ministers, and other important public figures were given titles (for example, Baroness Thatcher) and a seat in the House of Lords. But the relics of feudalism were still in the majority; and they were joined by many more Conservatives among the life peers. In the 1990s, the Lords consisted of about 750 hereditary peers, 26 bishops of the Church of England, nine senior judges and about 500 life peers. You can see from the figures that another problem was the size of the membership; luckily, only a small proportion of them ever came in to work.

A new constitution

The future of the House of Lords could be included in a new written constitution which would deal with all sorts of problems in one go; for example, the status of Scotland, Wales and Northern Ireland and the problem of the voting system. Now might be a good time to abolish or at least reform the monarchy, which has lost much of its popular support. The question of Britain's relations with the EU also needs to be resolved.

Also, there is a fundamental point missing from Britain's unwritten constitution – human rights. These rights only exist in a sort of negative form at present: you can do whatever you like if it is not against the law. In the Thatcher era some very basic rights seemed to be under threat; for example, unions were banned at GCHQ, the government's electronic spy centre, and in 1984–5 the police were used as a political force against striking miners.

- **Does your country's parliament have a second Chamber? What is its function?**
- **What is wrong with hereditary power?**

In 1988, a group called Charter 88 started a campaign for a written constitution, while others demanded a Bill of Rights and a Freedom of Information Act. At the beginning of the new millennium, the Labour Government was considering legislation on freedom of information, and was moving towards incorporating the European Convention on Human Rights into British law. But the idea of a written constitution is still rather alien to the British; perhaps it would actually make it harder to reform institutions rather than easier. At present Parliament is all-powerful, and can make any constitutional change it wishes to at any time. There may be dangers in this, but it is a quick and simple system.

A Hammersmith councillor with young unemployed people on a council training scheme.

The EU

There is very good reason for not writing a new constitution just yet. Obviously, as EU member countries move closer to merging into a single state, all their constitutions will need rewriting; in the end perhaps they will all make do with one big constitution. Britain signed the 1992 Maastricht Treaty, and some of its provisions now form part of UK law. In commercial areas, EU law has gradually replaced UK legislation; in criminal law, or civil law (divorce, libel and so on), Britain is still completely independent. It is a very complicated subject, but the general principle is clear: British law now comes under European law in those areas where treaties exist.

Local government

For people who live in, say, Hammersmith in the west of London, the decisions of Parliament in Westminster or of the Commission in Brussels are not always that important in their everyday lives. They have a local council which runs the schools, social services, roads, parks, rubbish collection and libraries.

The council also owns a lot of low-cost housing, and makes all the planning decisions for Hammersmith: where a new cinema can be built, and whether a club can serve alcohol, or have dancing. The councillors are party politicians who have won their seats in local elections. They also usually live in the borough and are known to the public, so there is a high degree of local democracy. The council is a Parliament in miniature, except that the councillors, unlike MPs in Parliament, are part-time and unpaid. This is the system in towns, cities and rural areas throughout the country.

Relations between the local council and central government are not always good: local leaders quite rightly want some power and independence, but Parliament feels that it must have the last word. Finance is at the root of the problem: 80 per cent of the councils' money comes directly from central government (they collect the rest through a local tax). Education is the biggest responsibility of local government, and it used to be very much in their hands; but over the last 15 years central government has intervened more and more in this area. The Conservatives started weakening local government, and Labour has not reversed the process.

- **Is there debate about human rights in your country?**
- **Where is your nearest local government? Are you interested in what it is doing?**

Devolution

Devolution of power from Westminster has, however, taken place in two very important areas: Scotland and Wales. In 1999, the Scottish Parliament and the Welsh Assembly came into being, and those two countries had a degree of self-rule for the first time in hundreds of years. The Scottish Parliament, as its name suggests, is the more powerful of the two bodies, having the ability to raise taxes. This reflects the fact that nationalism in Scotland is much stronger than it is in Wales. More than 50 per cent of Scots want full independence from England (or Britain), whereas in Wales not even the nationalist party *Plaid Cymru* talks in such terms.

Northern Ireland

In the case of Northern Ireland, devolution is on the political agenda, but it does not provide an easy solution to the problems. In fact, there was a devolved government there between 1921 and 1972, but it did not work out well. The Protestant majority ran the government as a sectarian regime, and discriminated against Catholics. In the end, the minority lost patience and started a civil-rights protest movement. There was violence, and British troops were sent in. The old IRA (Irish Republican Army), which had fought to free Ireland from the British 50 years earlier, was revived in a new form, the Provisional IRA, and started a guerrilla and terror campaign. In response, the Protestants formed their own paramilitary groups, the Ulster Defence Association, the Ulster Volunteer Force and the Ulster Freedom Fighters. More than 3,000 people died in the resulting war, known as the Troubles.

To the great relief of all the people of Northern Ireland, a peace agreement was made on Good Friday 1998. The aim was once more to devolve government to Belfast, with power shared between the rival groups. After long negotiations, a new executive, including both Protestants and Catholics, was formed in December 1999. At the same time the IRA agreed to discuss disarmament, and the Irish Republic changed its constitution to give up its claim to the North, as part of a united Ireland.

The position of the British government on Northern Ireland has always been difficult. Many outsiders consider it a colonial power, which should withdraw completely. But if that had been attempted, there was a real fear of Protestant violence – the same fear that led to the setting up of a Northern Ireland in 1921.

The British government says that it will agree to a united Ireland if a majority in Northern Ireland wants it. At present that is impossible as there is a Protestant majority, but the Catholic population is growing faster, so in the long term simple numbers may solve the problem.

The economy of the Irish Republic has also been growing faster than that of Northern Ireland, so there may be an economic incentive for change.

In 1998 a car bomb, planted by a Republican splinter group, killed 29 and injured 200 people in a crowded street in Omagh.

- **Is your country very centralised, or is there devolution to regions? Which do you prefer?**
- **How do you think the problems of Northern Ireland could be solved?**

🔊 📼 An interview with ...
the Right Honourable Betty Boothroyd

The Right Honourable Betty Boothroyd, MP, is the first woman to become Speaker of the House of Commons. Before that, Miss Boothroyd spent 18 years as a Labour Member of Parliament. Now as Madam Speaker, she has put party politics to one side, and become the Guardian of the Rights of the House of Commons and all its Members.

In terms of the British Constitution, how important is the role of the Speaker of the House of Commons?

Oh, it is an enormously important position is the Speaker. Of course, it is totally impartial: the speakership does not belong to any one political party. It's like being an umpire and keeping – not just keeping order – but in seeing that all the great rainbow of opinion in this House is properly heard.

On a day-to-day basis, how would you describe your job?

It's very demanding – from very early in the morning until late at night. There is much more to it than just simply going into the Chair of the Chamber and conducting business there. I am Chairman of the House of Commons Commission, this entire establishment of the House of Commons, which costs something like £200 million a year to operate through six large departments – so it is a very big business as well.

When you took office in 1992, you were the first woman to hold the position of Speaker. You also became the most important commoner – that is, a person who is not royal – after the Prime Minister. Did this overawe you and how did you feel about it?

It certainly did not overawe me. I regard it as a very great privilege, but that is quite different from being overawed by it. I think you have to keep in mind that I have been a Member of Parliament now for some 25 years. I love this place. I like the way our parliamentary system operates.

I never consider the fact that I am a woman. I am not treated in any way differently in my House as a woman.

But it is a very male-dominated House. So did you have a problem at all controlling this male-dominated House right at the beginning?

No, I didn't. Of course, you're quite right, it is male-dominated. But you must remember that since the 1997 General Election, far more women members have come in – but it is still male-dominated. I don't think that there is a real problem in controlling the male members here. It is a robust House; it is a confrontational House; it is not hemicycle like many parliaments are. By hemicycle, I mean like the shape of a horseshoe. Many parliaments throughout the world are sort of rounded: they are the shape of a horseshoe. The Chamber of the House of Commons is not – it has two distinct sides to it, the Opposition and the Government.

We have a green carpet on the floor of the Commons and in front of the two front-benches – the Government and the Opposition is a red stripe, and that is two sword-lengths and one foot apart from each other because hundreds of years ago, Members didn't necessarily just argue, they got out their swords and had a go at each other. And that is a tradition that we have.

You mention traditions. There is, of course, a great deal of ceremony associated with the British Parliament, such as the State Opening of Parliament. Now, you've been quoted as saying

---

• **Does your parliament have a Speaker, or similar role? Why is such a role important?**
• **How are women represented in your parliament? Is it male-dominated?**

that you rather like the traditions, and you'd like to keep them and this new wave of modernisation is not required.
There is no challenge at all to the State Opening. That is a tradition. I put on my gold robes at that stage, my Chaplain and my Secretary – and we go into the House of Lords to hear the Queen's Speech. The people of this country enjoy that enormously, no one seeks to challenge that.

In terms of modernisation, what we talk about is to modernise some of our procedures to get more brisk debate, greater scrutiny.

There is some concern about governments with large majorities failing to keep Parliament fully informed about their decisions and instead rushing to the press and public first. Why is this bad practice? Shouldn't a government be allowed to put its voters first?
No. In a parliamentary democracy, it is those who have been elected who must have the news first and when there is any change of policy or additional policy, it is right that the people who have been elected through the ballot be the first to question that. For example, the Foreign Secretary after he has just come back from his dealings in Kosovo.

You've been quoted as saying when you were elected Speaker that it would be a lonelier life than you'd ever known. Is that how it's been?
No, I'm not lonely. I suppose it is lonely to the extent that I'm gregarious and I am not allowed as Speaker to use the refreshment departments, the bars, the common areas of the House of Commons. And that is a good thing in many ways. Because what the House says to its Speaker is: "Look, we provide a home for you here at the Palace of Westminster. Go and live

there and keep out of our way, because if we wish to gossip about you, in the dining rooms, in the bars, in the tea rooms, we can do so very freely". That's fine for them. It's also fine for me because then I'm not button-holed by Members.

What have been the highlights of your time as Speaker?
I think every day presents something new. One that springs to mind right away, of course, was the visit of President Mandela, when we received the President in Westminster Hall, both Houses, the House of Commons and the House of Lords. We have a lot of steps, very difficult ones – into Westminster Hall, a hall that was built in the year 1080 – a great many steps. An elderly man, frail, he had, I think, difficulty walking down the steps and he took hold of my hand and we walked down together and that was a most thrilling occasion for me.

• **Are age-old traditions relevant to life today?**
• **Which roles in professional life do you think are lonely? Would you do Betty Bothroyd's job?**

The style of British politics

"All government, indeed every human benefit and enjoyment, every virtue, and every prudent act, is founded on compromise and barter," said the 18th century politician and philosopher Edmund Burke. This would perhaps do well as a maxim for political life in Britain. In general, the British are low on ideology and high on pragmatism. Within large political parties such as Labour or Conservative there are many different opinions, and the only way to agree on a policy is to compromise.

Uncompromising politicians have not done well in Britain. The parties on the extreme right and extreme left of the political spectrum are remarkable by their absence or by their small size. Sir Oswald Mosley led a group called the British Union of Fascists who used to dress up in Nazi-style uniforms in the 1930s. His anti-Jewish demonstrations got some support amongst unemployed workers in the east of London. The National Front (NF), with anti-immigration as its only policy, started to enjoy a degree of electoral success in the 1970s, getting up to 17 per cent of the vote in a few local council elections. It has since disappeared, but you can still occasionally see the initials NF written on walls in inner cities around the country. The NF was succeeded by the British National Party (BNP), which managed to have one candidate elected to a local council in 1993. Like other such groups, the BNP seems to thrive more in cyberspace than in real life – it has a website which concentrates exclusively on two issues: free speech (for people like its members), and what it calls anti-white racism.

The British Communist Party (CP) was set up in 1920, but never achieved what a workers' party needs most of all – mass membership. The majority of those sympathetic to communist ideas stayed with the Labour Party. In the radical times of the late 1960s, the CP and numerous other factions such as the International Marxist Group enjoyed a surge of popularity; but it was not maintained. After the collapse of the Russian communists, the CP in Britain went through the same crisis as similar parties throughout the world. In 1991, it changed its name to the Democratic Left, and has been rather quiet ever since.

Sir Oswald Mosley taking an oath of allegiance to the Italian fascist movement.

The most consistent and successful leftist group has for many years been the Socialist Workers Party (SWP), which is particularly strong among trade-unionists and sells its newspaper, *Socialist Worker*, on the streets. It receives very little attention from the media, but it is notable that at every demonstration for human rights or against racism and fascism the crowds carry *Socialist Worker* posters.

The smaller parties

The largest of the minority parties is the Liberal Democrats. They originate from the Liberal Party which formed the government for much of the 19th century. From 1914, they were replaced on the left by the Labour Party, and have occupied an

- **What attracts supporters to political extremes, such as fascism?**
- **Is the style of politics in your country the same as that in Britain?**

uncomfortable position in between Labour and the Conservatives ever since. Actually their policies – capitalism but with good social services and strong local government – have become more and more popular; but they have not benefited, as the big parties have moved onto their ground. Their constant problem has been the electoral system: MPs are elected on a first-past-the-post basis in each constituency, so that the third largest party rarely succeeds. It can appear very unfair: in 1983, the Liberal Democrats got 26 per cent of the vote in the general election, but won only 23 seats out of 650. Consequently, much of the Liberal Democrats' energy has been devoted to campaigning for a system of proportional representation (PR).

David Taylor, Principal Speaker of the Green Party, campaigning in the 1997 election.

The Green Party suffers from the same disadvantage as the Liberal Democrats – it cannot hope to get a candidate elected under the present system. In the European elections of 1989, two million people voted for the British Green Party but it did not win a single seat. The party has declined since that time, partly because of the frustration caused by such results and partly because of internal divisions. It has also lost support as the big parties have adopted, or pretended to adopt, green policies. It did, however, win a couple of seats in the European parliamentary elections of 1999, which were run on a form of proportional representation.

The political landscape in Wales and Scotland is always very different from that in England. The Conservatives do badly in both: they are perceived very much as an English party. Labour do well, but they are challenged by nationalist parties – *Plaid Cymru* and the Scottish Nationalist Party (SNP). These parties have campaigned for many years for more autonomy, and their work was rewarded in 1999, when the Scottish Parliament and the Welsh Assembly were established. The SNP is more interested in full-blown independence than the Welsh are, and has caused some panic about the break-up of the United Kingdom. Both parties are keen on the European Union as a counter weight to English influence.

The situation in Northern Ireland is unique. The normal patterns of politics just do not apply, and the mainland British parties have no role to play. The parties in Northern Ireland are split first and foremost on sectarian lines: the division between Catholics and Protestants. On both sides, some parties are more peaceful and compromising, others more violent. In favour of a united Ireland there is the Social Democratic and Labour Party (led by John Hume, who has worked hard to bring about a peaceful settlement), and *Sinn Féin* (led by Gerry Adams), the political wing of the paramilitary Provisional IRA (Irish Republican Army). On the other side, wanting to keep Northern Ireland in the United Kingdom, are numerous Protestant parties including the Ulster Unionists (led by David Trimble) and the Democratic Unionist Party.

The big two

When Britain changes its voting system, the political map will be dramatically re-drawn. But for almost 100 years Britain has had, in effect, a two-party state, with Labour and the Conservatives taking turns in government.

Labour, as its name suggests, originated as a working-class party. At the end of the 19th century, the Liberal Party was generally in favour of social reform, but in reality it did not represent workers and trade unionists. So the trade unions set up their own party in 1906, and in 1924, the Labour Party formed its first government. It has been in and out of power ever since. The trade union links have always been at the heart of the party: they have provided most of the money, they have sponsored MPs,

• Can social development occur without political change?
• In Britain people do not like to say who they vote for. Is this the same in your country? Why?

and they have been the source of policies and attitudes. Most importantly, the unions have politicised large groups of workers. Traditionally, Labour has been strong in the areas where the unions were strong, in the industrial parts of Scotland, Wales and the north of England.

Revolutionaries have always said that Labour is just another capitalist party, incapable, when in government, of doing anything different from the Conservatives. But actually it has a record of some very significant achievements: the National Health Service, National Insurance for pensions and benefits, the Race Relations Acts, equal pay for women, safety at work legislation, and a minimum wage in 1998.

The Conservatives have a longer history as a party than Labour. They were a continuation of the Tory Party which began in the 17th century, and in fact the Conservatives are still known by the nickname Tories today. They have always been supporters of the status quo, of tradition, and of the hierarchy of wealth and power. But over the last 150 years, they have shifted their allegiance from the aristocracy to the commercial middle classes. They obtain their funds from rich supporters in big business. In modern times, they have managed to attract voters and members from working-class backgrounds, who like their strict crime and immigration policies, and see themselves as moving into the middle class.

What have been the major policy differences between Labour and the Conservatives? It is interesting to look back to the mid-1980s, a time when the identities of the two parties were very clear and distinct. The Conservatives were in power. Mrs Thatcher was privatising everything in sight, trade unions were losing their legal rights, and the coal industry was being shut down. Income tax was being cut, and public spending was falling. Local authorities (which were mostly Labour) were being weakened, and a local poll tax, which even the poor would pay, was on the agenda. The British government supported the white regime in South Africa, America was allowed to base nuclear weapons in Britain, which in turn was building up its own nuclear arsenal. The Labour Party was in opposition, and opposed almost everything the Tory government did. Labour favoured nationalised industry and defended the coal miners. It fought to preserve trade union protection. It preferred a high-tax, high-spending system, and it believed in local authorities and bitterly opposed the poll tax. It supported Nelson Mandela and had a non-nuclear defence policy.

The Tory poll tax was highly unpopular.

Through the 1980s, Mrs Thatcher successfully waged a war against socialism and collectivism. The electorate chose the Conservatives in four consecutive general elections and Labour seemed consigned to the dustbin of history. In the end, Labour realised that it would have to move to the centre if it was ever to be elected again, and that is exactly what it did. The party decided that nuclear bombs were a good thing after all, that low taxes made sense, and that perhaps privatisation had been a success. The new leader, Neil Kinnock, started the process. But after another election defeat in 1992, Labour finally dropped all its old socialist style. It got rid of Kinnock with his Welsh accent and working-class background, and chose as its leader a public-school educated lawyer with a posh voice and a conservative upbringing: Tony Blair. The transformation was complete, and for the first time the Labour leader was more upper class than the Conservative leader. Predictably, Blair has done all in his power to cut Labour away from its trade-union roots.

- **Is your political system based on two main parties, or on coalitions?**
- **Do you feel that politics affects your everyday life?**

New Prime Minister Tony Blair after winning the election of May 2nd 1997.

While the Tories watched Labour adopt their policies, they managed to make a series of mistakes and suffered from the resulting bad publicity, from the BSE crisis to sex and financial scandals. As a result, they lost the 1997 election by a landslide: Labour with 419 seats, the Conservatives with only 165.

Political issues

British politics have changed in character, but they have not come to a complete full stop. Obviously there are always arguments, but these are as often within parties as between them. Europe is one such issue. When Britain joined the European Economic Community (EEC) 30 years ago, Labour was against and the Conservatives for membership. Since then, things have changed and the balance is now the other way round, with the keenest Eurosceptics on the Conservative side. In reality, Labour is divided on the issue too, especially among ordinary voters in the country. It is a question which causes more passionate debate than any other.

The question of the voting system does not go away. All the smaller parties continue their campaign for proportional representation, which would give them far more seats in Parliament. Labour has shown signs of favouring a change to that system, but it is very hard for a party in power to do something which might lose it that power. However, a semi-proportional system was introduced for the Scottish and Welsh elections of 1999 and the Euro elections of the same year.

The degree of autonomy of Wales and Scotland continues to be hotly debated, even within the nationalist parties. Educational methods have (rather strangely) become a regular topic of political discussion, with members of all parties giving their views on how to teach children reading and Maths.

Green issues are likely to be ever more important as political action on them becomes necessary. Genetically modified (GM) foods have been an issue, as the government has to decide whether to allow testing, production and sales. Many other major challenges, such as climate change and nuclear waste, keep returning to the political arena.

Both sides in the old political divide appear to have admitted defeat on one crucial question: how to deal with poverty and social exclusion. Socialists used to think that benefits would solve the problem. Conservatives thought that the wealth created by capital would trickle down to the poor. No party today is very confident about a solution.

According to a 1999 government report, one in three children in Britain will be born into poverty.

- What is political independence?
- What is liberalism? How does it differ from socialism?

[◦ ⊡] An interview with ...
the Right Honourable Dafydd Wigley, MP

Dafydd Wigley is a Member of Parliament at Westminster and the President of Plaid Cymru or Party of Wales. The Welsh nationalist party has long campaigned for devolution of political power, and for the three million Welsh people to have more rights and responsibilities for their own social and political affairs. The process began with the setting up, in May 1999, of a new Welsh Assembly. But Mr Wigley says he wants more.

How would you describe the recent political changes in the UK?

I think that we're moving into a new political era, not only in terms of the structural changes wrought around the Parliament of Scotland, the Assembly in Northern Ireland and the National Assembly of Wales, also the changes in London and possibly in the regions of England to follow. But there are also changes in terms of the reaction of the electorate to the Labour Government. New Labour has taken over a centrist role leaving a vacuum to the left, which in Wales we have moved in to fill, in part. Therefore, I believe that there is a sea change taking place. I also believe that the future politics of these islands is going to be largely determined by the European profile. Scotland and Wales make sense as units of government in a European context. If we're moving towards a United States of Europe, then Scotland and Wales would be very unhappy if we weren't constituent states within that United States of Europe, and having that framework makes it easier for us to talk in terms of self-government and autonomy where we're not needing to talk about customs posts and borders.

But will these changes really affect the United Kingdom in the near future?

Yes, yes, it's happening already. In pragmatic terms, it will affect the UK in policy delivery. Just to take three or four examples that are already happening in the first weeks of the establishment of the Scottish Parliament and the National Assembly of Wales. In Scotland, issues such as tuition fees; in Wales, issues such as beef-on-the-bone, CJD [Creutzfeldt-Jakob Disease] and BSE. In terms of the agenda in Wales, we're going to move forward to move back to free eye tests and dental checks – something which London had moved away from. If that happens in Wales,

---

- **Do you think devolution is a good idea? Or are some issues best left to a centralised government?**
- **Should a foreign government rule the lives of other countries' citizens?**

it inevitably is going to beg the question: "Well, if you can have them in Wales, why the hell aren't we having them in England?" Therefore, there is a movement in the balance, in the fulcrum of politics and those parts of these islands that have had a more radical agenda down the years; instead of having to wait for decade after decade to have a window of opportunity in Westminster, are going to be able to do it for themselves. Then people in England will ask the question: "Okay, why don't we?"

But is that really fair then, that the Welsh Assembly and the Scottish Parliament should be really influencing the lives of people in England?
Well, it's no less fair than that London should have told Wales and Scotland what to do down two or three centuries. The people of Wales and Scotland will not be doing it because they want the people of England to follow. They'll be doing it because it's what's right and wanted within our own communities. And if people in England see that and say for themselves: "Well yes, why not? – best of luck to them."

Is your party satisfied with the new arrangements for Wales?
No. The arrangements that we've got for Wales are substantially weaker than those for Scotland. Our National Assembly has no primary law-making powers and no tax-faring powers and that has to change. It's not going to change immediately. The first four-year period we're going to have to make it work on the basis that we had approved in the referendum by a hair's breadth. But when the assembly gets stuck into issues, and people from other political parties – not my own – who see that we can't deliver the goods in terms of social programmes, educational programmes, employment programmes, they will want more power to do so. It's human nature and it's, I believe, totally inevitable that Wales will have the same powers as the Scottish Parliament within the next five years.

Why do you think the Welsh Assembly has been given fewer powers than the Scottish Parliament? They often say that Wales has been kowtowing to England for so much longer than Scotland.
That is part of the psychological framework of the Welsh electorate that since 1536, we have been subject to a Union. And it was, in fact, not an Act of Union, but an Act of Incorporation, where the words were that Wales was united, incorporated and annexed and that very Act proscribed the use of the Welsh language, which was banned.
And the psychology that develops out of that is the psychology of a conquered people. It takes time to overcome that. And we want to overcome it in a constructive manner, where we are gradually rebuilding the confidence of people to do things for themselves rather than expecting other people to do it for them. What's really exciting since this project has been moving forward is first of all, the commercial and industrial part of Wales has been very much more positive towards it, people who are prepared to put their money where their mouths are; and secondly, that in Cardiff, our capital city, where people actually voted "no" in the referendum, that they have been rapidly changing their minds and saying that the project can be beneficial and exciting for them.

But how far do you think this process of devolution will really go – this project, as you refer to it?
It'll go as far and as fast as the people of Wales want and that may or may not be slower than the people of Scotland. I believe that it has to be in a European context. I believe that 19th century sovereignty is not what we're talking about. We're talking about getting the greatest degree of autonomy within a United Europe. I haven't the least interest in having a Welsh army, navy and airforce. For as long as they remain London functions, they're London functions. At some stage they'll become European functions. I am concerned about getting the right social and educational policies for our people.

- Why do you think Mr Wigley is not concerned about having a Welsh army?
- How does the political set-up in your country affect your life?

Europe

"Britain has lost an empire and not found a new role," said the American Dean Acheson in 1969.
The difficult transition from the position of great world power to ordinary, middle-sized country. A certain amount of indecision and confusion has perhaps been inevitable. The British have been faced with some hard choices, and have sometimes responded simply by not making up their minds.

Britain enters the Common Market: Prime Minister Edward Heath signs the Treaty, Brussels, in 1972.

Britain's closest links at the beginning of the new millennium are obviously with Europe. Britain signed the Single European Act at Maastricht, it elects members to the European Parliament in Strasbourg, its citizens are subject to European Union (EU) laws, and more than 50 per cent of trade is with EU members. There is free movement of labour – in fact, there are 450,000 young EU citizens living and working in London alone.
But membership of the EU is still not the answer to all Britain's foreign policy questions. Europe remains a trading partnership, not a military alliance. The member states are close friends, but Britain likes to feel free to go off and do things on its own.

British entry to the European Economic Community (EEC) was messy, and perhaps showed the way things were to continue. Although keen on the idea of the EEC from the beginning, Britain did not join the founding members in 1957. Soon, the Prime Minister, Harold Macmillan, saw how successful the Common Market was, and changed his mind. He applied to join in 1961, but France's President de Gaulle said "non", because British links with the USA and the Commonwealth were still

too strong. Britain finally joined in 1973, but public opinion on membership has been divided ever since. Generally, the political centre is in favour, while the right and the left are against. The right is nationalistic, and fears that the sovereignty and identity of Britain are threatened by a new super-state. The left considers the EU to be a creation of big business, designed to make it easier to move capital around, keep wages low and undermine the economies of poorer countries.

Whatever the differences of opinion within the country, Britain has consistently been against greater European integration, and in favour of enlargement: the addition to the EU of Eastern European countries, to produce a bigger and looser community.

The Commonwealth

Britain is unlikely, however, to lose its unique network of links with the countries of the Commonwealth. At the time of joining Europe, it looked as though Britain was turning its back on

• **What political, economic and social links does your country have with others?**
• **Do you think countries should integrate, or retain their individuality?**

the Commonwealth, which was expected by many to wither away. But the organisation has shown a surprising capacity to survive and reinvent itself.

A major part of Britain's modern history has been the withdrawal from the Empire. It started with a bang in 1947 when the Jewel in the Crown of the Empire, India, became independent. Then the union flag came down in one country after the other: Sri Lanka, Sudan, Cyprus, Jamaica, Kenya, Singapore, Papua New Guinea, Zimbabwe and many more. The final act of the drama was played out in 1997, when Hong Kong was handed back to the Chinese.

The Commonwealth started with the independent, predominantly white countries, such as Australia, which had been part of the Empire. As de-colonisation took place, most of the new states decided to join this club. Although the Queen was the symbolic head of the Commonwealth, Britain was, in fact, often obliged to accept the will of all the other members. In 1961, for example, South Africa under its apartheid regime was driven out of the Commonwealth by the hostility of many African and Asian countries, against Britain's wishes. Increasingly, the British government felt uncomfortable dealing with all these countries: they were troublesome, full of ideas of their own, and made the British feel guilty. Mrs Thatcher in particular seemed to have no idea what to say to them. Without Britain at the centre of the trading network, each region – Africa, the Caribbean, South-East Asia – was trading more locally. There did not seem much point in the Commonwealth any more.

South Africa rejoined in 1994, immediately after the election of President Mandela. That event seemed to give new life to the organisation: it was partly the pressure from Commonwealth peoples that led to the end of white rule. Since then, the profile of the Commonwealth has become ever higher. Teams of observers have been sent to various member states to check the conduct of elections. In 1995, Nigeria was suspended from membership because of human rights abuses; it has since rejoined. In the same year two new countries joined, Cameroon and Mozambique, the latter being the first non-English-speaking member (it is an ex-Portuguese colony). Rwanda, Yemen and the Palestine National Authority have expressed an interest in joining. Modern business people are keen on networking, making a wide circle of useful contacts. It may be that countries around the world are looking to the Commonwealth as an opportunity for international networking.

The last Governor of Hong Kong, Chris Patten, and Prince Charles prepare to hand the colony back to China.

- **Do you think white rule was/is necessary in certain countries? Why?**
- **What connections do you have with the rest of the world?**

NATO and the UN

Britain's principal military focus is NATO, the North Atlantic Treaty Organisation, which started in 1949 and includes the USA, Canada and most of the Western European countries. This alliance is very much dominated by its biggest member, the United States, and it was not easy for Britain to join and give up a long tradition of independence. Britain accepted a secondary role, and allowed the USA to use the country for its military bases, including, for a time, nuclear weapons facilities.

Britain has been involved in the United Nations (UN) since it was created in 1945. The British rather hoped at the time that, since they themselves were now too weak for the job, the UN would police the world, including the British Empire. It never worked quite like that, and in fact, as the colonies gained

their independence, they joined the UN and were able to vote against the richer, more powerful countries. Britain often found itself in a small minority, against the rest of the world; for example, only Britain, the USA and France voted against a nuclear test ban in 1987.

It is because of its nuclear weapons that Britain has a permanent seat on the UN Security Council, along with the United States, Russia, France and China. There are also ten non-permanent members of the Council. Decisions are based on a nine-out-of-fifteen majority vote, but permanent members have the right to veto proposals. Since the early days of the UN, Britain's international status has declined significantly. It now seems inappropriate that Britain should still have a permanent seat. Both Germany and Japan have applied for permanent seats, and it is likely that in the long run Britain will lose this privileged position.

Britain's new battle tank, Challenger 2

• **What are your views on nuclear weapons?**
• **If all arms factories were shut down, would the number of wars decrease?**

Arms and armed forces

Britain has about 200,000 men and women in the army, navy and airforce. This is a lower figure than many countries of similar size. But these are 100 per cent professional forces, made up of paid volunteers. Many other countries have a conscription system, while Britain abolished conscription in 1960.

Military spending has gone down steadily over the last 30 years, from a level which the country could not really afford. It has taken a long time for Britain to accept that it cannot be a super power. Today, the figure is around 3 per cent of Gross Domestic Product (GDP), still more than most European partners or Japan, but much less than many other countries.

A major component of this spending is nuclear weapons. Britain has over 50 American Trident missiles with British-made warheads, which are carried around the oceans in nuclear submarines. This is, of course, a massively expensive operation. The function of these weapons of mass destruction was to deter the Soviet Union from attacking Western Europe. Now that Britain is on friendly terms with Russia, it is very hard to see the point of the weapons.

Conventional (non-nuclear) forces have been involved in a number of conflicts around the world in recent years. Sadly, one constant theme has been the confrontation in Northern Ireland. British troops have been there almost continuously since the early 1970s, either keeping the peace between Catholics and Protestants, or maintaining British colonial rule, depending on your point of view. In 1982, Britain went to war with Argentina over the Falkland Islands (or Malvinas) in the south Atlantic. In 1991, British forces joined the Americans in the Gulf War against Iraq. From 1994, Britain provided a large proportion of the UN peace-keeping forces in Bosnia, and of the NATO troops in Kosovo after the 1999 war with Serbia.

The combination of a comparatively large army and a strong engineering industry means that Britain

An anti-nuclear protester is hauled aboard a dinghy as the Trident submarine HMS Victorious *cruises down the River Clyde.*

makes a lot of weapons. The British arms industry is an important part of the national economy, employing thousands of people and making huge sums of money from export sales. One single project, Yamamah, with the Saudi Arabian air force, has been worth almost £7 billion, and it employs 1,000 British workers in Saudi Arabia. British Aerospace is one of the largest world's largest arms manufacturers.

Supplying weapons, of course, does much to increase political influence. Apart from anything else, the buyers have to come back for spare parts: tanks and fighter aircraft need a great deal of servicing. Providing military training has a similar effect; officers who come to Britain for courses make friends and develop a positive attitude towards the country. Personnel from about 90 countries receive training in Britain.

Not everyone is happy about this arms dealing and training. Many of the countries Britain supplies are undemocratic, and some have very poor records on human rights. When they buy weapons, they always claim that these will be used for defence – that is, against foreign countries who attack. But quite often it turns out that the weapons are used within the country to suppress political opposition. Indonesia, for example, used British aircraft and weapons against the population of East Timor, an island which it had invaded and occupied.

- Is the spread of British culture a good thing?
- Are we becoming one world?

The USA

Relations with the United States started very badly indeed, with the war of Independence at the end of the 18th century, when the Americans defeated the British. But in the 20th century the two countries were close allies, first of all in both World Wars, then in the Cold War, and finally in a sort of international policing role. It has often been called a special relationship, although generally this has meant Britain doing whatever the USA wanted it to. Britain has given military support on several occasions, and has even more often given moral support. Britain was the only country to allow American planes to use its

The Blairs welcome the Clintons to a G8 meeting held in Birmingham.

airports on their way to bomb Libya in 1986, and the only country to support the American invasion of Panama in 1989. Similarly, the USA gave some helpful information to Britain during the Falklands War.

The relationship is not always special. The British did not really share the Americans' bitter anti-Communist feeling during the Cold War. Neither do they support Israel with the same unconditional enthusiasm. The British have resented American attempts to get involved in Northern Ireland, and been angry when Irish Americans have sent money to the IRA. There was a difficult moment in 1983 when the USA invaded the Caribbean island of Grenada to remove a left-wing government. This was an ex-British colony, but the Americans did not even tell the British that they were invading. More recently, Britain has been opening up commercial and tourist links with Cuba, in defiance of the American blockade.

In many ways Gibraltar is still very British.

Spain and The Rock

Britain and Spain are both members of the EU, which in a sense guarantees good relations. Lots of Spanish tourists come to Britain, and even more British tourists go to Spain; in fact, many British people have gone to live along the sunny Spanish coasts. There is, however, one little thing which makes for strained relations between the two countries – Gibraltar. This rock (it is often called The Rock) is just five kilometres long and one kilometre wide, but its importance is out of all proportion to its size. It dominates the straits which join the Mediterranean to the Atlantic, giving it a key strategic value. The English captured it from Spain in 1704, and have hung onto it ever since. Spain, quite understandably, wants Gibraltar back, and closed its border with The Rock between 1969 and 1985. The dispute bubbles along quietly while the two countries get on with everyday life. People forget about it for long periods and then the dispute surfaces again, as in 1999 when Spanish fishermen temporarily blocked the border. The people on The Rock have voted to remain British, so it is difficult to see how the problem will be resolved.

- **Should outside states interfere with other countries' wars? Who has the right to fight in a war?**
- **What relationship does your country have with the USA?**

Ireland

The Republic of Ireland gained independence from Britain in 1922. People in the new Republic were unhappy about the status of the six counties in the north of Ireland, which remained part of the UK under the name Northern Ireland. The constitution of the Republic of Ireland claimed the north as part of their country, so inevitably there was disagreement with Britain on this issue. Nevertheless, there were close links between the two countries: many Irish people came to Britain to live and work, and they have always had the right to vote on the mainland.

In 1985, there was a historic Anglo-Irish Agreement, in which both sides agreed to work together for a solution to the Northern Ireland question. Since then, co-operation between the two governments has been at the heart of the peace process.

Republican murals can be seen on many buildings in west Belfast.

Ayatollah Khomeini reviled the Western powers who had influenced Iran for so long.

The Middle East

Britain has taken an interest in the Middle East since the end of the 19th century; at first because of the strategically vital Suez Canal and later because of oil. At various times many states in the region were brought under British control or influence: Egypt, Iraq, Jordan, Palestine, Kuwait and the smaller Gulf states. The last to gain full independence were Bahrain, Qatar and the United Arab Emirates as late as 1971. Even outside her own sphere of influence, Britain has often intervened to make sure that oil supplies were secure and profitable. She did not like the Iranian government in the 1950s, because it was nationalising the oil industry. So, in co-operation with the Americans, the British helped to put their friend the Shah into power as a dictator. This kind of interference often leads to trouble. When the Shah was overthrown by the popular revolution of Ayatollah Khomeini in 1979, relations between Iran and Britain were very bad for a long time; they have only recently started to recover.

Today, Britain maintains strong commercial links with the area. British oil companies still operate there, and Middle Eastern countries are among the biggest customers for British weapons.

- **What conflicts has your country experienced? What were the reasons?**
- **Is world peace possible? Is war always inevitable?**

Free trade

For a very long time Britain has been a trading nation – importing, exporting, investing abroad and receiving foreign investment. The Scottish philosopher, Adam Smith, argued in *The Wealth of Nations* (1776) that protectionism, putting up trade barriers between countries, was bad for everyone in the end. His ideas became the accepted orthodoxy, and during the following 100 years Britain got rid of its protective tariffs, and embraced free trade. The national economy is still mainly based on free markets.

On board an oil production platform in the North Sea

One change in recent times is the list of Britain's trading partners. Joining the EU has meant a major move away from old markets and suppliers in the Commonwealth (members of Britain's ex-empire), and towards new markets closer at hand, though the USA is just as important as ever. Britain imports most goods from Germany and the USA (12–14 per cent each of the total), then France (10 per cent) and the Netherlands (7–8 per cent). The top four export destinations are the same countries in the same order. About half of Britain's visible trade is now with the EU.

There have been other changes in every sector of the British economy: in primary, secondary and tertiary industries.

Natural resources

Primary industries are those that exploit raw materials: agriculture, fishing, mining, oil extraction and so on. Agriculture is a small part of the economy, employing less than 2 per cent of the workforce, and producing less than 2 per cent of the Gross Domestic Product (GDP). The low level of employment in agriculture is explained by a high level of efficiency: British farms are big (though not by the standards of those in the USA or Australia) and highly mechanised. This efficiency has a downside. Parts of East Anglia have been turned into vast, featureless food-producing units, with an enormous reduction in wildlife populations.

Fishing has always been a natural activity for an island population. But this sector, too, employs only a fraction of the number of people it used to, due to increased mechanisation and bigger boats with smaller crews. However, there are other limiting factors which mean that the British fishing fleet only catches two-thirds of the fish eaten by the nation. Membership of the EU has obliged Britain to allow European partners to fish closer to British coasts and share the fish in nearby waters. Iceland has prevented foreign boats from fishing in its waters, which were important for the British. In addition to this, stocks have been depleted by pollution and over-fishing: there simply are not enough fish to meet the demand. Workers in the industry complain bitterly about quotas (official limits on the numbers which can be fished within a certain period), but if the industry is not carefully controlled, there will be no future for the workers and no fish left.

Cheap, available energy was a major contributor to the industrial revolution 200 years ago, and it is just as important today. Britain has more energy resources than any other EU country. Previously, that energy came from coal: at its peak in 1913, more than one million miners were employed in the coal industry.

- **What kind of economic issues are you aware of in your country?**
- **How do these affect your everyday life?**

Most of the mines have now been shut down: today about 18,000 miners are employed. However, since the 1970s huge quantities of gas and oil have been extracted from fields in the North Sea. The discovery of these fields was a stroke of luck for Britain, whose economy was, in other respects, doing rather poorly. Britain is now the world's sixth largest producer of oil, with an average output of over two million barrels per day, some of it exported. (Most of the oil comes from Scottish waters, and this has been a factor in Scotland's calls for independence.)

Manufacturing and services

The term secondary refers to manufacturing and construction, and tertiary to service industries. It is in the balance between these two industries that one of the most striking changes has occurred in the British economy. At one time one of the world's greatest manufacturing centres, Britain has largely given up producing goods in favour of other kinds of economic activity. In 1983, the country imported more manufactured goods than it produced for the first time since the industrial revolution.
As manufacturing declined, so the service industries expanded. Many people have been worried by this change: how can it be economically viable to stop building ships and open restaurants instead?
But tourism, transport and telecommunications are all important growth areas: in 1997, 25.5 million overseas visitors came to Britain.

Call centres make 24-hour banking services possible.

Financial services such as accountancy, insurance and banking are very big business too. Britain is now the world's second largest service exporter at 6 per cent of the total – ahead of both France and Germany, and just behind the USA. The contribution of service industries and their invisible exports means that the balance of trade (between imports and exports) is just about even, and the country is not heading for economic disaster – at least not in the short term.

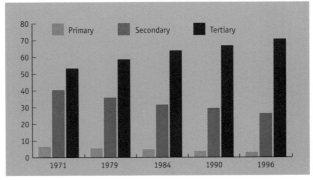

Percentage of total employment per sector of the economy

The loss of factory-based jobs has increased the old north-south divide – the disparity in wealth between the rich south of England and the less prosperous north of England and Scotland.
The heart of the prosperous zone is London itself, and in the heart of London is the headquarters of the successful financial services sector – the City. This is a confusing term: the whole of London is a city, but the City, originally surrounded by Roman walls and spelt with a capital C, refers to the approximate square mile of offices and banks around the Bank of England. This financial centre has expanded east into the developing docklands area of Canary Wharf, where 25,000 people now work. The City became globally important when Lloyds Register of Shipping started in 1760. Today, the City is one of the world's biggest financial centres, and handles 59 per cent of international equity (share) trading. In 1999, Peter Levene the lord mayor of London, said:
"The number of people involved in the financial services industry in London is greater than the whole population of Frankfurt."
Another huge change took place in the 1980s, under Margaret Thatcher's Conservative government:

- **Does increased mechanisation always result in more unemployment?**
- **In what ways do service industries contribute to the economy?**

the privatisation of certain state-owned companies. Previous Labour governments had been keen to nationalise parts of the economy – in some cases (as with the car industry), simply to save them from disappearing. This sort of interventionism was anathema to Margaret Thatcher and her free market philosophy. So she sold off car makers such as Jaguar, the steel and shipbuilding industries, the defence specialists British Aerospace, and the state-owned bus companies, including long-distance coach lines and local city buses. The Conservative Government also denationalised enterprises which were state owned in most countries (other than the USA): the telephones, railways and the national airlines, including British Airways. Finally, there was the unpopular sale of the public utilities: the gas, electricity and water suppliers became private companies, with their prices controlled by government regulators.

A fading economy?

Privatisation has caught on around the world. Margaret Thatcher and British business people are often given the credit for starting the trend (although in reality they were only following the American model). But in other respects the British economy is seen as a story of long-term decline interrupted by occasional bursts of recovery. Will Hutton, an economist, recently talked of "a fading, middle-sized economy protesting its Great Power ambitions" in his book, *The State of the Nation.*

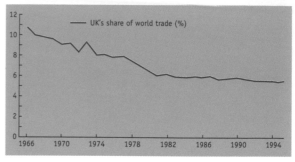

The UK's share of world trade in manufacturing

Two hundred years ago the British economy seemed invincible. Great wealth had been established from a protectionist market within its Empire, from the slave trade and colonial resources, and from the exploitation of workers and children. Using the capital built up in this way, and the huge wealth of the land-owning aristocracy, Britain managed to have its industrial revolution before any other country. By the time of the Great Exhibition of 1851, after decades of staggering economic growth, Britain was way ahead of its international competitors. Britain's railways, shipbuilding, and its coal, iron and textile production were all world leaders. But by the early 1870s, Germany and the USA were challenging this economic power, and Britain has never recovered its position. From having the world's highest GDP per capita, it fell to third place by 1913 and today hovers around seventeenth place. In 1913, it still had a 32 per cent share of the world's manufactured exports; today the figure is nearer to 5 per cent.

The reasons for economic decline have long been a

The British Department at the Great Exhibition of 1851, organised by Prince Albert to publicise the country's achievements.

• **Does free market trade exist in your country? Is it a good thing?**
• **Should prices of utilities, such as gas, be government controlled?**

Mapping genes on a chromosone at a Glaxo Wellcome research centre.

Risks and opportunities

For the British economy today the picture is a mixture of positive and negative. On the plus side, inflation seems to be under control at around 2.6 per cent, especially when compared to its high point in the 1970s of over 25 per cent per year! Productivity used to be rather low, but in recent years it has grown faster than in most countries. There is a great deal of inward investment: American, Japanese, Korean, French and German companies have bought British firms or set up their own factories. Some consider inward investment as a failure, with the issue of foreign control; but this must be weighed against outward investment. Britain is also a major investor overseas, and many British firms buy foreign companies. There are now no major British-owned car manufacturers, but British Petroleum (BP) recently bought Amoco, one of the largest American oil companies. The British mobile phone company, Vodaphone, paid £62 billion for a giant American rival; and, surprisingly, Burger King restaurants are owned by a British group, Diageo.

Pharmaceutical companies, such as Glaxo Wellcome, are world leaders; and SmithKline Beecham, which expects sales of over £614 million from a forthcoming diabetes drug Avandia, employs around 4,000 people at factories in Scotland and Sussex. The financial services are a strong point, as are creative industries such as publishing, TV and especially pop music: revenue from film and television exports (such as *Four Weddings and a Funeral*) has been increasing at around 7 per cent a year. In fact, in 1999 *Shakespeare in Love* and *Hilary and Jackie*, both widely acclaimed British films, were awarded certificates praising their British nature by the Department of Culture. Although *Shakespeare in Love* was financed by an American company, Miramax, much of the labour,

favourite topic of debate in Britain. It is a complex subject and several factors are commonly blamed. Not enough investment: industries have slowly but surely fallen behind the competition as they failed to take on or develop new methods and machinery. Short-termism and speculation: the money men in the City who make the investment decisions have looked for immediate profits worldwide, not the long-term development of local industry. Labour problems: in the 1960s and 70s, management and workers were often in conflict, and Britain, together with France and Italy, became associated with strikes and other types of industrial action, although this is no longer the case today. Welfare and military spending: in the middle years of the 20th century Britain had a more expensive health and welfare system than its competitors and, though defence commitments have diminished since the end of the Empire, funding for the military has remained high. Education: schools and universities have not given technology the attention and status it needs.

All these factors have probably played a part in the country's economic decline, but there is one other general point to remember: Britain started ahead of its rivals in the industrial race, and it was natural and inevitable that others would catch up and overtake.

• **Are your country's industries mainly privatised or state-owned? Do you agree with privatisation?**
• **Should more money be spent on health and education or on military spending?**

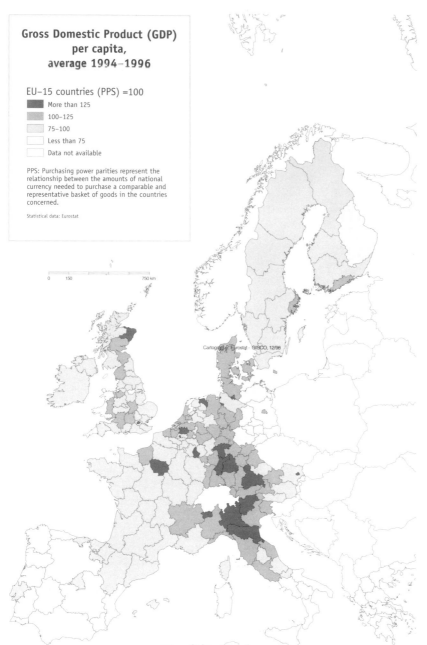

Gross Domestic Product (GDP) per capita, average 1994–1996

EU–15 countries (PPS) =100

- More than 125
- 100–125
- 75–100
- Less than 75
- Data not available

PPS: Purchasing power parities represent the relationship between the amounts of national currency needed to purchase a comparable and representative basket of goods in the countries concerned.

Statistical data: Eurostat

Cartography: Eurostat - GISCO, 12/98

0   150   750 km

Unemployment was, until recently, a major problem (as in most EU countries) with 10 per cent of the population remaining jobless for most of the past 15 years. Recent economic improvement, helped by a devaluation of the British pound in 1992, has reduced the unemployment rate to below 5 per cent for the first time in 20 years.

Among those with jobs, Britain has a relatively deregulated and flexible labour market, with trade unions weakened by tough laws introduced by the Conservatives, but left in place by the Labour government. However, whilst this flexibility may help to create employment, such jobs tend to be low paid and are often temporary contracts, leading to growing economic inequality and uncertainty for many working people. A minimum wage (£3.60 for those aged 22 or over) introduced in 1999 may help to prevent very low levels of pay.

One interesting aspect of Britain's long-term economic position is revealed on the economic map of Europe (left). The areas with the highest levels of prosperity are concentrated around the centre of the map, in Germany and northern Italy, while the periphery is doing noticeably

talent and locations were British, with four-fifths of the budget being spent in the UK.

On the minus side, manufacturing shows little sign of re-establishing itself as the powerhouse of the economy. In most areas the technology has fallen behind that of Britain's main competitors.

less well – although London is one notable exception. Some economists feel that Britain's behaviour as a peripheral, rather reluctant, member of the EU (as when Britain failed to join the first wave of monetary union in the 1990s) has contributed to the economic problems.

- **Which countries have relationships with ex-colonial powers? Why do these links still exist today?**
- **In which ways is flexibility in employment good or bad?**

Women in the workforce

For a long time the number of women in paid work has been high in Britain. Right through the 19th century women went out to jobs in factories and offices. But that did not mean that they worked on equal terms with men – far from it. Women finally got the vote in 1918 (subject to certain restrictions), after repeated campaigns by the suffragette movement in the 19th century. But it was not until 1975 that employers' unfair treatment of women was outlawed by the Equal Pay Act and the Sex Discrimination Act. The latter also protected women

Women have gradually broken down traditional barriers in the workplace.

in education, housing and other aspects of life. The legal changes have been reflected in social life, with women asserting themselves in all sorts of ways, and challenging traditional gender roles. Unemployment among women is now lower than among men.

However, there is still a very clear-cut division between the sexes in some areas. The sciences, for example, are male dominated: only 5 per cent of university physics teachers are women; and around 20 per cent of women hold positions in government and parliament – approximately half as many as in Scandinavian countries. In most areas of work, women are still not getting the best jobs.

There is often said to be a glass ceiling, an invisible barrier to promotion. This fact is reflected in average earnings: women only receive 73 per cent of the average man's pay. Women also often have two full-time jobs: one at home with a family and house to look after, and one to bring in a second income.

A different perspective

In looking at economic statistics, it is easy to forget the wider picture. Growth is, of course, important to the economy: the twin aims are always higher efficiency and higher production. Efficiency is a good thing in itself, if it means that work is done as cost-effectively as possible. But what if improved efficiency is at the expense of jobs, so that some benefit from it at others' expense?

The great American economist J.K. Galbraith has admired the British for choosing quality of life rather than maximum economic growth. The government has taken up this idea and started to publish annual quality of life indicators – these are similar to economic statistics but cover such things as education, health, housing quality, pollution and diversity of wildlife. In 1998, the best places to live in England, according to these indicators, were North Yorkshire and the north-east. The idea is to measure things other than GDP which positively contribute to people's lives.

North Yorkshire: the highest quality of life in the UK

- Is gender the only factor which contributes to the glass ceiling?
- Are quality of life and economic growth compatible?

User-friendly police?

On three evenings each week a British TV channel shows an extremely popular police drama called *The Bill* (which is a slang word for the police). It is a fairly realistic soap opera, with a group of characters that viewers know well. The police officers are not perfect, and they make mistakes; but in general they are good, honest and hard-working.

No task is too small; policemen rounding up some ducks left outside the Prime Minister's home at No. 10 Downing Street.

Some might say that this kind of programme is just propaganda for the police, an attempt to improve their image. But actually, it is in line with public attitudes; in a survey, 75 per cent of people in Britain considered that the police were doing a good job. In fact, the police in Britain have enjoyed a positive public image for a long time. They are approachable – you can ask them the way in the street. Police officers visit primary schools to give talks and meet the children – trying to ensure that the next generation grows up with the same pro-police view as their parents. They are better paid than teachers, and much better paid than nurses; this helps to prevent corruption, and they very rarely accept bribes. Of course, the fact that they are unarmed is good for their public image; they look less threatening.

The organisation used to be called the Police Force, but it has now decided to call itself the Police Service. This reflects its desire to be part of modern society – serving people rather than controlling them. However, it is no use pretending that the British police are absolutely perfect. Especially in the last few years, there have been quite a lot of problems. The most common complaint about the police is that they are incompetent. Victims of crime often say that it is not worth calling the police because they will do nothing. There has been a big increase in some types of crime such as car theft (Britain now has the highest rate in Europe), and people have the impression that the battle is being lost. Even with very serious crimes, the police appear to make mistakes. The serial killer Fred West was known to

the police for 20 years but they never took his record of petty crimes seriously. During that time he killed ten young women, including his own daughter. Even when they had caught him, they failed to bring him to court; he managed to kill himself in prison before the trial began.

It is even more serious when the police intentionally do things wrong. There have been a number of celebrated cases of miscarriages of justice, where, by lying or concealing evidence, the police have managed to have innocent people sent to prison. They apparently wanted to show results, even if the wrong people suffered. The two most notorious cases of this type involved suspected IRA terrorists – the Guildford Four and the Birmingham Six. These Irishmen were convicted of planting bombs and killing people in the mid-70s, and some spent 17 years in prison, until the courts accepted that a mistake had been made.

The overwhelming majority of police officers are white males, and there is a persistent problem of sexism and racism. If you are a young black man, you are far more likely to be stopped in the street by the police. And sometimes these attitudes among officers have even more serious results. In 1993, a black 18 year-old called Stephen Lawrence was stabbed to death at a bus stop in south London. The attackers were a group of white men, and there were witnesses. But the police did not seem very interested in doing anything about the crime, and no-one was ever convicted for his murder. In the end, the case attracted huge publicity, and an official report accused the police of racism.

- **What is the public attitude to the police in your country? What is your attitude?**
- **How can we make sure that the police behave in an acceptable way?**

Bobbies

Before 1829, there were no police anywhere in Britain. In that year, the Prime Minister, Robert Peel, set up a force in London; they were often called bobbies, and the nickname is still occasionally used today. (Bobby is the familiar form of the name Robert.)

There was considerable resistance to the idea of a permanent police force, rather than groups of citizens brought together to deal with particular problems. The early 19th century was a time of political unrest in Britain as elsewhere in Europe, and workers suspected (rightly, as it turned out) that the police would be used against them. A writer named J.P. Smith warned in 1812 that the police would mean: "... a system of tyranny; an organised army of spies and informers, for the destruction of all public liberty, and the disturbance of all private happiness."

There is no national police service in Britain. Each region has its own independent service; for example, the West Midlands Police, Devon and Cornwall Police, or (in London) the Metropolitan Police. If there are serious complaints about one service, an officer from another service is brought in to investigate.

Police without guns

One of the first things that visitors to Britain notice is that the police are unarmed. Britain is one of the few countries in the world (Norway and New Zealand are others) where the police do not normally carry guns. Most people in Britain, including the police, are happy with this. They feel that if the police were armed, criminals too would always carry guns, and the cycle of violence would increase.

A comparison is often made with the USA, where the rate of murder by firearms is almost ten times the UK rate. It would be fairer to look at a country like Belgium, where the police are armed but the murder rate is not much higher than in Britain.

The trouble with comparisons with the USA is that it is a very different sort of society. Above all,

there are 250 million handguns in the USA, whereas in Britain it is illegal to own a handgun; you can keep a shotgun or a hunting rifle, but even for these it is quite difficult to get a licence.

Actually the first impression of an unarmed police service is not quite accurate. Some officers do have guns, but they do not patrol the streets with them. There are a number of police cars known as Armed Response Vehicles (ARVs), which contain guns locked in boxes. These are called in when necessary. In London, for example, there are 12 such ARVs, and they go into action about 25 times per day.

Zero tolerance

In 1994, the Mayor of New York, Rudolph Giuliani, decided to tackle crime in his city with a radical new approach which has come to be known as zero tolerance. Although the problems were not nearly so great, this was being tried at the same time in Hartlepool, a small town in northern England.

The essence of the idea is this: instead of ignoring minor crimes, you treat them very seriously – and in this way you prevent young criminals from going on to more serious crimes. So, for example, the police always stop and question or arrest teenagers who break windows or write graffiti on walls. As a result, the atmosphere in public places changes; people feel safer, and they go out more. Then it is more difficult for groups of young boys to dominate the area and terrorise older or weaker people. In New York the effect was dramatic; car theft, for example, fell by 56 per cent.

Zero tolerance has proved quite popular, and other parts of the UK have been experimenting with it. In Strathclyde, the area which includes Glasgow, they used to have a lot of alcohol-related problems, especially with young people. The local council has now made it illegal to drink alcohol in public places, and the police enforce the rule strictly. It has also tried a curfew for children in certain problem parts of town; anyone under the age of 16 on the streets after 7.30 p.m. can be taken home or to a police station.

The danger with zero tolerance is that the effect may wear off after a period of time. It may only be the initial shock which has the good effect.

- **Do you think it is ridiculous for the police to be unarmed, or is it a good idea?**
- **Would you like to be a police officer?**

The police are not allowed to arrest people without good reason.

The English legal system

The word English, rather than British, is used here because Scottish law is different from English, and they have separate courts and many of their own laws.

In England the most basic distinction is between the criminal law system and the civil law system. Civil law involves disputes between people about, for example, contracts. In this chapter we will concentrate on criminal law – where the police and the State take action against a criminal who breaks the law of the country.

Actually, criminal law in England operates rather like two people arguing with each other. It is called the adversarial system, and involves two sides arguing about the guilt of a person. If you are accused of a crime, you have a defence lawyer who argues with the prosecution lawyer. The court decides which side is right. This is very different from the inquisitorial system in many countries, where the judges simply try to find the truth by investigating and asking questions.

Types of courts

Less serious crimes, or offences, are dealt with in a Magistrates' Court. The person in charge is a magistrate, who is not normally a professional lawyer but a suitable member of the public. It is an unpaid, part-time job, and magistrates can be from any profession. The magistrates (there are usually three of them in the court) decide whether the defendant is guilty of the crime, and they fix the punishment, or sentence. They deal with cases such as driving offences, shoplifting or vandalism, and the maximum sentences they can give are six months in prison or a £5,000 fine.

In fact, all cases go first to the Magistrates' Court, but more serious ones are then referred to the Crown Court. In the Crown Court the person in charge is a professional judge. The judge decides on the sentence: there are limits for each type of crime, and the maximum penalty for murder is life imprisonment. The judge does not decide whether the defendant is guilty; that is done by a jury of 12 ordinary citizens. The jurors are chosen at random from the population between the ages of 18 and 70, but police officers, lawyers and criminals cannot sit on a jury. The idea is that the public should take part in the judicial system. This ensures that the law cannot be dominated by a small group of professionals, and it gives the public confidence. Very importantly, it makes it very difficult for criminals to avoid punishment by bribery.

Of course, there are problems with the jury system. If all 12 jurors are white, they may be prejudiced against a black defendant. If they are all middle class, they may be unfair to a working-class defendant. But statistically it is quite unlikely that 12 prejudiced people would be selected. It is more of a danger that in complicated cases some of the jurors will not be intelligent enough to follow the arguments.

Is the law accessible?

It is often said that the English legal system looks very fair in theory, but in practice it is difficult for ordinary people to use. Firstly, it is extremely expensive: a good lawyer costs £200 per hour (however, poor defendants are given free legal aid).

Secondly, it is very formal and frightening for members of the public. There are all sorts of

- **What sort of minor crimes are ignored by the police in your country?**
- **Which seems better to you – the adversarial or the inquisitorial system?**

rules in court. The judge and the lawyers wear extraordinary old-fashioned costumes: black robes, high white collars and (most surprisingly) powdered white wigs. The inside of the court is rather like a church, with the judge looking down from a seat above the court. This creates an atmosphere which can be quite intimidating.

Thirdly, there is the problem of language. You would expect lawyers to speak in a careful and formal way, using a lot of legal jargon. But besides this they use many Latin expressions; the law is based on tradition, and this language has survived for hundreds of years. If you visit an English court, be prepared to hear such terms as *mens rea, sub judice* and *obiter dicta*.

The price of crime

What sort of sentences can you receive if you are found guilty? The English system gives the magistrate or the judge a lot of freedom in deciding on the sentence, depending on the exact circumstances of the crime and criminal; for example, is it your first offence, did you really understand what you were doing, are you a danger to society?

The lightest sentence possible is community service. This means that you do unpaid work for a fixed number of hours (between 40 and 240), on jobs such as painting hospital buildings or gardening for elderly people.

You can be put on probation for a certain period of time. You have to visit your probation officer every week, and keep out of trouble. There can be other conditions; for example, you have to accept treatment for drug addiction.

You may have to pay a fine. For smaller things like driving offences, the fines are usually fixed amounts – perhaps £40 for parking in the wrong place.

But fines can be used for serious crimes if prison is not appropriate – for example, when a company breaks the law. Then the fine depends on ability to pay: rich people or organisations sometimes pay millions of pounds.

The standard punishment for serious offences is prison. You will probably go to prison if you commit burglary (breaking into houses and stealing things), robbery (stealing with force or violence), battery (using violence on a person), rape or murder. For criminals between the ages of 15 and 20, there are special young offenders' institutions.

Many people feel that criminals should go to prison, but it is far from the perfect answer to the problem. When prisoners are released, they often carry on with their lives of crime; in fact, they meet other criminals inside, get ideas from them, and make useful contacts. There is quite a lot of drug abuse and violence in English prisons. It is an extremely expensive system. Yet judges continue to send large numbers of people there: the United Kingdom has a higher percentage of its population in prison than any other European country, and the prisons are very overcrowded. A useful alternative to a prison sentence is a suspended sentence. You remain free for a certain period, and if you behave well, you will never have to serve your sentence. But if you commit another crime in the fixed period, your suspended sentence is added to your new one. An example would be one year in prison, suspended for two years.

The death penalty was abolished in 1965. Although there are often calls for it to be re-introduced, it is unlikely that it will ever be reinstated in Britain.

High Court judges' procession at the beginning of the legal year

• **Is the law accessible to ordinary people in your country?**
• **What do you think of the sentences in the English legal system?**

A look at history

As in other countries, the vast majority of people in medieval Britain were illiterate. Written texts were in Latin, and apart from churchmen, there was only a small group of professional clerks who could read and write; if you needed something written down, you had to pay one of these clerks to do it for you.

After the Norman invasion in 1066, Britain started to join the mainstream of European intellectual life. Rich families employed clerks to teach children at home. The Church set up small schools for ordinary people, especially choir schools where boys learned to read and write and to sing in the church choir. By the year 1200, there were the beginnings of a university in Oxford – at least a community of masters and scholars living and working together.

In 1440, England's most famous school, Eton, was founded by King Henry VI. (It is still regarded by many as the top school in the country – it was chosen by Prince Charles and Princess Diana for their sons William and Harry.) In its early days it was a mix of rich and poor students: the rich paid, and the poor worked in the school, cooking and cleaning to pay for their education.

By the middle of the 17th century there were a number of charity schools around the country, paid for by committees of rich subscribers. Of course, they were almost exclusively for boys. Some aristocratic girls were well educated, speaking French, and Latin, and reading music. But they were taught by private teachers at home.

There was always a basic problem with education for the poor: when they had got it, what could they do with it? In a very static, rigid society, it was almost impossible to change your position. Status was based on family, on birth – not on brains, energy or talent. Poor people who became educated, it was said, would get ideas above themselves, and feel dissatisfied and frustrated.

However, with the industrial revolution from the middle of the 18th century, British society began to change radically. People in business made huge amounts of money, and the old aristocrats lost much of their power and influence. The pressure for universal education increased. So for the first time in history, ordinary working people had the chance to get an education – and the motivation of a more meritocratic society in which they could make use of it.

The French Revolution brought ideas of social equality and a belief that all human beings could perfect themselves through education. Women started to demand greater freedom, respect and access to education. There was still a tendency to teach girls particularly feminine subjects, such as cooking, sewing, art and music. But later in the 19th century, girls began to receive the same sort of education as boys. In 1874, Girton College, Cambridge, offered the first university places for women.

A woodcut of a Victorian grammar school classroom

- **Can you imagine a time before there were schools? Would you like to have lived then?**
- **Do you think that the spread of education was important for economic development?**

Through the 19th century more and more children went to school, and in 1880 education was made compulsory up to the age of 13. A few years later about 97 per cent of girls and boys were literate – a situation unimaginable in most of the rest of the world. The school-leaving age continued to go up in steps until it reached 16 in 1972.

The system today

In this section we will look at education in England and Wales; the system is different in Scotland. The chart below shows the general structure of the English/Welsh system.

A primary school class listening to a story.

	Age 17–18	6th form A level exams
	Age 16–17	
	Age 15–16	Year 11 GCSE exams, after which you can leave school.
SECONDARY SCHOOL	Age 14–15	Year 10
	Age 13–14	Year 9
	Age 12–13	Year 8
	Age 11–12	Year 7
	Age 10–11	Year 6
	Age 9–10	Year 5
PRIMARY SCHOOL	Age 8–9	Year 4
	Age 7–8	Year 3
	Age 6–7	Year 2
	Age 5–6	Year 1

- Local, not central, government runs the state schools. Traditionally, schools have had a great deal of independence about what to teach and how to teach it. But in the last ten years the government has introduced a National Curriculum; this means that every pupil in the country does more or less the same work, especially in primary schools.
- Pupils cannot repeat a year in this system, which is based strictly on age. However badly they do, pupils go up to the next year. The only exception is GCSEs and A levels, which pupils can repeat if they need better results; for example, to get into a university.
- League tables are published in the national press showing the exam results of each school. Consequently, some schools are more popular with parents than others.
- Many secondary schools are single-sex rather than co-educational. Statistics show that girls get better results when they are separated from boys.
- There has been much debate in recent years about teaching style: is it better for the teacher to stand at the front of the class and lecture (in the old-fashioned way), or to set up a variety of learning activities for pupils to do individually or in groups? Traditionalists claim that the latter method, originating in the liberal 1960s, has failed.
- About 7 per cent of children in Britain go to private/independent schools. The fees are between £5,000 and £15,000 per year; the main advantage of these schools is that discipline is better, so teachers and pupils waste less time.
- The school year is divided into three terms. Schools have 13 weeks' holiday per year: six weeks in the summer, two weeks each at Christmas and Easter, and three half-term weeks. The year starts early in September.

- **What are the differences between the English system of education and your own?**
- **What is better about the English system, and what is worse?**

CHISWICK COMMUNITY SCHOOL

Chiswick School is a large secondary school in West London. It is co-educational (i.e. not single-sex) and has about 1,250 pupils between the ages of 11 and 19. In most ways it is a typical English school. It has a good reputation and is very popular with local people. Parents have to apply to the London Borough of Hounslow, the local government authority, if they want their daughter or son to go to the school. There are always more applicants than places, so some children have to go to other, less popular schools in Hounslow.

In the first three years (Years seven to nine), all pupils study the same subjects, following the National Curriculum:

- English
- Maths
- Science
- Religious Studies including Christianity and other religions
- Geography
- History
- Technology
- Art
- Music
- Drama
- Physical Education
- Personal and Social Education including Sex Education
- Information Technology
- Two from: French, German or Latin

Then in Years 10 and 11 pupils work for their GCSE exams – usually taking about nine subjects. Everyone takes English, Maths and Science, but there is quite a wide choice of other subjects. The exams are in May or June of Year 11, but there is also coursework in which pupils get marks for pieces of work throughout the two years. Because of coursework, the result does not depend entirely on the exam.

After the GCSE exams, some pupils leave and get jobs; others go on to do their A levels at other schools or further education colleges (which specialise in adult and evening classes). Chiswick School encourages as many as possible to stay on in the sixth form. It is considered good for the atmosphere of the school to have these more mature pupils around and the teachers enjoy working with them.

Most pupils take three or four A levels. Typical combinations would be Maths, Physics and Chemistry, or English, French and History. But the school also offers a range of extra subjects which pupils can start in the sixth form: Economics, Food Technology, Government and Politics, Photography, Psychology and Theatre Studies.

Facilities

The school has very good sports facilities: six tennis courts, a gym, two squash courts and a large games field, where boys and girls play football and hockey. Pupils can also row on the nearby River Thames.

There are three main computer centres, and most subjects (such as Chemistry or Languages) have their own computers. All pupils study Information Technology.

There is a large library run by a professional librarian, and a Learning Resources Centre with photocopying facilities, computer scanners and printers.

Art is a popular option, even at GCSE and A level.

- **Does your country have a National Curriculum?**
- **Are the subjects in your school similar to those at Chiswick? How do they differ?**

The school has an excellent library.

you were present and behaved well. If you do anything wrong at this stage, you are out; you have to go to the hall to join any other pupils in trouble. In the hall, you all work in silence under the supervision of a teacher.

For persistent offenders, there is a system of detentions, when pupils are kept in for an hour after school. In really serious cases, it is possible to exclude pupils for a period of time from the school, or to expel them permanently.

As in most schools in Britain, pupils have to wear a uniform. There is some resistance to this rule, but generally teachers and parents agree that the uniform is good for discipline, gives the school an identity and avoids the problem of competition among the pupils to be fashionable.

Extracurricular activities

Extracurricular means outside the normal curriculum. Chiswick School provides lots of activities at lunch time and after school. There is judo, trampolining, dance, cooking and chess. There are music and photography clubs. There is a theatre group which puts on a play at the end of each year.

The school organises foreign exchanges, in which French or German schoolchildren come to stay with Chiswick pupils, and vice versa.

In the holidays, the school organises trips such as camping in Wales or skiing in Switzerland.

Discipline

There is one basic rule in the school: to respect others and their property and behave in a normal, sensible way, with due consideration for the health and safety of all. If, as a pupil, you misbehave there is a system known as WRO – Warning, Report, Out. First you get a warning from your teacher. Then you are put on report; you have to carry a form around with you and the teacher signs it after each lesson – to show that

The management

Like most schools in Britain, Chiswick is under the control of elected local government – not the central government in Westminster. The council of the London Borough of Hounslow pays for the school, and makes general policies for it – for example, the council decided that it should be co-educational and not single-sex. Hounslow is the employer of the teachers and other staff, such as cleaners. The council is a democratic body, with elections every five years. So if the people of Hounslow do not like the way the Labour Party runs their schools, they can vote Conservative or Liberal Democrat.

More directly in control of the school are the governors – a committee including councillors, the head teacher, a parent, a teacher and a representative from the Church. They meet about once a month. On a day-to-day basis the head teacher runs the school.

- **How important are sport and music in education? Would you like to do more of these subjects?**
- **Do you have a uniform at your school? How do you feel about wearing a school uniform?**

Universities

British universities are not open to everyone. To get a place, you normally apply in your last year at school, before you have taken your A levels. The university makes you an offer; for example, it will give you a place if you get at least one grade A and two Bs in your A levels. The offer depends on market forces; for popular, high-prestige courses, the university will ask for very good A level results.

The number of students on a particular course (for example, Economics at Cardiff University) is strictly limited. The system does not allow students to follow full-time courses in a casual way, having a job or living in another town as they study. Students are quite closely monitored, and have to see their teachers regularly. Consequently, drop-out and failure rates are low.

The negative side of the system was that, compared with other countries, a rather small percentage of British school-leavers actually went on to university.

But there has been a dramatic improvement; the numbers have doubled over the last 20 years. One explanation of this is that in the 1980s many polytechnics and higher education colleges were given university status. As a result, many cities now have two universities – an old one and a new one. For example, in Bristol there is Bristol University and the University of the West of England; in Oxford there is Oxford University and Oxford Brookes University.

Officially, all universities in the country are equal in status. But they differ greatly in reputation and public image. In general, the older a university is, the higher its status. So the most prestigious are the ancient ones – Oxford and Cambridge – followed by long-established ones such as London, Manchester and Edinburgh.

Some of this is just based on tradition and snobbery. In fact, each university has strengths and weaknesses, and sensible students make their choices according to their own particular needs and priorities.

Oxford, Britain's oldest university, is trying to throw off its élitist image.

- **Which is better – to have a more selective university system, or more students?**
- **What are the differences between the universities in your country?**

About half of British students go away to university, rather than attend the one closest to home. This is an expensive thing to do; the government used to give grants (money to live on during studies), whereas now students have to borrow money or get their parents to pay. But still many students find that combining study and family life is impossible.

British universities are very popular with overseas students. There are about 70,000 – mostly from Africa, the Arab world and Far Eastern countries such as Malaysia and Indonesia. The Erasmus programme arranges exchanges (from three months to one year) for students and teachers between universities in 24 countries including all the members of the European Union. In fact, the UK is the most popular destination, receiving over 25 per cent of all Erasmus students.

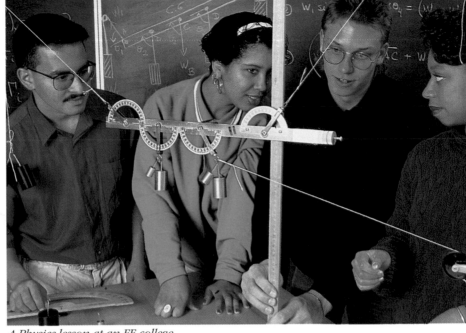
A Physics lesson at an FE college

Further education

Apart from schools and universities there is another sector, which often gets forgotten – a sort of Cinderella of the education system. In fact, there are almost as many students at further education colleges as at university, and these colleges perform some very important functions.

We mentioned that some pupils from Chiswick School prefer not to stay there to do their A levels, but to move to a nearby FE college such as Ealing Tertiary College (ETC). Going to ETC has two main attractions. First, there is a wider choice of A level subjects, including Law, Computing and Sociology; and second, there is a much freer, more adult atmosphere than at school.

Another group of ex-Chiswick students may also go to ETC – those who are not happy with the academic study involved in A levels, and who want to do a vocational course which leads quickly to a job. FE colleges offer all sorts of work-related courses, from Car Mechanics to Dental Nursing, which give students NVQs (National Vocational Qualifications).

Then there are those who leave school at age 16 and go straight into a job, but later on realise that they need higher qualifications. Quite a lot of people in their mid-20s or older come back into education at an FE college and take a one-year Access course; this gets them into university, where they are often more successful than younger students because they are more serious and focused.

FE colleges like ETC also offer English-language courses for foreign visitors; in some ways they are a better learning environment than specialist language schools, as the visitors mix with all the British students around them.

- **Would you rather live at home or go away for your university course?**
- **Is there a system similar to the English FE colleges in your country?**

An interview with ... Mavis Grant

Mavis Grant was born and brought up in Newcastle-upon-Tyne in the north-east of England. Fifteen years ago, she became head teacher of Mary Trevelyan Primary School in one of its most deprived areas. She has to deal daily with the problems of high crime and unemployment rates, poverty and family breakdown.

You run a school in what is known as a difficult area. Why is it difficult?

Difficult isn't my description of the area but it's one that's often applied to the area. It's because it's got very high levels of unemployment and lots of social problems. The unemployment rate in the area is well above national average as it's round about 40 per cent in this part of the city. And we have 88 per cent of the children in the school who receive free school meals. The family's qualification for that has to be that they're on very low incomes or they're in receipt of state benefits, mostly through unemployment. The area itself has quite significant levels of crime, of all sorts of crime, and a very difficult problem with families who move house very frequently. The impact of that on the school is that the children can move from school to school every few months even at a very young age. We have a lot of lone-parent families, a lot of families where the mother has had her first child at a very young age, often mid-teens, so lots of problems with family breakdown, social exclusion, that is people who are not part of the mainstream, often through unemployment, not involved in community life.

How does this affect the teaching?

I think we have to have far more awareness of the children's individual needs and the problems that they've encountered at home or in the local community. We have to have a lot more patience and be able to establish very positive relationships with the children very quickly, particularly children where there has been a family breakdown or they've been subjected to a violent background. Sometimes that's in their own home,

quite often it's in the community at large. I think you have to have teachers who are, if anything, more skilled than you would expect in other schools. The teaching has to be very high quality particularly with literacy because a lot of the children who are admitted into the school consistently come out in the bottom 10 per cent on entry into school. We had to develop teaching strategies where literacy has the main emphasis. It's obviously not the only thing that we concentrate on, but it is of prime importance in terms of early skills in the school. And it does pay off, because by the time they come to the end of the first key stage in primary schools: that is, by the time they're about seven years old, when they're tested – although many of them are still below national averages of what you would expect of a seven-year-old in Maths and in English and literacy, they have made huge gains from where they were on entry. And then by the time they leave the school at age 11, our children for the last three or four years have been achieving at or about national averages. It also means we've got to support the parents and the families more than some schools need to do.

So what do you do with that?

We've run workshops for parents, you know, to show them what we do in the literacy hour. We do run a home-loan scheme, where we lend story tapes, story books, poetry books, reference books to the parents and to the children. We run a homework club as a support to the children and the parents actually, one night a week after school, which the staff and I have been doing. This is the fourth year now. It's available to every child in the

• **Does this school sound similar to yours in any way?**
• **Should the government give more funding to this kind of school?**

school from the four-year-olds up to the 11-year-olds; it's free, we don't make any charge for that; the staff give up their time voluntarily. It's hugely successful. We've always had between 50 and 70 per cent of the children who come to the school attend every week. We also provide support for the parents by running a bus service of our own, which we call the *Ticket to Learn* bus, sort of an adaptation of the title of a Beatles' song. One of the problems we had was in poor attendance rates in the school. It was largely down to issues to do with single parents, poverty: couldn't afford bus fares. Parents who had a sick baby and there was no one else to bring the older children in to school. And also, the fear in the area of crime – the parents will not leave their homes unattended. And I felt that if we could provide some transport for these families then the children would come to school more regularly and, consequently, their education would improve. But also some of the stresses on the families would be relieved to some extent.

Did this problem – that is, schools in difficult areas – always exist or do you think it is more recent?

Oh, I think it's always existed. I think if you go back to pre-war, 1920s–1930s, schools in areas of poverty around the country have always had more problems to deal with and more acute problems to deal with than schools in more affluent areas. I think what has changed is that schools are more accountable now: they're under the microscope a lot more. There's more of a demand for national standards, in everything, not just in education and therefore, there's more emphasis put upon schools in areas of difficulty, who are seen to be underachieving. I think some of the social problems that we deal with have become more acute, more difficult in recent years.

What is the government doing? What can it do to help?

I think this government is doing more to help. It's not that I would be arguing for other schools to get less; I think there needs to be new, additional funding for schools in the highest areas of poverty and deprivation. I think there needs to be a recognition that where there are huge pockets of underachievement, which educationally in my view is linked to continuing social problems as those children become adults, it has a cost in terms of higher crime. I think people need to make the connection, local government needs to make the connection, and national government needs to make the connection.

• **Do you agree that educational underachievement is linked to higher crime and other social problems? What can governments do to help?**

The NHS: pride and despair

The National Health Service (NHS) is a very emotive subject for the British. It looks after them "from the cradle to the grave". But they despair about its apparent decline and inability to cope with demand. Politicians profess an almost religious faith in the NHS: "We founded it," say the Labour Party. "But it is safe in our hands," say the Conservatives. There are constant arguments about how best to run it, but no-one ever proposes to scrap the whole thing and replace it with something else.

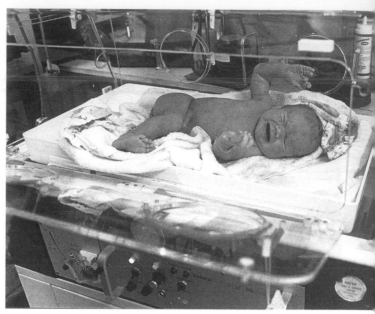

Today 98 per cent of British babies are born in hospital.

The British system is special in a number of ways. Its most distinctive feature is that it is universal, and free at the point of use: everybody can use it, and they do not have to pay when they use it. Unlike most systems in other countries, it is funded from general taxation, rather than being an insurance scheme. This has two great benefits: it is simple to administer, and it gives people peace of mind – they do not have to worry about money when they are sick.

Another unusual feature of the system is the role of the GP, the general practitioner. When you are ill in Britain, you normally go to your GP in a small surgery near your home. You are registered with that practice, or team of doctors, and they keep your medical records. Each GP has about 2,000 people on the books. If you suffer from a lot of illness (or are a hypochondriac) your own doctor will know you personally. If you need specialist care from, for example, a dermatologist, an ophthalmologist or an obstetrician, the GP will refer you to a hospital. All specialists work in hospitals, and you cannot see them without a letter from your GP.

The advantage of this arrangement is that the specialist's time is not wasted by inappropriate inquiries, as the GP acts as a sort of gate keeper. Also the patient does not have to make difficult decisions about which specialist to go to. GPs are able to deal with the great majority of problems themselves; if you have a cold, you do not need an ear-nose-and-throat specialist to tell you to go home and keep warm. And GPs are more likely to take a holistic approach, having knowledge of the patient's character and lifestyle.

The origins of the present NHS system can be traced back to the beginning of the 20th century. The national health insurance, which was introduced in 1911, gave benefits to 16 million workers. By stages, access to doctors was extended to more of the population, and in 1946, the newly-elected socialist Labour Government passed the National Health Service Act. There were many obstacles to this great reform – in particular the doctors themselves were against it. In return for their co-operation they had to be allowed to continue seeing private patients, and they had to be offered lots of money. The founding father of the NHS, Aneurin Bevan, said that he "stuffed their mouths with gold".

It was assumed in the early days that the system would be expensive at first, and then become cheaper as the whole population became healthier and used the system less. As it turned out, this optimism was unrealistic. In fact, expectations

- **How does your health-care system differ from the British NHS?**
- **Do you often waste your doctor's time? Or do you avoid going even if you need to?**

increased, creating massive new demand. So vaccination brought about a reduction in measles, tuberculosis and rubella. But people began to expect to have their failing sight improved by eye operations, and their damaged hips replaced with metal implants.

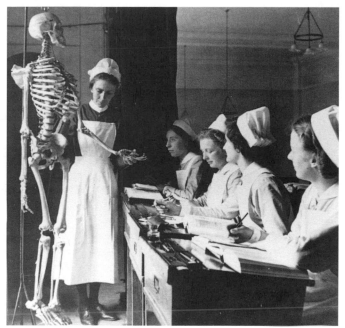

Student nurses from Guy's Hospital at the Preliminary Training School, in the 1950s

As a result, the system is chronically under-funded. There are long waiting lists for surgery; when there is a flu epidemic (which happens quite often) there are not enough beds in hospitals; nurses are under paid, which inevitably leads to a shortage of nurses; hospital food is often disgusting. There is always debate about a regular dilemma faced by the free NHS: which non-essential treatments to offer? Should people expect the right to tattoo-removal, or sex changes, or fertility treatment? And does the tax payer have to fund all essential treatment – for example, should the tobacco companies pay for the treatment of smoking-related diseases?

Certainly the UK spends less on health than most comparable countries. This can be explained partly by the cost-effective structure of the NHS. For example, the United States' largely private system is wasteful, with much duplication of services and competition in high-tech equipment between neighbouring private clinics. But it is also a result of the British public's unwillingness to pay higher taxes. In surveys, people always say they are prepared to pay more for a better service,

Often new technology is highly efficient and cost-saving. For example, patients with kidney stones used to be cut open and then kept in hospital for a week, but now a device called a lithotripter breaks up the stones with high energy shock waves and the patient can go home hours later. However, some of the new machines are very expensive indeed, and they do things which in the past were simply not done. A Royal Commission report said in 1979: "The demand for health care is always likely to outstrip supply, and the capacity of health services to absorb resources is almost unlimited."

PROTECT CHILDREN FROM PASSIVE SMOKING

HELP THOSE WHO DEPEND ON YOU THE MOST

Health Authority leaflets inform the public about healthy lifestyles.

- **Which non-essential treatments do you think a free health service should offer?**
- **What would you like or dislike about being a doctor?**

but when it comes to an election, they vote for the party that promises tax cuts.

As an alternative to the NHS you can use the private healthcare system. Many people now take out private health insurance, or receive health insurance as a benefit of their employment. If you use private healthcare, you will probably be able to get an appointment to see a specialist much more quickly than with the NHS.

Health problems

Two statistics stand out in comparisons between Britain and other European countries. Heart disease and cancers, in particular breast cancer, seem to be bigger killers here than elsewhere. What could be the reasons? In the case of breast cancer there is one clear factor – there is less screening and fewer regular checks. Heart problems are made worse by various aspects of lifestyle: diet, lack of exercise, stress, smoking and drinking. Of course, the British are famous for getting drunk, especially on holiday or after football matches, but the statistics do not support this negative image, and in reality, the British drink less alcohol per person than in any European country except Sweden and Finland.

British children eat a lot of sweets and chocolate.

About 28 per cent of the adult population smokes and that is very close to the European average. So perhaps diet is the key: it is often said that the British eat too much unhealthy food like sugar and animal fat, especially compared to the healthy Mediterranean diet. This argument is supported by comparative statistics within the UK, which show more heart disease in the north of England and in Scotland than in the south-east – Northerners and Scots eat more sausages, chips and chocolate.

Another remarkable fact emerges from the statistics: in spite of more than half a century of socialist-style medicine, health differences between the social classes are as great as ever. Almost every health indicator tells the same story – you are much more likely to die early from disease if you are working class. A poor unemployed woman is a staggering seven times more likely to die of cervical cancer than a well-paid professional woman. One common measure of public health is the infant mortality rate; that is, how many babies die within their first year. Amazingly, this rate still shows huge differences between the social classes in Britain.

There are all sorts of explanations for these class-based differences. Again, one obvious factor is lifestyle: working-class people smoke much more, and their diet is more unhealthy. It also seems that doctors pay more attention to richer people, and take their illnesses more seriously. But there are real problems in interpreting the statistics; for example, if your health is bad, you are more likely to become unemployed, and so you will go down the class ladder. In this case, class status is the result of illness, not one of its causes.

Social protection

What happens when people lose their jobs, or retire, or do not make enough money to support themselves and their families? There are welfare benefits: some flat rate, which provide the same amount of money for everybody who claims them, and some means-tested, meaning they vary according to the needs of the individual person. Among the former are unemployment benefit (now under the more positive name of Jobseeker's Allowance), child benefit and the old age pension.

- **Which health problems are especially common in your country?**
- **What can governments do to improve the health of poor people?**

So everyone in Britain receives child benefit for their children and a pension when they are 65 years old. The state pension, at around £70 per week, is a very modest amount of money, and in fact most people make sure that they have another pension so as to avoid poverty in old age. As they work, they put money into pension funds arranged by their employers – some of these pension funds contain billions of pounds and are very important players in the British financial system.

For those who are unemployed for a long time (the Jobseeker's Allowance stops after one year), or whose pay is too little to live on, there are means-tested benefits such as Income Support and Family Credit. To get these, you have to prove that you need them and that you do not have a lot of savings hidden in a bank.

A big issue

Homelessness has increased dramatically in recent years. A visitor to London today cannot help seeing people lying in the street in sleeping bags or wrapped in newspapers. It is estimated that there are more than 100,000 homeless people in the capital city, and of course many more across Britain. *The Big Issue* is a magazine sold only by the homeless, who keep the profits. It has been a great success in practical terms and in giving homeless people a sense of identity and dignity.

Charities

A striking feature of life in Britain is the amount of fund-raising for charities which is undertaken. These are voluntary non-government organisations which help people in need, and so replace or supplement the official welfare system. There is Help the Aged, Save the Children, Imperial Cancer Research, the Terence Higgins Trust (for people with AIDS), the British Heart Foundation, the Guide Dogs for the Blind Association and hundreds more.

The biggest organisation is Oxfam, founded in Oxford in 1942 to feed the hungry children of Greece during the war. Today, it collects about £120 million per year to spend on famine relief around the world. These charities collect money through high street second-hand shops, through adverts, sales of Christmas cards and through volunteers who rattle collecting boxes on the street. Film stars, pop musicians and the royal family all identify themselves with particular charities. Princess Diana regarded charity fund-raising as her full-time job – she was specially associated with AIDS charities, the homeless and victims of land-mines.

This all seems very positive, but some people question the role of charities. For example, Help the Aged collects about £65 million per year to help old people in need. But that raises the question, why doesn't the state look after old people adequately? Wouldn't it be better to improve the system than to supplement it with all this voluntary work? Perhaps giving to charity just makes people feel better, but has little overall effect.

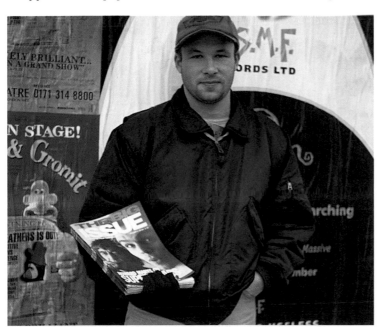

The Big Issue *is sold on the streets.*

• **Should people give money to charities? Do you?**
• **What would upset you most if you were homeless?**

An interview with ... John McFadzean

John McFadzean is called Kiwi John. He left his native New Zealand 14 years ago to come to Britain. After losing his job and becoming homeless, he wandered the streets of London for four years. Now, he works with The Big Issue, *a magazine that was set up to help homeless people.*

John, how did you become homeless?

I was sacked by a brewery basically, through a disagreement, if you like. But because they supplied me with my housing – the room over the pub, etc. As a manager, once they sack you, they just don't want you there so you're out, as simple as that. Having no family – I had some friends – but not immediately obtainable, I had nowhere to go. I immediately found myself on the streets. For a very short period of time I stayed at some friends' place, but they didn't have the room, it was just impossible for them. And there I was; it's quite frightening how quickly it can happen.

What was it like to literally have no home?

Well, it's frightening, it's shocking; and it's also possibly, what you say, a rude awakening, if you like. I didn't know the system at all, so I didn't know what was available to me, what wasn't, like simple things about feeding myself. Originally, I had no access to money, I had a little bit of savings, it certainly didn't last long, I used that to stay in bed-and-breakfasts and so on, but at like £35–40 a night, my money quickly disappeared.

What was your first night like, do you remember?

Oh yeah. Wet and cold. It was December, very cold. It was in the open. I managed to doze off, woke up at say about 5 o'clock or whatever time it was, it was raining, I had to look for shelter, I was frozen. I was confused but ending it all, heaven, no, I never thought of that, never would, I don't think.

But when you were homeless what did you think would happen to you eventually, or did you not think about the future at all?

No, I thought from day to day. What plans I made were the plans of trying to go to places where I could get on to housing lists, contact anybody I may know to see if they could perhaps put me up. Some people I didn't want to contact, I was too embarrassed. It then becomes a day-to-day existence really. You're thinking, how am I going to survive today, how am I going to feed myself today, where am I going to stay tonight and you just have to get through it as best as you can.

- **Have you or anyone you know ever been homeless?**
- **For what reasons do you think people become homeless?**

Then what happened?

I was sleeping rough under Waterloo station. Surviving then was hard. I just happened to see one day a woman that was selling a magazine. We got to chat because I knew her to actually be sleeping rough herself and found out that this was *The Big Issue* magazine. That's when things started to get better.

What is *The Big Issue* magazine?

It's a magazine that's sold by homeless people in the sense of giving them a hand-up and not a hand-out. The design of it is to hopefully make people motivate themselves to do something and the idea of *The Big Issue* magazine is that you would go and you would buy it and sell it. Initially, they will give you so many copies free to set you up, so you can walk in there completely flat-broke and then work your way from there.

So what exactly happened?

I sold *The Big Issue* magazine for about two-and-a-half years roughly. During that time I got to know the people in the office, as you do, you're going there daily to buy your magazines and so on. They must have liked what they'd seen; they asked me to do part-time work for them, which I did for two days of a week and stuff, a vacancy came up in the side that I would have liked to have been involved in, which was in the support side. Having had, if you like the experience, unwanted as it was, I had the experience by then of what it was like to be on the streets, of how hard it was to exist. So I could empathise, if you like, with those people, so I also felt what *The Big Issue* had given me was the opportunity to lead a normal life again as such.

How did you overcome homelessness?

Through *The Big Issue* housing team. They have two sides – they have a business side and they have a charity side or the foundation as they call it. The foundation, because it's got charity status,

they collect money. They use that money to set up services. We have a mental health worker, a drug and alcohol worker, a housing team; we have a jobs, education and training unit.

I'd been on the housing list with *The Big Issue* housing team for probably only about four months. They made references for me and I got a flat, which I can happily say is my own. This was that particular point in time when I took control of my own life again – none of it was left in somebody else's hands.

Why do you think homelessness has become such a fact of life in modern Britain?

I think there's so many reasons. From young people who have horrific family backgrounds who run away; young people who run away from good family backgrounds and don't know when they've got it good; through to drugs, to alcohol; I think, the education system. I think it's a little bit of everything that applies. There are people who have chosen that way of life, but they're a minority. The majority don't want it, I hear different reasons almost daily. Some of them are new.

What do you think society should be doing to help? Is enough being done?

I'd like the government for example – they could go a long way to making accessible housing easier to come by. For instance, all the military, all the army houses – there're thousands and thousands and thousands of houses that sit free through Britain that are under some form of local government or government control and nothing is being done with them.

I think they could also go a long way further to a little bit more funding. Funding of charities, day centres, the cold weather shelters that set up over the Christmas period, and some of them now stay open till Easter – if they had the funding, they'd stay open all year.

- **Is society or are the individuals themselves to blame for homelessness?**
- **In which ways does a magazine such as *The Big Issue* help?**

The Church of England

There is a paradox about religion in Britain. On the one hand this is officially a Christian country, where Church and state are linked. On the other, Hindus, Muslims and Sikhs form quite a large part of the population, and the British pride themselves in tolerance and adaptability.
At the same time, many small religious groups and sects appear to be growing, while most young people have no religious beliefs at all.

The link between Church and state is something unique to Britain; no other Western country has anything quite like it. The Queen is not only the symbolic head of state, but she is also the head of the Church of England; British coins have a portrait of the monarch with the letters FD (from the Latin *fidei defensor*, Defender of the Faith). In most modern countries there is a strict separation between the government and religion. How did this strange situation come about in Britain?

It was partly the result of a historical accident. King Henry VIII wanted to divorce his first wife, Catherine of Aragon, in order to marry again but the Pope would not agree. So, in the early 1530s, Henry broke away from Rome, and the Church of England became independent. It was still Catholic, but it then began to adopt many of the new Protestant ideas from Germany, such as man's ability to speak to God without the intercession of priests.
Under Queen Elizabeth I, the Church became officially Protestant, and Roman Catholics were persecuted – they were forced to go to Protestant church services, and much of their money was confiscated. Even today a Catholic may not become king or queen.

As a result, bishops of the Church of England are appointed by the Queen, even if she does not use her own judgement but always accepts the advice of those in the Church. The bishops sit in the House of Lords, the upper house of the UK Parliament – so, in theory at least, they are part of the government of the country. Prayers are said at the Opening of Parliament in November each year. Religious education is compulsory in schools, and one quarter of all primary schools are Church schools. All state schools are required by law to have a collective act of worship which is predominantly Christian.

Of course, organised Christianity is in decline in most countries. The Church of England is no exception. A hundred years ago about 60 per cent of the population went to church on a Sunday, and today the figure is less than 10 per cent. People used to know the Bible so well that their everyday language was full of quotations from it; British children at the beginning of the third millennium do not even know the simplest Bible stories. The Church itself has quietly given up talking about many of its own basic beliefs: the virgin birth, heaven and hell, the resurrection of the body.

The Church is trying to adapt to the modern world and attract young people to it.

- **What, if anything, is wrong with the State and the Church being combined?**
- **Should the Church be responsible for schools?**

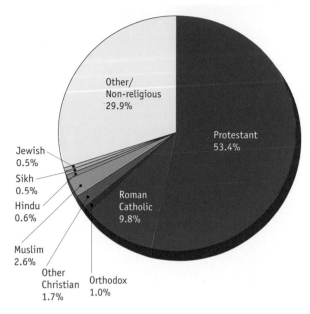

Other/
Non-religious
29.9%

Protestant
53.4%

Jewish
0.5%

Sikh
0.5%

Hindu
0.6%

Roman
Catholic
9.8%

Muslim
2.6%

Other
Christian
1.7%

Orthodox
1.0%

Religions in Britain
Source: Office for National Statistics

Britain's other churches

Of course Christianity in this country does not begin and end with the Church of England. There is quite a strong Roman Catholic community – many Irish, Italian and Polish immigrants, but also English Catholics who kept their faith through the persecution during the 16th and 17th centuries. The Greeks and Russians in Britain have brought with them their own orthodox churches.

In addition, there are numerous smaller Christian groups and churches; in fact there are more than in any other country – even the USA has only half as many as Britain. The older ones are the Quakers, Baptists, Presbyterians, Methodists and the Scottish Free Church. Newer ones include the Mormons, Jehovah's Witnesses and Christian Scientists. African-Caribbean people are particularly attracted to the Pentecostal churches and the Seventh Day Adventists.

The Church of England has tried to modernise itself in various ways. Vicars no longer condemn gay men or lesbians, or couples who live together without being married. Rock music sometimes replaces the traditional organ-played hymns. And very significantly, since 1994 women can become priests; this question caused serious division within the Church, and some members left and joined the Roman Catholics.

British people have not given up the Church altogether. There is still a sort of nostalgic respect for the music, the buildings and the ritual. At Christmas, groups of people go out singing carols, and the churches fill up for midnight mass on Christmas Eve. About half of all weddings still take place in church, and a quarter of all children are baptised. Almost all funerals have a Christian element, at least some prayers and hymns.

Easter is the most important festival in the Greek Orthodox year.

- **What can the Church do to attract more young people?**
- **Is religion declining in importance in your country?**

The New Age

Many religions, including Christianity, are declining in popularity. Yet, in a recent government survey, only 10 per cent of the population claimed to be atheist: that is, not believing in God; and only 13 per cent called themselves agnostics, who think that it is impossible to know the truth.

Many people looking for an alternative to traditional, official religions have moved towards something called New Age. The term comes from astrology – we are passing from the previous age of Pisces, which has lasted 2,000 years since the birth of Christ, into the new age of Aquarius.

Astrology is very popular with New Age people, as is fortune telling by all sorts of means: tarot cards, tealeaves, *I Ching* and palm reading. Old non-Christian beliefs have been revived: magic, the occult, and the powers of witches.

Islam

The great majority of Muslims in this country are Pakistani or Bangladeshi; although they read the holy book, the Qur'an, in its original Arabic, they speak mainly Urdu and Bengali. Young Muslims, like all young people, tend to rebel against the beliefs of their parents. But Islam seems to be surviving much more successfully than Christianity. Mosques in London and other big cities are full on Fridays. Many schools and colleges have a special room for Muslims to pray. New all-Muslim schools are being set up.

Why is Islam in such a healthy state, compared to other religions? There are probably two main reasons.

One is that it is natural for an immigrant group to hang on to its religion; it is an important way of maintaining its identity. The other reason is that Islam all over the world has been very strong and dynamic in recent years.

There was a difficult moment for Muslims in Britain when a small number of them supported the *fatwa* against the British writer Salman Rushdie. (This was the death sentence issued by the Iranian government on the grounds that Rushdie had insulted Islam in his 1988 book *The Satanic Verses*.) The press, which tends to be anti-Islamic, took advantage of this to create a picture of Muslim assassins waiting for a chance to kill the author. More than a million ordinary, peaceful Muslims suffered the effects of this negative image.

Muslims praying at the Regent's Park mosque in London.

Judaism

The Jewish community has been in Britain for much longer than the Hindus or Sikhs. In fact, some Jews came here with the Norman invasion in 1066; but 200 years later their property was confiscated and they were expelled from the country. (Britain has not always deserved its reputation for racial and religious tolerance.) When they were expelled from Spain in the 15th century, Jews once again came

• **Which religions are important in your country?**
• **Do many people get interested in other religions, study them, or even convert to them?**

The huge Hindu temple in Neasden, North London

Hinduism

The names Hindu and India are just two forms of the same word, and Hindu was first used by outsiders to mean any religion in India which was not Islam, Sikhism or Buddhism.

This is perhaps why it is difficult to describe and define Hinduism. It is over 8,500 years old and has no single founder. There are a number of gods, like Vishnu, Rama and Shiva; but each individual Hindu only prays to one of these gods, and they think of themselves as monotheists.

Hindu culture has rather a good image among the British as a whole. The music is lovely, the pictures of gods are strange and pretty, and the character of religious Hindus seems very gentle and attractive. Although he struggled against British imperialism, the Indian leader Gandhi has been admired, even revered, by the British people for his non-violence and spirituality. In reality, not all Hindus deserve this positive image: Hindu extremists in India have been as violent as Islamic extremists.

Sikhism

The Sikhs come from the Punjab in the north-east of India, and they speak Punjabi. The more traditional men are easily recognisable, as they wear turbans and have beards. The religion is monotheistic, and similar in some ways to Hinduism. But it is centred around the teachings of ten gurus, who lived between the 15th and the 18th centuries. The greatest of these was the first, Guru Nanek, and it is his portrait that you see in Sikh shops and houses. There are about 400,000 Sikhs in the UK.

The London suburb of Southall, near Heathrow airport, is a very interesting place to visit – full of Punjabi shops and restaurants, and with an important Gurdwara (a Sikh temple).

to live in this country, and have been here ever since. Many more came from Russia and Eastern Europe 100 years ago, and then from Central Europe in the 1930s.

For Jews, who had no national homeland for so many centuries, religion has been an essential way of expressing their sense of community and their identity. Without their religion, would they be Jews at all? Today, you can still see orthodox Jews who wear special clothes, observe the Sabbath (Saturday) strictly, and follow the kosher rules about food (such as not eating pork). But as among Christians, many younger people are drifting away from religion. They do not attend the synagogue regularly, they eat forbidden foods, and marry non-Jews.

Their elders are worried; they say that Judaism used to be threatened by persecution but now it is threatened by indifference.

The Sikh flagpole ceremony

• How important is religion in people's sense of national or ethnic identity?
• Is it important to you in that way?

▶ ▭ An interview with ... the Right Reverend Dr Michael Nazir-Ali

The Right Reverend Dr Michael Nazir-Ali is the Bishop of Rochester, a title that goes back nearly 1,400 years. Born and brought up in Pakistan, the Bishop understands multi-culturalism in Britain better than most people.
He advises the heir to the British throne, Prince Charles, on the issue.

Bishop Michael, how religious is Britain today?
Well, it depends on how you measure religion. About 70 per cent of the population say that they believe in God; about 60 per cent belong to some Christian church or other; and then, of course, there are people of other faiths: like Muslims, Hindus, Buddhists, Jews, Sikhs, and they have to be added, of course, to that number to show what the practice of religion is like. Now, when that translates into going to church on a Sunday, then, of course, the figures are much lower. About 14 per cent of the population go to church weekly, but that doubles if you think about people going monthly, and it increases with people going once or twice a year.

Should there be a state religion?
Well, if you mean by that the Church of England: the Church of England is not a state church in the sense that they have, for example, on the continent of Europe. It is an Established Church. It is not a state church in the sense that its clergy are not paid by the state. But it is an Established Church and by that what is meant, I suppose, is that the state has decided through its official organs, like Parliament, that a particular church should have a special voice in the affairs of the nation. Now, naturally, when the Church is asked to do this, it would be very foolish to refuse because the Church has a whole range of interests – not only in religious matters, but in things like education, aspects of medicine, social policy and so forth. So the Church naturally values being asked to have a voice. But, of course, we live in a developing situation and the state may feel that in addition to the voice of the Church of England, it may also want to hear the voices of other churches and indeed people of other faiths.

• **Are people in your country religious? Is there a state or established religion?**
• **How many religions or religious denominations exist in your country?**

What advice do you give the heir to the British throne, considering he's going to be king of a country which has large numbers of religious minorities?

Well, I don't think that the heir to the British throne, the Prince of Wales, actually needs advice; because he's fully aware – more than aware – of the situation in this country and, indeed, generally throughout the world. He has said that he wants to be Defender of Faith rather than Defender of the Faith. And if by that he means that he wants to defend the rights of all the citizens of this country to practise and to propagate whatever faith they choose, then I think that is quite a noble ambition.

Do you sometimes feel personally that you're caught in a very tricky situation, being a South Asian immigrant who belongs to a family that was originally Muslim and you're now in a predominantly Christian country?

Yes, I think there are dilemmas, but there can be creative dilemmas. I think every society needs a perspective from the outside, if one can put it like that, though that perspective should also be informed by what is going on inside. Most of my ministry has been not only in South Asia but in the Middle East and indeed in Africa.
So, I have some experience of what the world looks like outside. I think it was Kipling who said: "Those who only England know, How can England know?" I never thought that I would be a minister in this country. All my preparation, all my study had been for a ministry in South Asia and the Middle East.

But God works in surprising ways and so I accept this calling, which, as you say, is not always easy, but it can be very creative.

What role is there for religion in a society that looks to science for answers?

Well, science can give you certain kinds of answers. Science is concerned with quantity, with the behaviour of objects; it can increase our understanding about how the physical world works.

It can answer questions like 'what' and 'how', but it cannot answer questions like 'why'. And, of course, for that we need a spiritual vision.

You belong to a family that was originally Muslim. What do you think of the prospects for a dialogue between Islam and Christianity?

Well, I still have many Muslim relatives and many more Muslim friends in many parts of the world, and I've been engaged in conversation with them on all sorts of issues for many years.

Some of those issues have to do with belief, with the nature of God, how God reveals Himself in this world. Some have to do with questions about society – how human societies are to be shaped in today's world; some have to do with rights and responsibilities of people – not only with religious freedom but other kinds of freedom. For instance, the place of women in society. Those are all matters for dialogue and they have continued for a very long time.

What is the Church doing to make itself relevant to people in modern Britain?

The Church has many opportunities to address particular social and political issues. But there are many issues locally. For instance, some years ago, our own local authority decided to make some cuts in the budget, and there was an uproar by all sorts of people, some of whom had considerable clout in the community and were able to make their voices heard. But I realised that there were some people being affected who did not have a voice.

It is very important for the Church to organise its worship and its teaching in such a way that it is accessible to people. This is where we have not been very successful in the past. Accessible not only in terms of language and music and so forth, but, for instance, access to the disabled, access for those who have impaired hearing.

So I think we have to be mission-minded, outward-going, to reach people and to show them how faith relates to their daily life.

- **Do you agree that every society needs a perspective from the outside?**
- **What do religions, such as Christianity and Islam, have in common?**

Newspapers

The British are great newspaper readers. They used to read even more 50 years ago, when there was no competition from television, but even so almost every adult in the country reads, or at least glances at, a daily newspaper. The sales and readership figures are tremendous (see chart below).

	Sales per day (millions)	Readers per day (millions)
The Sun	3.7	9.9
The Mirror	2.3	6.3
Daily Mail	2.2	5.1
The Express	1.1	2.6
The Daily Telegraph	1.0	2.5
The Times	0.7	2.0
Daily Star	0.6	1.9
The Guardian	0.4	1.2
The Independent	0.2	0.7
Financial Times	0.2	0.6

Sales and readership of national daily newspapers, 1998.
Source: National Readership Surveys Ltd.

The high numbers reflect the fact that newspapers are not only popular with educated middle-class but also with working-class people. The more serious, weightier papers are known as broadsheets, a term which refers to their big page size. The lighter, easier-to-read papers have a page size half as big, and are called tabloids. *The Times*, *Daily Telegraph*, *Guardian* and *Independent* are broadsheets; *The Sun*, *Mirror* and *Star* are tabloids. *The Express* and *Mail* are in between – tabloid in size, but semi-broadsheet in content.

The cultural gulf between the broadsheets and the tabloids is enormous; it almost seems strange to call them both newspapers. A serious paper like *The Independent* gives long, detailed news stories with historical analysis, and carefully balanced comment which is usually separate from the news reporting. It has a lot of foreign news; it has sections on books, education and computers; it rarely mentions the National Lottery except to discuss its organisation. The lightest of the tabloids, *The Sun*, has very short items on politics and world events in which it freely mixes facts and comment; it has many pages of gossip about TV celebrities and lots of sex stories; it has competitions and horoscopes and semi-pornographic photos of women; it is obsessed with the lottery and lottery winners.

In spite of the apparently light content of the tabloids, they appear to have as much if not more political influence than the broadsheets. Although television has taken over as the main news provider, the law prevents TV from taking sides in politics. So it is left to the newspapers to support parties and give interpretations of the news. None of the daily papers is actually run by the political parties, however. Several are owned by companies controlled by individuals: there is a tradition of rich and powerful press barons. Viscount Rothermere dominates the *Mail*; Lord Hollick, *The Express*. Some of these press barons are not English but from Commonwealth countries: Conrad Black of *The Daily Telegraph* is Canadian; Rupert Murdoch of *The Sun* is Australian. Actually, Murdoch's multinational company, News Corporation, also owns *The Times*, *The Sunday Times* and the massively popular Sunday paper *News of the World*; it also controls the satellite TV channel BSkyB, various media companies in the USA, a satellite TV service based in Hong Kong and 70 per cent of all Australian newspapers. Many observers are concerned that with all these media interests Murdoch has bought himself too much influence in politics.

The Sun is by far the biggest-selling paper in Britain, and it always has a clear political line. In addition, many of its readers are the floating voters who change their minds at election time and so decide the results. Throughout the 80s and early 90s it gave solid support to Mrs Thatcher, and the Conservatives won four elections in succession. As the Labour Party moved to the political right, Murdoch deserted his old allies and switched his

- **Are any British newspapers available in your country? Have you read any of them?**
- **What is the advantage of newspapers over TV for news?**

The Sun *Tuesday March 18th 1997*

support to Tony Blair in 1997, so once again *The Sun* was on the winning side. It is not possible to say that Murdoch actually delivered these election results, but in some cases his intervention made a very great impact.

As in all democratic countries, press freedom is an important aspect of British life. In this country, without a written constitution, such freedom is not actually set down in the law, but there are no laws restricting it, so the end result is much the same. In fact, it is fairer to say that there are very few laws restricting it; for example, it is illegal to incite racial hatred. Recent discussion of press freedom has been around the question of privacy: how far should the press be permitted to investigate and report people's private lives? Things have changed a lot since the 1930s, when King Edward VIII was having a love affair with a divorced American woman, Mrs Simpson, and the press agreed not to report it. In the 1990s, an embarrassing phone conversation between Prince Charles and his mistress Camilla Parker-Bowles was illegally recorded and then

splashed all over the newspapers. The sex lives or financial dealings of politicians became one of the journalists' most popular topics. The paparazzi, mainly photographers with long lenses, were a very international group, but one of their biggest markets was the British tabloid press. There were many proposals to limit invasions of privacy, but without result: it always appeared impossible to distinguish between pure gossip and items of real public importance.

The issue came to a head in 1997 with the deaths of Princess Diana and her lover Dodi Al Fayed while their car was being chased through Paris by a pack of paparazzi on motorcycles. Had she, in effect, been killed by the media? Were the newspaper readers in some way to blame for the tragedy? The shock of her death was something unique in British life: the whole country seemed to come to a standstill for several weeks. For a full month, 35 per cent of newspaper stories were devoted to the Princess – more than to any news event in history. One reason for this was the feeling of collective guilt. Although it became clear that the paparazzi in Paris were not directly to blame for the accident, Diana's brother, Earl Spencer, in his speech at the funeral blamed the press. There were loud calls for more regulation. Many said that the voluntary code of practice operated by the Press Complaints Commission was not enough. But in the end, the only action was an agreement from the newspapers not to harass Diana's sons, Prince William and Prince Harry.

A line of paparazzi photographers in action

- **What is the relationship between newspapers and political parties in your country?**
- **Should newspapers report on the private lives of politicians?**

Television

Regulation of TV in Britain is very different from regulation of the press. Whereas newspapers are mostly about news, the TV is mostly entertainment and so is subject to more rules on sex, violence and bad language. As watchdogs, there are the Broadcasting Standards Council and the Broadcasting Complaints Commission. They make sure, for example, that there is very little pornography on TV; and they police the 9 p.m. watershed: the time before which all programmes must be suitable for children. Strangely, more complaints are received from the public about bad language – swearing – than anything else; the British seem to be particularly sensitive to this rather superficial issue.

It is on the question of politics that TV rules differ most from those which apply to newspapers. While newspapers can express any political views, or support any political party they wish to, TV channels are not permitted such freedom; they are obliged to maintain a strict balance between the political parties, to be impartial. One programme which shows the Conservatives in a good light must be followed soon after by one which favours Labour. The system seems quite heavy-handed, but it is easy to see why it has come into being.

Tony Blair in the hot seat on BBC's Question Time.

Although newspaper readership is high, people actually tend to get most of their news from television: a recent survey showed that 62 per cent rely on TV and only 17 per cent on newspapers as their main source of national news. At the same time, there are only five terrestrial TV channels – so without regulation, one rich political party could completely dominate the news on the commercial channels. The government of the day, of whichever party, could manipulate the state-owned company, the BBC.

The BBC is not an organ of the government; it is run by governors, some of whom are appointed by the government, but there is little political control. All political parties complain sometimes about the BBC's treatment of them, and that includes the party in power: the last Conservative Government often said that the BBC was against it. The BBC is funded by a TV licence fee; everyone with a TV has to buy one each year for just over £100. The system means that the BBC can put on educational material which would not be commercially viable; it fulfils the role of a public-service broadcaster. And many feel that it is worth £2 per week to be able to watch films which are not interrupted by advertisements!

Viewers trust TV news partly because they know that it is not in the hands of one political party, and partly because it is much harder to tell lies with live interviews and filmed reports of events than on the pages of newspapers. Still photos are easy to manipulate on a computer, but video is far more difficult. Seeing the faces of politicians as they speak, and hearing their voices, helps the viewer to identify the truth. However, the truth is not really quite so easy to obtain. In reality, politicians still manage to manipulate their TV messages in all sorts of ways. Each interview is planned in advance; the TV presenter and the politician agree on rules of engagement: questions will be asked on the economy but not on Northern Ireland, for example.

The overall political agenda is created by politicians, not by TV or the press. An interesting case is that of green issues and Mrs Thatcher. She had not been at all interested in climate change, until one day she decided it might be a vote winner, so she started talking about it. The media picked this up and suddenly employed environment correspondents to cover the green stories.

- **Is there a lot of sex and violence on your country's TV? Who decides what is allowed?**
- **Is it a good idea to have public-service broadcasting without advertising?**

An array of satellite dishes on a block of flats

Then in the European Parliament elections in 1987, the Green Party won 2.3 million votes, and Mrs Thatcher realised that she was actually losing votes as people became interested in the environment. She dropped the topic, and the media followed her lead. Reporting of green issues in the newspapers and on TV went back to the same low level as before, and has stayed there ever since.

With only five terrestrial channels available, it is not surprising that many people have switched on to satellite TV. One of the biggest visual changes in British cities in the last ten years has been the appearance of satellite dishes on houses and flats, especially in working-class areas; more than a quarter of all households have one. In addition, about 7 per cent have cable TV. Both of these systems offer lots of channels – Sky Movies, Sky Sports, Cartoon Network, Discovery, UK Style and many more. These channels make their money by charging subscriptions and through advertising, and they are doing very well commercially. But their contribution to the quality of TV is questionable: they make their own news and sports programmes, but very little else. Unlike the five terrestrial channels they do not invest in original programme making; they recycle material made by others.

Radio

Radio is, in a sense, the Cinderella of the media: it is often left out of discussions, or, as in this chapter, left until last. Television is more glamorous, and everyone watches it. But 90 per cent of people say that they listen to the radio in their spare time – in fact, it is the third most popular leisure activity after watching TV and visiting friends. But in spite of predictions when television first arrived, radio has not died, in fact its popularity has risen.

Because radio is comparatively inexpensive, it can fill far more niches than television: there is local radio even in small communities, and there are hundreds of specialist stations. People living in Birmingham, for example, can receive 27 stations on FM, including no fewer than nine BBC stations (national and local), a Welsh language station, and a variety for pop music. At one time, the BBC had a monopoly on radio in Britain, whereas today it has to compete with lots of commercial stations, both local and nationwide. Radio 3, the BBC's classical music station, is very academic and serious, but it used to do quite well because it had no competition. Then in 1992, Classic FM came on the air, with Vivaldi, Mozart, jokes and recipes all day long, and Radio 3 lost most of its audience. Surprisingly, however, in the pop-music field, BBC Radio 1 fought back against fierce competition, and it remains the favourite music station for young people in Britain.

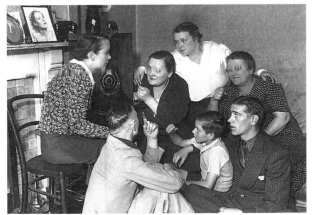

Fifty years ago, families listened to the radio together.

• Is there any disadvantage in having lots of TV channels?
• Do you listen to the radio much? What sort of programmes work well on the radio?

Getting around

Britain has almost the same population as France but less than half the space. With 238 people per square kilometre, it is a densely populated country. So it is not surprising that the transport system is fairly comprehensive. With the notable exception of the Highlands of Scotland, almost every square centimetre of the map of Britain is covered by a network of roads and railways.

As in most countries of the world, roads have taken over from rail as the major transport system. But trains in Britain are still a safe, fast and comfortable way of travelling. There is one big problem which deters many people from using them: the price. British trains are very expensive to travel on, at least if you do not know how to get the best deals. If you simply go into a station, buy a ticket and get on the train, you may end up paying a small fortune. To avoid a nasty shock, there are two secrets: one, get a full list of all the special types of tickets available; and two, book in advance. As an example, in 1999 the full price of a London to Manchester return ticket was £119; a Super Saver ticket, which cannot be used in the rush hour, was £48; and a Virgin Value ticket, which has to be booked a minimum of three days in advance, was only £19 – saving exactly £100. If you are travelling from London, there is one other useful piece of advice: make sure you go to the right station, as there are seven major and many smaller ones!

Much cheaper, and without all the restrictions about advanced booking and rush hours, are coach services. Of course, there are disadvantages: no restaurant, no room to walk around and no tables. The worst drawback is that the coach station is usually in the middle of town, so there is a long struggle through traffic before your coach gets out onto the motorway.

Road rage

Forty years ago, private car ownership was growing rapidly, and public transport was losing its dominant role. The process seemed quite natural and, on the whole, a good thing. In the 1960s, British Railways cut hundreds of lines and stations. It was painful for small rural communities at the time, but, as car ownership spread, they adjusted to the situation.

Governments were happy to see the hugely expensive state-owned railway wither away.

Roads became over-crowded, of course, and the solution to that problem was simple – build more roads. A massive new motorway around Outer London, the M25, was opened in 1986. However, this provided a dramatic example of a phenomenon which had been noticed by experts many times before: building new roads appears to generate new traffic. The M25 was overloaded immediately, and now it is the site of some of the country's worst traffic jams almost every day.

It has long been noted that car driving has some strange psychological effects on human beings. The Canadian philosopher Marshall McLuhan said: "The car has become the carapace, the protective and aggressive shell, of urban man." People who are normally quiet and pleasant are often transformed when they get behind the wheel of a car. As in the R. L. Stevenson story, the good Dr Jekyll becomes the evil Mr Hyde. The idea used to be a common

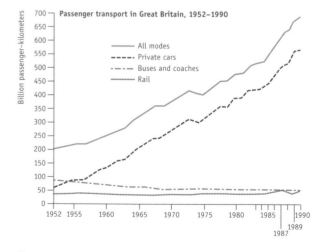

Passenger transport 1952–1980
Source: Transport statistics 1981–91, Department of transport

• **What are the advantages of trains for the traveller and for the environment?**
• **What is your favourite form of transport?**

The Humber bridge, near Hull in the north-east of England, has a total length of more than two kilometres.

The problems of public transport

However crowded the roads are, British car owners usually find a reason not to switch to public transport. The buses are too slow, or the trains are too expensive, or no public services actually take them where they want to go. In many cases, these are just the excuses of people who really want to sit in their own cars with the radio on, and who blame others for creating the traffic jams. But there is also some truth in their criticisms. There has been a serious lack of government investment in transport, with predictable consequences.

An interesting example is that of the London Underground. The Tube, as Londoners call it, started in 1863 as the first underground line in the world, and is still the longest, with over 400 kilometres of lines. When it is working well, it is extremely quick and efficient. But those who use it every day complain of terrible delays when things go wrong. The electrical engineering is old, and it breaks down frequently. In 1987, 30 people died in a fire at King's

theme for comedians. By the 1990s, however, it was no longer a joke, and a new phrase was coined: road rage. More and more often, people were getting out of their cars and starting fights with other drivers; murders have been committed. Hours of isolation, competition and frustration, while breathing in exhaust fumes, are obviously not good for people.

Road accident figures, on the other hand, have not increased with the number of vehicles on the road; in fact they have decreased. Various reasons are suggested for this: modern cars have better lights and brakes, and the culture of driving has become more mature. One obvious reason is the slowness of city traffic – nobody gets killed when the cars are standing still. Whatever the reasons, Britain has a better record than most European neighbours; the number of deaths per 10,000 vehicles is less than half that of France, for example. Another significant factor is that seat belt laws for vehicle drivers and passengers are respected by almost everyone.

Britain is one of the few countries in the world (Japan is another) where cars drive on the left. It would be possible to change: they used to drive on the left in Sweden. But, like Japan, Britain is an island nation, so there is not much road traffic across its borders. In any case, many British people are rather proud of little oddities like this. There are no plans to change.

The latest addition to the Tube system: the Jubilee Line extension was completed in 1999.

- Is road rage a problem in your country? Have you ever suffered from it?
- Why are governments starting to think about limiting the number of cars on the road?

Cross station. Since then a lot of money has been spent on safety, and the record has been good. But reliability has not improved. Successive governments have simply failed to invest the huge sums of money which would be needed to bring the Tube up to 21st century standards.

The London Underground is one of the only parts of the transport system which is still in the hands of the state. The Conservative Government in the 1980s and 90s thought that the problems of under-investment could be solved by privatisation. Buses outside London, and the whole of the railway system, passed into private ownership. The idea was that, with profits to be made, private finance would come in and rebuild the system. So far, however, the results have been disappointing. Public use of buses

The Eurostar at its specially-built London terminus.

has continued to decline. Train fares are so high that they deter passengers, and in most parts of the country trains are less reliable now than before.

One particular failure has been a cause of considerable embarrassment to the British since the opening of the Channel Tunnel. Eurostar trains from Paris travel at up to 300 kilometres per hour in France, but have to slow down to 80 kilometres per hour once in Britain because the high-speed line has not yet been built. Parliament only made the decision to build the line after the tunnel had opened. This sad story seems to symbolise all the country's transport problems.

Integrated transport?

The government has recently started talking about the ultimate solution to the problems – an integrated transport system. This means improving public services and making sure that they all work together as a system, rather than a series of disconnected parts. At present, if you need to take a train, a bus and a ferry for your journey, you will often find that the bus station is kilometres away from the train station, and the bus timetable does not match the ferry timetable. You end up taking taxis between stations, and spending hours sitting in waiting rooms. In many parts of the country, trains and buses compete with each other on one route, while another route has no service at all. An integrated transport system is urgently needed to address all these problems. But it will take a great deal of time, money and political will to achieve such a system.

London Heathrow is the world's busiest international airport. It handles over 58 million passengers per year.

A solution?

Rush hour is when traffic really becomes a problem. Millions of people commuting to work by road every day create jams. These create pollution, waste time and cause stress. A very simple solution would

- **Can market forces solve transport problems – or must governments intervene?**
- **How well integrated is transport in your country?**

be not to go to work. Of course, if you are a police officer, a builder or a surgeon, this is not a very practical idea. But for many professionals, including designers, engineers, accountants, writers and software specialists, it is now possible to get connected and work from a virtual office. It is sometimes called teleworking, and it can be done from home, wherever your home happens to be. A teleworker can sit in a cottage on a beautiful little island off the west coast of Scotland and send all work via the Internet straight to an employer in Birmingham or a client in Cardiff. A few years ago this was only a dream, but now several million people in Britain are making the dream come true. In the long term, this could bring about the economic regeneration of country areas which have been suffering from unemployment. It could also go some way to solving Britain's transport and pollution problems.

Snail mail

Snail mail is the humorous term coined by e-mail users for the old-fashioned letters-in-envelopes postal system. The implication is that such letters travel very slowly, but actually that is rather unfair. In Britain you can send letters first or second class; the first class ones normally get to their destination, anywhere in the country, the next morning. The efficiency of the service is one of the reasons that it did not get privatised along with most other state-owned enterprises in the 1980s and 90s. Another reason is the British love of tradition. The service is called the Royal Mail, and all British stamps have the head of the Queen on them. The royal crest appears on the classic red pillar boxes.

Telephones

Like the old red pillar boxes, another traditional feature of British streets is the red phone box – but they are something of an endangered species these days. The telephone system, which used to be part of the Post Office, was privatised in 1984. The new company, British Telecom (BT), proceeded to replace the old boxes with a more modern steel and glass design. Before they had finished the job,

the public started to protest and some of the old style boxes were preserved.

The monopoly of the state system was not preserved, but it has been hard for new competitors to get a share of the market, and BT continues with a quasi-monopoly. The company makes huge profits, often around £4 billion per year. Its huge size has enabled it to make major deals with overseas companies, such as Spain's Banco Santander. In 1998, it set up a joint venture with the American giant AT&T worth $10 billion per year.

BT's competitors have been much more successful in the new market for mobile phones. Mobiles have increased massively in Britain just as in the rest of the world. They are to be seen absolutely everywhere – in schools, restaurants, theatres and even churches. They ring during lectures, meetings and the quiet bits in classical music concerts. In a recent opinion poll, 62 per cent of people said that the most annoying thing in their lives was mobile phones on the train!

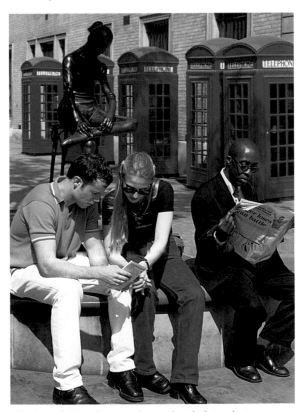

The British love their traditional red phone boxes.

- **Do you use/like e-mail? Does snail mail still have some advantages?**
- **How widespread are mobile phones in your country? Do they annoy you?**

An interview with ...
St George Alphonse

St George Alphonse originally comes from a tiny Caribbean island called St Lucia, which is one of Britain's 14 remaining dependent territories. He is a courier – ferrying documents from the airport and between offices. With the help of his son, Wayne, he runs his own small courier company, which is made up of one van and three cars.

How would you describe a typical day of work?
I've got a motto of mine: "If you know you got so many jobs to do the following day, if you get up early, you're on top of the job. But if you get up late, you're flat out". And I've tried to instigate that to my son but he's got a different line of thinking to mine. My typical day is starting early, do all the jobs I got to do and fit other jobs in between. To me that is the most beautiful day I can ever have, in any day of work. On a typical day of work I do a combination of things. I start with the airline for the press material coming in, which is required by the BBC at a certain time. Then after that, I fit in doing a friend a favour by moving a chair or doing some, work we call, "unpack" for people coming here from abroad. They need their personal belongings taking to their home and so on. Then, if I can, I try and pop into my local, have a bite to eat, but if I can't, I usually pick up a sandwich and eat as I go along. And you'll find, come the afternoon, there'll be the usual pick-up in London to take back to the airport for export. My hours vary. For example, yesterday, I had a 16-hour day. I started at nine o'clock and I didn't get indoors last night until two o'clock. Because of this Kosovo war, a certain BBC reporter wanted a bullet-proof jacket and helmet picked up from Hereford, and I'd just finished my day and it was six o'clock and that phone call comes through – could we do it?

What's it like being a courier?
It's a great job. I've been doing it from '65 and the buzz I get out of it is to be able to deliver the press material or the document to the people concerned so that they could then get on with their job. At the end of it all, they show their appreciation, say, "You're a star", and that's what I like about a courier.

Have things changed a lot since you started?
Yes, it has. There's not as much work as there used to be. I think one of the main reasons is the satellite thing which the Third World countries are having installed, which the BBC is doing quite a bit as well. And the programmes now are being put on mostly video tapes and there's very, very few press materials. But I still get quite a lot of bits and pieces coming through but not as much as there used to be. A perfect example: the BBC used to use a laboratory in north London which, back in the '60s, I used to do, in a day, five-six trips to. Now, I'm lucky if I do one in three months. It seems to be dying because of the modern technology, with the video being used continuously, and of course satellites from the different countries being used more and more. News material, like big accidents, the trouble in Kosovo or so on and so forth – the majority of it is beamed straight across and some of it is sent by video, which is for them to keep or the shots they couldn't get live, we handle that part of it. And, of course, there's still the camera equipment, there's still the programmes they sell abroad which we pick up and deliver back to the airport to be shipped abroad. Before the mobile phone came, we used to get to our destination, ring office and say, "Is there anything else you need to be picked up or need to be done?" But now the mobile phone is there, you'll be on your way

• **Would you be prepared to work long hours like St George?**
• **What would your ideal working day be?**

leaving Heathrow with one urgent package and another one comes up; you do a U-turn, go back for it; and you kill two birds with one stone.

Are there any in-built problems with all these new developments in technology, for example, the use of mobile phones?

Well, I can't confirm that for sure, but from what I've been reading, I think there is something to be feared about mobile phones. Me, personally, I notice my left ear – which is the one I use a lot for my mobile phone – there always seems to be an itching. What I've discovered recently is that burning sensation round my eyes. OK, I know when I haven't had enough sleep my eyes tend to irritate. But it's happening more often now than it used to. Even when I have enough sleep. So I still think until someone comes out and say, "Right, this is such and such wrong with it", which I don't think they will, because if they was to tell you the truth, I think the whole set-up would collapse. Now I must admit I'm getting a bit worried because if there is something genuinely wrong, we need to know now rather to let it go on and at a later stage discover it's gone to the point of no return.

I started using a mobile phone in the '80s when they first came out. My first mobile phone was a P3, which was the rather heavy object. I read about them and they had a salesman who came into the BBC Shipping at the time, who was trying to sell to the BBC and the manager called me and said, "I think this would be very helpful to communication", – between BBC Shipping and myself *en route* from home or going on a job and, of course, we went into it there and then. Nothing was explained to us, all the salesman was interested in was to get the sale. So because I wanted to give the BBC the best service as I can I then went into it. And it's been a good piece of technology, but the problem is worrying – about the end, the damage it might be doing to us individually and we don't know about it yet.

Going by the pace of change, do you think you'll still have a job in 20 years' time?

It's difficult. I don't think so. Personally, I don't think so. With the technology and communication at the moment – I don't think it will. Because I heard you could see whoever you speak to on the phone in some parts of the States. If that can happen, who knows what else could come true in 20 years' time. Don't forget the courier's main stuff is usually printed matter. The videos – usually you could pick it up by satellite, which a lot of Third World countries are installing anyway.

Do you ever worry that your son is in the same job and such a job may not even exist tomorrow?

Yes, I worry and he made me know that he doesn't see anything in it for him. I was having a general chat. He wanted to call it a day because he said he was going away and there was nothing in it for him. I tried to say to him: "a job like this, because you don't expand, you've just got to stick to it to cover the daily costs". He'll be 36 this year, and I said to him: "You left it a bit late to say something like that. You should have made provision that if you didn't like it after so many years, you could always go and try your hand at something else."

• **Do you think mobile phones are dangerous?**
• **Can you think of any other jobs that might disappear in the next 20 years?**

TV, drama and comedy

We have already looked at TV as a news medium, but of course it is much more than that. British people do not spend an average of 3.5 hours in front of the television every night watching the news. Most of the favourite programmes are drama in one form or another: films, serials, series or soaps. Quite a lot of these are American, as you might expect: not only films but comedy series such as *Friends*, and action series such as *ER* or the *X Files*. British children have no problem imitating American accents. For some reason there are no American soaps, but there are two massively successful Australian ones – *Home and Away* and *Neighbours*. An impressive amount of programmes may be exported from Britain, but almost twice that amount are imported.

There is, however, a tradition of quality home-grown drama which is different in character from the American product. Much of it is socially realistic. Two of the top soaps – *EastEnders* and *Coronation Street* – are set in working-class communities and reflect the very unglamorous lives of ordinary people; *EastEnders* often deals with serious issues such as racism, drug addiction and sexual abuse. Later in the evening, there is sometimes serious drama in the form of TV films or serials. The BBC had a name for making this sort of material – often uncompromising, radical and highly original drama by writers such as Dennis Potter and Alan Bleasdale. But there is an economic problem with these programmes: they are hard to sell to foreign markets. So these days the BBC, which has changed very much in character and become a highly commercial enterprise, prefers to make costume drama: adaptations of classic novels by Jane Austen and so on, which it can sell to the USA and elsewhere.

Fortunately, Channel 4 has taken over the BBC's old role as sponsor of quality television drama, and does a lot to finance new filmmakers. Mike Leigh, Stephen Frears and Peter Greenaway all started with Channel 4. Michael Radford, the English director of the wonderful Italian film *Il Postino*, made his first film for Channel 4 – a realistic, romantic tragedy about Italian prisoners of war in Scotland in 1944, titled *Another Time, Another Place*.

Both the BBC and the independent stations produce a lot of good (as well as quite a lot of bad) comedy. Of course, humour is especially hard to export, and in fact many shows are remade with different actors for the American market. But surprisingly, some humour does seem to travel. The comic Benny Hill, although considered hopelessly unfunny by many British viewers, enjoyed

Much of the drama in the popular soap EastEnders takes place in a pub in London's East End.

- **How many American programmes are shown on your country's TV? Do you feel there are too many?**
- **Does TV have a serious role to play, or is it just entertainment?**

Comedian Eddie Izzard is a major hit on stage and TV.

worldwide commercial success. *Monty Python*, in spite of seeming completely surreal when it first appeared, became a cult classic. Then there was the phenomenon of Britain's new Charlie Chaplin – great for international audiences, as he hardly speaks – Rowan Atkinson, in *Mr Bean*. A problem with a lot of older comedy was that it was based on sexist and racist jokes about women drivers, stupid Irishmen, mean Jews and so on. The last ten years have seen the growth of alternative comedy which manages to avoid, and in fact often attacks those old stereotypes. Eddie Izzard, for example, is a brilliant alternative comedian who also succeeds in communicating with overseas audiences.

Theatre

Film and TV drama have their roots in the theatre, and theatre has long been important in British cultural life. After all, the most celebrated creative export of all

time is Shakespeare. Actually Shakespeare, although uniquely talented, was not the only dramatist of his time; he had competition from Christopher Marlowe, Ben Jonson and others. The theatre flowered quickly and gloriously in the Elizabethan and Jacobean periods. It was suppressed briefly by the Puritans in the 17th century, but since then it has been a vibrant and popular art form right up to the present day. Most periods have had their great playwrights: William Congreve, Oliver Goldsmith, Sheridan, Oscar Wilde, George Bernard Shaw, Harold Pinter. Even when, as in the mid 19th century, there was a lack of major dramatists, the theatre thrived on European drama or revivals of classics.

Cinema has not destroyed live theatre, as some thought it would. Theatre-going actually increased during the 20th century, the age of film. In London today there are over 100 theatres, which is more than any other city in the world, including New York. Of course, the audiences are not all Londoners; the majority are foreign tourists. But the British are still very theatre-minded, and there are no fewer than 17,000 amateur theatre groups in the country. Every school does drama – the school play is an institution, and can be extremely well-produced with good lighting, music and costumes.

The theatre and the cinema have a sort of symbiotic relationship, with many actors, directors and writers doing both. Sir Anthony Hopkins, Kenneth Branagh and Emma Thompson all had careers on the stage before going into films.

London's theatreland buzzes with action in the early evening.

- **Are there theatres in your town or city? Do you ever go?**
- **Can you see any advantage of theatre over film, or is theatre just old-fashioned?**

The theatre writer Tom Stoppard wrote the screenplay for the hugely successful *Shakespeare in Love*. Actors in the theatre quite often go into films for the money and fame, and later come back to the stage for the pleasure and artistic satisfaction of it. So Hollywood stars like Nicole Kidman or Dustin Hoffman occasionally appear in small London theatres.

Film

The reason why Hollywood dominates the world's film industry is a long and complicated story. It can be traced back to the very beginnings of film technology 100 years ago, when Americans such as Thomas Edison fought hard to get a monopoly on the hardware of film making. At that time the French Lumière brothers, George Méliès and the Pathé brothers were leading the way, and the Germans and Italians soon had thriving film industries. The Americans also had a more aggressive approach to the business, and understood that distribution was the key to success; cinemas in Britain today are 80 per cent owned by Hollywood companies such as Warner and Buena Vista.

Shakespeare in Love: *the playwright is the star in this highly original film.*

World War I undermined the economies of the European countries at a crucial time, and the American movie industry was never seriously challenged again. Even now, through the GATT (General Agreement on Tariffs and Trade) agreements, US negotiators are fighting any attempts by Europeans to protect their small film industries with subsidies or quotas.

Quite a lot of films are made in Britain today, even if many of them are not strictly British. There is a solid base of excellent technical staff – the lighting and sound engineers, camera operators and so on – which attracts American and other filmmakers to this country. There are some good studios: Shepperton, Pinewood, and Elstree, where Steven Spielberg directed *Raiders of the Lost Ark* and the other two Indiana Jones films; he called it "the best studio in the world". The great American director Stanley Kubrick (*A Clockwork Orange, 2001 A Space Odyssey, The Shining*) lived and worked in Britain,

Harrison Ford in Raiders of the Lost Ark, *an American film made in Britain.*

- **Has your country got a strong film industry? If so, what are its strengths?**
- **Which British films have you seen? What was good or bad about them?**

and even made his wonderful Vietnam war film *Full Metal Jacket* on bits of waste ground in East London.

In the last few years, a series of films with a strong British character has done well internationally. The Scottish director Danny Boyle made a name for himself with two shockingly realistic, violent and funny films, *Shallow Grave* (about getting rid of a dead body) and *Trainspotting* (about heroin addicts). A simple romantic comedy, *Four Weddings and a Funeral* was a big hit, as was another funny film on the rather unfunny theme of unemployment, *The Full Monty*. Rowan Atkinson managed to translate his great comic character from the small to the big screen with the film *Bean*. A highly original director who lets his actors improvise and so obtains extremely natural performances, Mike Leigh, won critical acclaim at the Cannes festival with *Secrets and Lies*. To crown it all, *Shakespeare in Love* won seven Oscars (film – industry awards) in 1999, including Best Picture.

Of course, the *James Bond* films have always been popular around the world, and so was the *Pink Panther* series 30 years ago. But most good British films have been more artistic and obscure, getting shown only in film clubs and art cinemas. Ken Loach has made a number of films with serious social and political themes, starting with *Poor Cow* about homelessness in 1967; *Hidden Agenda* is critical of the British role in the Northern Ireland troubles; *Raining Stones* is a touching story of a poor unemployed man's desperate attempts to get money to buy a dress for his daughter; *Land and Freedom* is about an English communist who goes to fight in the Spanish Civil War, and the terrible disappointment he suffers. Peter Greenaway is more interested in acting, sets and visual effects – a more theatrical approach. His adaptation of Shakespeare's *The Tempest*, a film called *Prospero's Books*, is an extraordinary feast of sound and pictures; his most popular film *The Cook, The Thief, His Wife, and Her Lover* is a witty, beautifully acted story which ends with a shocking act of cannibalism. The gay director Derek Jarman made films with a strong homoerotic element but they are serious comments on sexuality, rather than pornography. As he was dying of AIDS, he made *Blue*, a film consisting of a plain blue screen throughout, with a soundtrack of Jarman's own feelings about his illness.

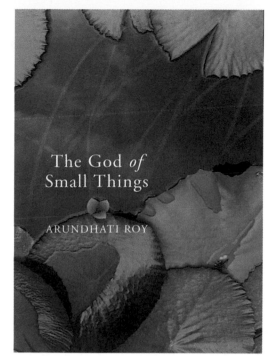

Arundhati Roy won the 1997 Booker Prize with her first novel The God of Small Things.

Literature

It is difficult to sum up British literature in a few paragraphs. After all, this is the country's greatest contribution to the world's culture. Whatever else is wrong with Britain, it has produced a large number of plays, poems and novels that are worth reading. The status of British writers around the world might seem to be connected to the spread of English as an international language. But actually much of the best writing dates from a time before globalisation, and Britain exports less literature today than ever before.

Also there is something of an identity problem for British literature: it is seen more often as just a part of worldwide literature in English. The school subject used to be called English Literature; but that term seems to exclude not only the Americans, but the Welsh and Scots too. In fact, people in this country are just as happy to read novels by the American, E. Annie Proulx, the Indian, Arundhati Roy, the Canadian, Margaret Atwood, or the Australian, Peter Carey.

• **Do you prefer the literature of your own country or foreign literature?**
• **Would you say that reading is an important part of your national culture?**

Books are still popular in Britain. Publishers and bookshops are doing very good business, and reading comes fifth on people's favourite home-based leisure activities (60 per cent of men and 70 per cent of women are readers). There is lots of media attention for the Booker Prize for the best novel each year – there is even betting on the result. The election of the new Poet Laureate (the official national poet) in 1999 created massive interest, with many newspaper articles supporting one candidate or another.

The novelists who are considered for the Booker Prize are the more original or intellectual ones. The best-seller lists are dominated by books written for a mass readership. The numbers of copies sold are sometimes staggering: *The Secret Diary of Adrian Mole Aged 13¾*, the comedy for teenagers by Sue Townsend, has sold over 3 million copies, while Barbara Cartland wrote about 500 romantic novels and sold an estimated 500 million copies worldwide.

Public libraries are an important part of British life. They are run by local councils, they are free, and you are never far away from one. (In the countryside there is often a library bus which comes once a week.) Old ladies take out popular novels, young children get piles of books and audio-cassettes, students find research materials and meet each other in the reference section, and lonely people go to read the newspapers; 40 per cent of people use public libraries. You might think that authors would be against free libraries, which readers can use instead of buying their books.
But actually the opposite is the case for two reasons: firstly, it seems that libraries actually encourage people to buy books as well as borrow them; and secondly, there is a system called the PLR (Public Lending Right) whereby authors get a small payment each time their book is lent by a library.

These days, many libraries have videos, CD-ROMs and Internet access. There is often discussion about computer technology replacing libraries and, indeed, books. But for most purposes, a reference library is still quicker and more effective for finding information than the Internet, not to mention more pleasant to use; you can actually ask a friendly and knowledgeable assistant for help, and walk around a little as you work. As for reading novels – well, you can't curl up in bed with a computer, can you?

Romantic poetry

English Romanticism effectively begins with the publication of the *Lyrical Ballads* by William Wordsworth (1770–1850) and Samuel Coleridge (1772–1834). These poems demonstrate the principal concerns of Romanticism: a love of nature, and a defence of a rural way of life threatened by both the agricultural and industrial revolutions.

An important aspect of the Romantic movement was the poets' reactions to the failure of the French Revolution. Wordsworth and Coleridge gradually became more conservative. Byron (1788–1824), Shelley (1792–1822) and Keats (1795–1821) grew up in the repressive atmosphere of the Napoleonic Wars and were, to varying degrees, radicalised by the events of 1789.

The themes of Romanticism – for example, powerful warnings against tyranny and destruction of the environment – are still relevant. The poems communicate a belief in human spirituality and a desire for social justice as powerfully today as they did 200 years ago.

Percy Bysshe Shelley

• **Do you have access to public libraries or school libraries? Do you think they are important?**
• **Which of the authors on this page have you read? Which would you like to read?**

The 19th century novel

Verse and drama had been the dominant literary forms of previous times, but the novel, which started in the first half of the 18th century, came very quickly to maturity. In the hands of Jane Austen (1775–1817) the novel already seems exquisitely developed and sophisticated. She wrote only about the middle classes, but within that restricted area she was very realistic (which was something new) and humorous; these qualities make her just as popular today as ever.

George Eliot

Although women writers still had difficulty being taken on by serious publishers, Austen was followed by a line of great female novelists. The sisters Charlotte (1816–1855) and Emily (1818–1848) Brontë created two of the most perfect Romantic novels – *Jane Eyre* and *Wuthering Heights*. George Eliot (1819–1890), who was in fact Mary Ann Evans writing under a man's name, tackled moral issues such as women's rights and anti-Semitism with insight and satire; she is considered by some modern critics to be the greatest novelist of her time.

The most popular novelist of the century was Charles Dickens (1812–1870), who wrote in such detail about every aspect of Victorian life, including the virtues and vices of all social classes, that today we often see that period through his eyes. These great names, and many others (such as Thackeray, Trollope, Mrs Gaskell, Hardy, Stevenson) made the 19th century the golden age of the novel.

The 20th century

The novel became the strongest literary form in the 19th century (and it has remained so ever since), but poetry did not die out. Time and again in the last 100 years there have been bursts of poetic creativity and public interest in it. World War I put so many young men through the most extreme of experiences and emotions; and it gave rise to some wonderful verse – philosophical, nostalgic, political, hopeful and despairing. Among these young men were Wilfred Owen, Siegfried Sassoon and Edward Thomas.

Then T.S. Eliot (1888–1965), an American in Britain, took poetry in the direction of experimentation and intellectualism. A fiery Welshman, Dylan Thomas (1914–1953), put the passion back into poetry, and won a new audience through radio. Today, very few people actually buy books of poetry,

Benjamin Zephaniah

but, through public readings and the media, there is still intense interest in original poets like Seamus Heaney, Ursula Fanthorpe and rap poet Benjamin Zephaniah. And, of course, there is the massively successful and popular world of the song lyric.

The novel, surprisingly, was subjected to extreme experimentation early in the century and then later returned to more traditional forms. The Irish writer James Joyce (1882–1941) shocked the literary world with his extraordinary novel *Ulysses*; it is long but has very little plot – its powerful effect is created by the continuous interior monologue of the central character, and by endless changes of style. In his next novel, *Finnegan's Wake*, the experimental style becomes almost incomprehensible.

Virginia Woolf (1882–1941) also concentrated more on the interior life of her characters than plot; her writing is light and delicate, almost poetry rather than prose. D.H. Lawrence (1885–1930), with his passionate analysis of relations between men and women, and his love of nature, seems to look back to the Romantics. In recent years there has been an explosion in the publishing of novels – thousands per year; the form is fairly unchanging, but the variety in content and intention is almost limitless.

• What, if anything, is interesting or valuable about poetry? Do you like it?
• Do you think you could write a novel? If so, what sort of novel would you like to write?

Buildings: first impressions

What makes the look of British towns and cities distinctive? The most striking feature is the lack of blocks of flats. People prefer to live in individual houses – units with their own front doors and sometimes gardens. Perhaps this says something about the national character; a love of privacy and a lack of interest in the wider community. There is a proverb: "An Englishman's home is his castle."

Whatever the deeper reasons for it, the result is that British towns and cities are full of two or three-storey houses. Only in the 1950s and 60s did councils start building tall blocks of flats in the American style; but these have been very unpopular, and the cheaper ones are now being demolished.

Another distinctive feature of British buildings is the use of brick. Some of the oldest monuments, like Hampton Court Palace or Queens' College, Cambridge, are made of brick. It remains the favourite material for new houses today. While the rest of the world prefers concrete, for some reason the British taste is for brick, at least in smaller buildings.

British architecture

Apart from some ancient churches, the oldest buildings you will see in Britain are castles. They are dotted all over the country, with many beautiful examples in Scotland and Wales. They were first built by the Normans after their invasion of England in 1066. The Tower of London dates from about 1078. Because of the Normans' desire to control the population, they started to build castles everywhere, but especially in the more restless regions. For example, King Edward I built a series of massive castles in Wales at the end of the 13th century; his aim was to keep the lawless Welsh under English rule.

As the dominance of the English crown was established, the need for castles diminished. Then the use of gunpowder meant that they could no longer resist attack. So by the 15th century the castle-building age was over. Many Scottish castles are from a later period, but these are not military buildings; they are aristocratic family houses that imitated older styles.

Caernarfon Castle in North Wales, still in perfect condition after 700 years

Since the Middle Ages, architecture in Britain (as in most of Europe) has been based on three major styles: Gothic, classical, and modern. The great early cathedrals and churches are in Gothic style – tall, with pointed arches and highly decorated; they are covered in sculptures of people, animals and plants. The buildings are fantastic engineering achievements, constructed with very little machinery and designed by architects whose names have been forgotten. The tallest spire in Britain, at Salisbury Cathedral, is 123 metres high and was built in the 1330s. It is incredible that such size and perfection were achieved without a single crane or computer!

- **Which are more common in your area – houses or flats? Which do you prefer?**
- **Do you enjoy walking round old buildings such as castles? If so, why?**

Salisbury Cathedral, built 1220–66, has exquisite proportions and lovely surroundings.

Castle Howard, North Yorkshire, is a fine example of 18th century classical architecture.

After the Gothic period, architectural fashion looked back to the classical age of Greece and Rome for its inspiration. So we see columns and triangular pediments as on Greek temples; round arches, domes and perfect Latin lettering as on Roman public buildings. Many of the finest London churches are in this style; St Paul's Cathedral (built by Sir Christopher Wren between 1675 and 1710) is the biggest and most celebrated, but there are many more all over the city.

Not only churches were in the classical style. Rich aristocrats built huge and impressive houses surrounded by parkland; they are on such a grand scale that it is difficult to imagine that they were once private homes, but of course they had dozens and sometimes hundreds of servants.

Many of the most beautiful parts of British cities consist of houses in this style. The period of kings George I to George IV is known as the Georgian period, and cities such as London, Edinburgh, Bristol and Bath still today have large numbers of elegant Georgian houses, which give the streets a striking sense of unity and design.

In the 19th century, during the Victorian age (taking its name from Queen Victoria), architects went back to medieval Gothic ideas for their inspiration. At first sight it is sometimes difficult to tell whether a Victorian church is 100 or 500 years old! At the same time, classical styles did not disappear altogether. In fact, there was a "Battle of the Styles" between classical and Gothic. The British Museum (1823) was a victory for the classical, and the Houses of Parliament (1836) for the Gothic. There was also debate about the use of iron and steel: should these new materials be visible, as in the new bridges and railway stations, or hidden, as in the Natural History Museum, London, where the metal frame is covered by coloured brick and stonework?

From the 1920s on, new ideas were transforming art and music, and architecture, too, was caught up in the modernising culture. People wanted buildings which were not just copies of the past. Having abandoned both classical and Gothic styles, the challenge was to create – to invent – something really new. Luckily, this change in attitude came at the same time as exciting new engineering materials were becoming available.

• **Is the architecture in your country very different from that in Britain?**
• **Why do you think architectural styles change from time to time?**

The city of Bath is famous for its Georgian terraces.

can it make the most of natural light, and can it function without wasteful air conditioning? He is keen to make London a better place to live in, with less traffic and more spaces in which people can enjoy city life. Talking about famous parts of the city like Oxford Circus, Parliament Square and Marble Arch, he says: "They are dangerous, degrading, inhuman and unnecessary spaces where vehicles have replaced people, and the servant has become the master. ... clean, live-work cities based upon the bicycle and upon walking, are absolutely possible." Happily, the government is beginning to follow Rogers' advice and the future of London is looking brighter; there are, for example, plans for a car-free Trafalgar Square.

With concrete and steel together, and new types of glass, it was possible to escape from the traditional forms. For the first time in history, architects were free to make almost any shapes they liked.

Richard Rogers

British architecture is going through a dynamic period, with several big international names such as James Stirling and Norman Foster. Perhaps the architect best known in Britain is the designer of the Millennium Dome, Richard Rogers. He too, has carried out many major projects abroad. He was responsible for the airport in Marseille, numerous office complexes in Japan and the USA, and (with an Italian, Renzo Piano) for the great Centre Pompidou in Paris. In his own country he has worked on many smaller projects, such as the flats shown in the photograph on the right. But he is best known for the most spectacular modern building in the financial centre of London – the Lloyd's Building. Although it contains a very conservative insurance business, and is in the oldest part of London, it is an extraordinary and daring piece of modern architecture – all steel and glass, with pipes and lifts on the outside.

Richard Rogers is also modern in his philosophy. He is extremely concerned about the environmental aspects of design: can a building use solar power,

Richard Rogers designed these flats overlooking the River Thames in Fulham, West London.

- **Do you take notice of new buildings around you? Which ones do you admire?**
- **What should be the priorities of architects today – beauty, environmental factors or what?**

Painting

It is sometimes possible to see the national character in painters or groups of painters. But the visual language of art travels quickly and easily, and artists are influenced by things they see all over the world. Painters themselves also travel a great deal, and one of the first important periods of English painting was started by a German visitor. Hans Holbein the Younger lived in London between 1527 and 1543, and painted wonderful portraits of the rich and famous around the court of King Henry VIII.
He had learned from Italian painters – which shows how international the art world was, even at that time, when travel was slow and difficult.
Inspired by Holbein, a school of portrait painters developed in England. The result was that there are many lovely pictures of Queen Elizabeth I and those who surrounded her. One of the most famous of

William Blake's Infant Joy from Songs of Innocence and of Experience,

An unknown youth leaning against a tree among roses *by Nicholas Hilliard*.

these painters was Nicholas Hilliard, who specialised in miniatures: very small, beautifully coloured paintings.

Another great portrait painter, Joshua Reynolds (1723–92), spent time studying in Italy in the 18th century. Of course, from the viewer's perspective, portraits are a strange art form. As with photographs, why should you be interested if you do not know the person in the picture? But, like that of his contemporaries William Hogarth and Thomas Gainsborough, the quality of Reynolds' painting is enough in itself; the expression in the faces, and the insights into character are fascinating.

One of Reynolds' students was as much a writer and poet as a painter. The mystic William Blake (1757–1827) had extraordinary religious dreams and visions, which he expressed in poetry, drawings and paintings.

Although there have been brilliant British painters, few of them have achieved an international reputation. However, there is at least one notable exception – J.M.W. Turner (1775–1851). His paintings were years ahead of their time. He was working in the first half of the 19th century, but his work seems to look forward to the impressionism of 75 years later. While almost all other paintings of his period were realistic and detailed, Turner's were free, daring and impressionistic.

- **What are your reactions to the paintings on this page? Which do you prefer and why?**
- **For portraits, does painting have any advantages over photography?**

Rain, steam and speed – the Great Western Railway, *painted by Turner in 1844.*

In fact, the genius of Turner was not really appreciated in his own time. Only more recently has he come to be regarded as the greatest of British painters. Much of Turner's work is at the Tate Gallery in London, which is also the best place in the country to see modern art.

The 20th century was an extremely busy and exciting time for British painting. At first the tendency was, as often in the past, to imitate the big names from Europe. The French impressionists had taken the art world by storm, and there was little to do but try to copy them. Then Picasso and Braque came up with something completely new – cubism; again British painters followed.

British art history books are therefore pleased to report that in the middle of the 20th century a new movement actually started in this country. In the 1950s and 60s, Britain was in many ways a very fashionable place: British pop music and clothes were big news all over the world. The visual arts too joined in this successful piece of marketing. Pop art in particular caught the imagination of young people.

This movement dropped almost all previous ideas about painting, and picked up the images of advertising, pop music and cheap everyday objects. The first artists to do this were Richard Hamilton, Eduardo Paolozzi (who is Scottish, in spite of his Italian name) and Peter Blake (who did the famous cover of the Beatles album *Sergeant Pepper*). In 1957, Hamilton said that pop art should be: "Popular, expendable, low cost, mass produced, young, witty, sexy, glamorous".

The same feeling of confidence, freshness and innovation gave rise to other styles, too. In her accurate, beautifully designed paintings, Bridget Riley made images which created interesting optical effects – and as a result came to be known as op art. One surprise was that at first she used only black and white, a very unusual thing for a painter to do!

David Hockney

One of the members of the 60s pop art movement has gone on to become Britain's favourite modern painter. At the time, David Hockney (born 1937) fitted perfectly into that new, fashionable London scene.

David Hockney at the opening of an exhibition of his work, November 1995

• **Which countries have produced the greatest painters? Is Britain one of them?**
• **What do you think of Hamilton's statement about pop art? Should all art be like that?**

Damien Hirst's Mother and Child Divided *caused great controversy when it won the 1995 Turner Prize.*

He was young, well-dressed and gay, but came from a working-class background in Bradford in the north of England; so for rich Londoners he was a breath of fresh air. But, having followed a fashionable style at the beginning of his career, he has developed a very personal way of painting which puts him outside any modern art movement.

While younger artists have been playing around with all sorts of theories, political statements and attempts to shock the public, Hockney has just continued to produce lovely paintings with fabulous design sense and colours.

Like all great artists, Hockney had been through a number of periods in which he changed his style and experimented. For example, in the 1980s he did clever montages using photographs. He would take a lot of pictures of details of a person, an object or a scene. Then he reassembled all the photos in a free and inventive way, so that you can see the scene broken up – almost as in cubism.

But generally his work has been painting, often mixing graphic design with realism, and always with a supremely modern sense of colour. This is what has made him so popular with the public. His work can be seen everywhere: on posters, postcards, calendars and T-shirts as well as in art books, museums and galleries.

The latest in British art

For some years now, young British artists seem to have given up the traditional forms of drawing, painting and sculpture. If you go to an art college exhibition, you will probably see photos, videos, constructions with lights and sounds, live people performing, found objects and philosophical statements. Media attention is always on the new, the daring and the shocking, and art prizes often reward originality rather than old-fashioned taste and skill.

One of the current celebrities is Mona Hatoum, who made a video with tiny medical cameras inside her own body. Tracy Emin became quite famous for making a small gallery entirely devoted to things about herself: pictures of her, bits of her hair and objects of importance to her.

But unquestionably the biggest name is Damien Hirst, who won the important Turner Prize in 1995. He is a joker who actually makes fun of those who pay high prices for his work. His best-known piece was a 4.5-metre shark in a tank of formaldehyde. The prize-winning piece was a cow and its calf, both cut down the middle, amusingly entitled *Mother and Child Divided.*

- **Is it important for an artist to do something new and original?**
- **Do you create any kind of art works? If not, what would you like to create?**

Pop and rock in Britain

In the 1950s, American popular music spread all over the world. Together with film, it was part of the USAs cultural imperialism which had started earlier in the century and was now advancing on all fronts. Because of the shared language, it made more of an impact on Britain than on most other countries. People listened with pleasure to Bing Crosby, Frank Sinatra and Doris Day; then with shock, horror and delight to Chuck Berry, Buddy Holly and Elvis Presley. Whatever the Americans produced, Britain enjoyed.

Rock 'n' roll caught on in a very big way in Britain, and in fact some American rockers like Eddie Cochran had more fanatical fans here than at home. Although Elvis only set foot on British soil once (at a military airport, on his way to Germany), he was the King as much in Britain as anywhere. But the interest in rock 'n' roll extended beyond listening to it; the British began to imitate it, sometimes quite successfully. Amateurish skiffle groups gave way to classy rock 'n' roll acts. The Beatles had their first hit, *Love Me Do*, in 1962 and it was not long before they turned the tables on the Americans; they were the first British artists to break into the US market, and they were the vanguard of a real invasion. Soon there was international success for the Rolling Stones, the Animals, the Kinks, the Dave Clark Five, Herman's Hermits, Gerry and the Pacemakers, Freddie and the Dreamers, and others.

Since that time, pop music in Britain has been a mix of American and British. However, in more than any other aspect of the culture, pop seems to be xenophobic: foreign artists just cannot break into the market. Of course, there are exceptions, including a few from English-speaking countries: Australians

The Beatles were top of the pops in Britain, then America and then the rest of the world.

- **Why do you think American pop music has tended to dominate the world market?**
- **Does your country produce good pop music? How much British music do you listen to?**

Punk bands like The Sex Pistols, introduced a new, anarchic style.

the expensive sounds of high-tech studio production. This inspired the creation of a lot of new bands by people without much money (or talent in some cases). But punk did not last long.

The pop business is driven by the need for change and innovation; the economics of it simply do not work if the public listens to the same thing all the time. The result of all this innovation is the massive variety of pop music today. Some styles, like punk, appear and then disappear. Some, like country music, stay and are added to the ever-growing pop menu. Others split into subgroups, as has happened to dance music. In the 70s, when the Bee Gees wrote the soundtrack for the film *Saturday Night Fever*, there was just disco. As it got heavier and funkier, it was known as house, or acid house. Out of house in the USA came techno and garage, and in Britain, jungle, which in turn gave birth to ragga jungle and drum 'n' bass. Then the earlier house music had a revival under the name old skool.

In spite of all the fashionable rebellion, mainstream pop is still doing extremely well. Actually, the term pop itself needs some explanation. So far, it has been used here to mean popular music in general, including rock, dance and rap. But young people use it more often in the more restricted sense of chart music: ordinary, middle-of-the-road tunes with a big audience – the sort of thing that is shown on TV in the early evening. In this sense, it is often a term of abuse. But in reality, not many people follow all the latest developments in drum 'n' bass; it is only accessible to 15 to 25-year-olds who go dancing. Most of the population listens to pop music – to Boyzone-type boy bands and Spicegirl-type girl bands, to Robbie Williams and Celine Dion.

Kylie Minogue and INXS, Canadians Bryan Adams and k.d. lang, Irish bands U2 and the Cranberries, and great reggae artists like Bob Marley from Jamaica. Occasionally north-European voices manage to get heard: A-Ha, Kraftwerk, Björk, the ever-popular Abba, and recently the highly entertaining Aqua.

The pop music world moves very fast. By the end of the 1960s, rock 'n' roll seemed a fully mature art form, with a whole range of variants. From then through to the late 1970s, there was a wide variety of popular music styles from psychedelic, folk rock, glam rock and progressive rock to funk and reggae. By the late 70s, some people were beginning to tire of the smooth professional style of the rock industry It had become a rich show-business phenomenon and had lost touch with its working-class roots. In Britain a few young musicians (with the help of some marketing experts) started the punk revolution. It was pure anti-establishment, and that included the rock 'n' roll establishment. The Sex Pistols, Siouxsie and the Banshees, the Clash and the Buzzcocks hated or pretended to hate middle-class society and the pop super-stars. They also made rock music cheaper to produce, getting away from

• **Does pop music change because of its youth and vitality, or just for commercial reasons?**
• **Which pop styles, past or present, do you like best? Why?**

Classical

Classical music is big in Britain. Every evening in London there is a huge choice of concerts to go to. There are many full-time professional orchestras, and hundreds of amateur ones including the National Youth Orchestra. Most secondary schools have their own orchestras. There are two dedicated classical radio stations – BBC Radio 3 and the much newer Classic FM. The sales of classical CDs are enormous, sometimes rivalling pop sales; the young violinist Nigel Kennedy's recording of Vivaldi's *Four Seasons* sold more than one million copies.

But in spite of all this, the history of British classical music is very uneven. It started well, and is thriving today, but in between it went through a long, unsuccessful period. Medieval churches had highly-trained choirs which were part of the European Catholic tradition, and after King Henry

Henry Purcell, 1659–1695 wrote King James II's coronation music.

VIII broke away from Rome, lots of new choral music was written in English. Thomas Tallis, William Byrd and Orlando Gibbons are great names from this period. Henry VIII also sang, played the keyboard and composed; he is said to have written the very popular song *Greensleeves*, still played today by ice-cream vans and telephone waiting systems. Henry's daughter, Elizabeth I, also loved music, and so the royal palace encouraged a thriving musical culture. At the same time as the flowering of drama with Shakespeare and his contemporaries, there was a fabulous Golden Age of English keyboard and lute music and song. John Dowland, Thomas Morley and John Bull wrote exquisite material, which is not just of historical interest – it is really worth listening to. This wonderful period came to an end in the 1620s. However, the close of the same century produced the man generally considered to be Britain's greatest composer – Henry Purcell. He wrote choral and instrumental works, many of them for the church and for King Charles II, but one of his best-loved works was composed for Chelsea Girls' School – the first English opera, *Dido and Aeneas*.

Purcell died in 1695, only 36 years old, and so began a 200 year gap in British musical creativity. The next home-grown composer of international status was to be Edward Elgar, whose music flourished at the beginning of the 20th century. A 200 year gap is bad enough, but consider what was happening in the rest of Europe during that time: Britain managed to miss out on the whole of the high baroque, classical and romantic periods of Western music. No wonder his compatriots were so delighted with Elgar (1857–1934). He had absorbed the new harmonies of Liszt and Wagner, but in an indefinable way he succeeded in evoking his native landscape near the Welsh border and the rather nostalgic mood in England at the time. Among his loveliest pieces are the cello concerto, the violin concerto and the songs called *Sea Pictures*.

The musical scene in Britain, which had seemed so dead, now burst into life. Elgar had several notable younger contemporaries: Delius, Vaughan Williams and Holst. They were followed by William Walton, who composed some great film music, and several important women composers – Elizabeth Lutyens, Elizabeth Maconchy and Thea Musgrave.

- **What did you know about British classical music before you read this section?**
- **How popular is classical music in your country? Do you listen to it?**

Sir Georg Solti K.B.E. was music director of the Royal Opera, Covent Garden, London from 1961–71.

way, Hændel, or pronouncing it accordingly. One of J.S. Bach's many sons, J.C. Bach came to live in London in 1762 and became known as the English Bach. The Italian Luigi Cherubini became court composer to King George III. In the 20th century, the Spanish composer Roberto Gerhard settled in England and is thought of as British. Many great instrumental players and conductors have lived or worked in Britain: Vladimir Ashkenazy, Yehudi Menuhin, Mstislav Rostropovich, the Amadeus Quartet, Yo Yo Ma, Mitsuko Uchida, Otto Klemperer and Georg Solti.

Attitudes to classical music are strangely contradictory. Many young people learn to play instruments like the piano, the violin or the flute at school. This is nearly always in a classical context; they learn to read music and play in the orchestra, with teachers who are essentially classical musicians. But the same 16-year-old boy who studies the cello every week, and practises Brahms for the school concert, comes home and listens to Oasis and Radiohead. With his friends he talks about guitar riffs and drum machines, and has strong ideas about the quality of the DJs in the local dance clubs.

There was a flowering of opera in the hands of Michael Tippett and the biggest British star of 20th century classical music, Benjamin Britten. Having missed the 19th century, when Italy and Germany were producing a great number of operas, Britain made quite a good attempt to catch up.

Of course, it is rather inappropriate to talk about classical music in nationalistic terms; more than perhaps any other art form, it is international. British musicians work all over the world, and the music scene in Britain is, and always has been, full of foreign talent. Handel has not so far been mentioned; he did not strictly fit the criteria, since he was German by birth. But he settled in England in 1712 at the age of 27, became a British subject, wrote a large number of works (such as *Messiah*) in English, and has been Britain's favourite composer ever since; the British long ago gave up writing his name in the correct

Jacqueline Du Pré's passionate interpretation of the Elgar cello concerto in 1965 made this one of Elgar's most loved pieces.

- **Why do you think classical musicians are more international than pop musicians?**
- **Do students learn to play musical instruments at your school? If not, do you think they should?**

Disney's The Lion King, *which opened in London in 1999, has attracted audiences of all ages.*

He likes Puccini, but he does not buy *La bohème* on CD; he buys Blur.

Pop and classical seem to exist in completely different worlds, with only occasional and rather embarrassed contact. You will never hear a classical piece played on a pop radio station, or vice versa. Hardly any musicians actually manage to sing or play in both styles. The divide is a subject of jokes: when Beatle Ringo Starr was asked what he thought of Beethoven, he said: "I love him, especially his poems."

Actually there is one area of crossover, the musical: in the Andrew Lloyd Webber-type stage shows, such as *Cats, Starlight Express* or *The Lion King*, easy-listening pop songs are accompanied by a classical orchestra. But it is interesting that both serious classical musicians and serious pop fans despise the musical: it is too anodyne, too middle-of-the-road.

As with so many aspects of life in Britain, social class comes into the question of musical tastes. If you mingle with the crowd coming out of the Royal Opera House, Covent Garden, you will see (and hear, if you are sensitive to accents) that they are middle class. Pop musicians, on the other hand, are expected to be working-class heroes. Mick Jagger came from a middle-class background, but does not like to admit it; so he tries to speak with a cockney accent and sing with an American one.

Of course, talented musicians see past the class stereotypes, and are able to appreciate what is good, whether it is pop, classical, jazz or world music. It seems that the less musical you are, the more partisan you become. Tone-deaf middle-class people support classical as though it were a football team, and dismiss pop as rubbish and noise; unmusical working-class people treat classical as though it were purely an expression of snobbery.

- **What is the difference between classical and pop music? Is it possible to like both?**
- **Is there a connection between music and social class in your country?**

Folk, world music and all that jazz

Pop and classical may dominate the market, but there are alternatives. The big folk revival of the 1960s seems a long time ago, and few people today sing Joan Baez songs or early Bob Dylan. But there is something of a craze for folk dancing. Instead of the more common mini-disco and strobe lights, big parties often have a guitar, a violin and a caller, who shouts instructions for square or barn dancing. There has also been an explosion of Irish music. It is not surprising that Irish is the most vigorous folk scene: English folk was a modern revival, but in Ireland the tradition of folk song and dance never really died out.

There has long been an interest in folk and classical music from around the world. People came back from various places around the old Empire with strange instruments, and later, recordings. There was a burst of popularity for Indian music after the Beatles went there and George Harrison learnt to play the sitar; in the early 70s the sitar virtuoso Ravi Shankar became a star in Britain.

Of course, the Asian communities keep music from their homelands alive, and mixed styles have also emerged: in the 1980s and 90s Punjabi instruments were blended with pop and dance music to produce Bhangra. African drums and song, of course, keep returning to the music scene; the amazing beat and harmony of the big vocal group Ladysmith Black Mambazo have made an impact. Every year styles from all over the world are celebrated at a huge open-air festival called WOMAD (World of Music, Arts and Dance). All these styles have now been given a marketing identity under the name world music.

Somewhere between pop and classical and world music, there is a musical tradition whose importance is far greater than its low profile would suggest. Jazz came from America, but today it is thoroughly international and Britain has a small but powerful jazz scene. You can hear it in small venues – pubs and clubs – all over the country, and the brilliance of the musicianship is all the more exciting since you can get up close to it. Some great English jazz names are John McCloughlin (guitar), Django Bates (keyboards) and Geoff Simkins (saxophone). The future for jazz looks good as there is a generation of new talent now emerging, including, for the first time, some excellent young black players like Courtney Pine and Steve Williamson.

Young black British musicians like Courtney Pine are producing some of the most exciting jazz in Britain.

• **Does your country have a living folk-music tradition? Do you like it?**
• **Some music is difficult to understand. Is it worth trying to appreciate it?**

The fashion industry

English jackets and blazers have been an international fashion theme for a very long time. So have brogues: the heavy brown leather shoes, handmade with a pattern of little holes, which are the favourite footwear of the English gentleman. So, too, has tweed, that classic woollen cloth with rich colours and traditional patterns, woven in the Scottish islands. But in spite of the enduring popularity of a few items like these, Britain used to be something of a backwater in terms of fashion, known mostly for conservatism in clothes, as in other aspects of life.

This all changed dramatically in the mid-60s, when boring old London discovered pop music and became Swinging London. Suddenly the city, which had always looked to Paris as the capital of taste and style, realised that it did not have to try to imitate *haute couture*. Cheaper, younger, livelier clothes took centre stage as popular culture emerged with an unprecedented self-confidence. Fashion historians always look for meaning in clothing styles: the state of the economy affects colours and skirt lengths, and social relations are reflected in the way people dress. Seen in this light, the new style of the 1960s was very significant.

English style – classic quality, or boring and old-fashioned?

It was a time when the old hierarchy of Britain was crumbling. From 1964, the Labour Party was in power and ordinary people were rapidly losing their respect for the out dated aristocratic ruling class.

New materials like jersey and PVC were used in the fashion industry for the first time. Design ideas came from lots of different sources: circles and stripes, for example, were taken from the Op Art of the painter Bridget Riley. Clothes became daring and sexy as never before: the young designer

The 1960s: dresses had never been this short.

- **Do you ever see people wearing traditional English clothes? Do you like them?**
- **Do you think fashion tells us something about society?**

Kate Moss wearing a cardigan designed by Vivienne Westwood.

Mary Quant introduced the miniskirt and later hot pants, which would have been quite unthinkable just a decade earlier.

From that time on, the British fashion industry has been in and out of favour many times. The punk look came out of London in the mid-70s, and achieved worldwide recognition. In the early 80s, there was the new romantic look, as worn by Boy George and Culture Club. These were young, radical, pop music-based styles. Building on such successes, London developed a new image. Since the 1970s, the city has joined Paris, Milan and New York as a fully-fledged fashion capital, with top foreign designers showing their collections there, and London-based British designers moving around the world to work for all the big international names. French Nicole Farhi and Turkish Rifat Ozbek came to work in London. Significantly, a number of the supermodels have been British, too – Naomi Campbell, Kirsty Hume, Stella Tennant and Kate Moss among others.

There has been success, but there is also a feeling of insecurity, as though the whole fragile structure could collapse at any time. One year the headlines say London is booming, and the next it all goes quiet again. A regular pattern is that a young designer makes a huge name, is hailed as the saviour of British fashion, and then goes off to work for a big French fashion house. John Galliano was the London hero of the mid-80s, but then started showing his collections in Paris and finally went to work for Givenchy and Dior. The next big name, Alexander McQueen, followed exactly the same route and replaced Galliano at Givenchy. In 1997, Stella McCartney closed her London company and went to Paris to design for Chlöé. One great exception and an almost permanent fixture is the wonderful originator of punk, new romantic and lots of fabulous ideas since then, Vivienne Westwood. But even she has to go to New York to find customers who can afford her prices.

Real life

Outside the world of the designers, what do ordinary British people wear? Of course, the answer is that, as in most countries, they are a collection of tribes, each with its own dress code. Age, class, race, religion and even politics come into it. If we really want to generalise, it is probably true to say that the British are rather careless about clothes. Smart suits are rarely worn outside working hours. No-one minds very much if you have a hole in your sweater. Even the designers themselves tend to wear jeans and T-shirts most of the time.

Some rich girls think it is smart to wear second-hand clothes.

- **What do you think of high fashion? Is it art, or just a game for rich people?**
- **If you were a fashion designer, what sort of clothes would you create?**

The look says it all – a woman in London's upper-class Sloane Square.

On the plus side, young people tend to be daring and inventive, and the level of public tolerance is high. In London at least, you can wear whatever you like – nobody looks twice.

Upper-class young people, in spite of their money, often prefer a rougher, cheaper grunge look. The term grunge actually came from America in the early 1990s, and was associated with bands like Nirvana and Pearl Jam. Classic grunge includes torn jeans, a plaid flannel shirt and heavy Doc Marten-type boots. But a very similar dress style had been around in the UK for some years. Every high street has charity shops with second-hand clothes, and chic teenagers, whose parents could easily afford smart new clothes, are among the regular customers. Working-class young people tend to dress more carefully in sports gear or designer labels. It can be confusing for foreign visitors in Britain to see rich people looking poor and vice versa!

Enthusiasm for smartness and sports gear is particularly noticeable among young black men. There appears to be an American link here: all the latest, coolest street-fashion trends from New York or California are picked up first by them. The fashion points are quite subtle – minor variations in haircut, the designer name on the sweat shirt, a particular model of trainer, or even a way of tying the laces. To the uninformed observer, the general impression seems unchanged over the years – the baseball caps, the glossy new sports outfits, the uncompromisingly state-of-the-art modern look. Some white kids adopt the same style, but never with quite the same total conviction and confidence.

Once you start to study the subject, it is extraordinary how much you can tell about British people from their clothes. Look at the woman in the picture on the left. You can see that she is quite well-off, but can you tell (as most British people can) that she almost certainly speaks with an upper-class accent and is probably a Conservative? Each social tribe in the country has a range of little identity markers. Conservative upper-class women like pearls, silk head scarves, shirt

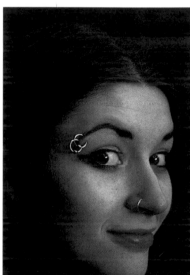

Piercing looks very good on some people.

collars worn up, green waistcoats in the cold, and green rubber boots in the wet. They drive Volvos or Range-Rovers.

A fashion trend that cuts across class barriers is piercing. Earrings, of course, have been with us since time immemorial; they are popular with females between the ages of five and 105, and in recent years they have also caught on with young men. Nose rings and studs started to appear about 20 years ago. But it is only since the late-80s that the

- **In your country, how much can you tell about a person from their clothes?**
- **How would you describe your own clothes? How much freedom do you have to dress as you like?**

trend for really original, imaginative, all-over-your-body piercing has taken off. Now some brave (or crazy) people wear metal in their eyebrows, tongues, teeth, nipples and even genitals; nowhere is off limits. Piercing has become a leading cause of family disputes, which is probably part of its attraction. Parents do not like it, basically because it is new. This is reflected in illogical school rules which allow earrings but forbid nose rings. There is a real question of hygiene, however: you must only have piercing done in clean, well-managed shops. Doctors take the risk of infection seriously, and you are not allowed to be a blood donor for 12 months after piercing.

Serious about fashion?

Surveys show that most British people claim not to care very much about fashion. But look beneath those stated views, and you will find that the reality is rather different. In all sorts of everyday situations powerful prejudices about dress codes manifest themselves. Most schools in Britain have uniforms, and most parents support this policy. Offices are just as strict about suits and ties as ever, even if women can nowadays wear trousers. Some offices have recently adopted the American custom of a dress-down Friday, when employees can wear more casual clothes for one day a week.

Even away from the world of work, there are lots of subtle rules in operation: the bouncers on the doors of dance clubs are brutal in their enforcement of standards – if you do not look cool, you just will not get in.

There are also some serious issues which cannot be avoided, however carefree and fun-loving the attitude to fashion.

We are unlikely to revive the 1960s enthusiasm for PVC now that its damaging environmental side effects are known. In fact, there are problems caused by wasteful use of clothes in general: cotton, wool and synthetic fibres are all environmentally destructive in different ways during their production. The whole fashion industry is, for obvious economic reasons, geared to encouraging waste: it wants us to throw away our clothes before they are worn out, and buy new ones.

Very few people are so politically green that they avoid buying new clothes, but there is a consensus in Britain about buying fur. Hardly anybody does. The anti-fur campaigners have been so successful that the fur shops have all closed down, and women who have fur coats keep them for walks in the country where they will not be seen. You can still see a few furs around the smarter parts of London, but they are usually keeping Italian or Japanese women warm. The fashion industry generally supported the campaign, given that fur was viewed as old-fashioned anyway. Famously, a group of super models including Naomi Campbell appeared in an advert wearing nothing at all, with the slogan, "We would rather go naked than wear fur."

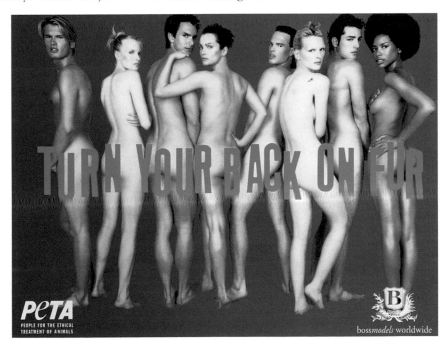

Turn Your Back on Fur: *some supermodels joined the campaign against fur.*

• **Is piercing popular in your country? Is there a difference between an earring and a lip stud?**
• **How do you feel about people wearing fur? Do you agree with the anti-fur campaigners?**

An image problem

British food has an image problem. Every other country seems to have an established national cuisine, and to be proud of it. India has curries, Italy has pizza and pasta, Turkey has kebabs, Germany has tasty sausages, China has all sorts of stir-fried delicacies. So what is Britain famous for? It used to be renowned for roast beef but even that has gone out of fashion.

The sad truth is that most of the British gave up cooking a long time ago and started buying ready-made meals from the shops. They love tins, tubes, packets and frozen foods of all kinds.

One children's favourite is baked beans on toast. There is some logic in tinned beans, as cooking beans at home takes a long time. Rather stranger is tinned spaghetti, another kids' classic. Spaghetti really is better freshly cooked, but young people seem to be addicted to something in processed food. If you take away the stabiliser, colour, emulsifying agent, antioxidant, E101, tartaric acid, sodium diacetate and monosodium glutamate, it just does not taste right!

Of course, convenience food is an international phenomenon, but it started earlier and has gone further in Britain than in most countries.

What they used to eat

British food did not always suffer from an inferiority complex. If you go back to the time of Queen Elizabeth I (1558–1603), people really knew how to eat and drink. Country houses had special herb gardens full of rosemary, thyme, parsley, garlic, fennel and basil. (These herbs were very important as they were used in medicine as well as in cooking.) Chefs used to travel around Europe to get new ideas and ingredients.

The reign of Elizabeth I was also the time when British explorers sailed all over the world. They brought back all sorts of exotic foods: rice and tea from China, spices such as cumin and cardamom from India, coffee and dates from Arabia.

Roast beef and Yorkshire pudding – a typical Sunday lunch

In the Americas they found tomatoes, maize, peanuts, pineapples, sugar cane, hot chillies and vanilla.

Perhaps the most important American vegetable is the potato, but there is a mystery about when it came to Europe, and who brought it there. The British claim it was the Elizabethan explorer, Sir Walter Raleigh, around 1585. In the town of Offenburg in Baden, Germany, there is a monument to another English sea captain, Sir Francis Drake, with the inscription: "... introducer of the potato into Europe in the year of our Lord 1580". In fact, it originates in Peru, and it was probably introduced by the Spanish. Whoever it was deserves a big thank-you. What would the British do without mashed, boiled and roast potato, chips and crisps?

So what happened?

In the past, without cookbooks and TV programmes, women learnt from their mothers and grandmothers; and spent hours every day in the kitchen. But then, around the end of the 18th century, life in Britain changed dramatically. The industrial revolution took families from farms in the country, and put them into small houses in crowded, new cities like Manchester and Birmingham. Men and women (and often children, too) worked long hours in factories.

- **How would you describe your own national cuisine? What are the best things about it?**
- **Does it really matter if fast food and processed food take over?**

So they no longer had the time or the energy to cook properly at home.

There was already an interest in fast food. In 1762, the Earl of Sandwich had invented a snack consisting of two pieces of bread and something in the middle. He was a keen card-player and did not like wasting time on meals. Sandwiches became popular with busy working people. So did fried fish and bread, and in 1870 a French invention caught on in Britain – *pommes de terre à la mode*. Under the new term chips, they were very popular indeed, and fish 'n' chips became Britain's first great fast-food classic.

It is still a big favourite, but now has a lot of competition from those thoroughly international fast foods – pizzas and hamburgers. As in the rest of the world, American giants like McDonald's and Pizza Hut have spread to every corner of the British Isles. If you are in this country, why not take a break from burgers at least once and try fish 'n' chips? It is very simple food, but quite healthy (the fish comes straight from the Atlantic Ocean), and very filling.

Deep-fried cod and potato chips – the nation's favourite

Things are looking up

We have talked about strange new foods being brought here from other continents. Another result of British adventures overseas was that in the 20th century lots of people came to the UK from the colonies and ex-colonies: India, Pakistan, Bangladesh and Sri Lanka, from West Africa and the Caribbean, from Hong Kong and the Greek-Turkish island of Cyprus. There were already many other immigrants living in Britain, especially Irish, Jews and Italians. All these people brought with them their own ways of eating, and they did not simply give them up on arrival in their new home. Far from it. Immigrants are usually keen to preserve their own traditions, and food is one of the most powerful parts of a culture. You may stop wearing the traditional clothes, you may forget your music, your language, even your religion; but when you see and smell a dish that your grandmother used to make, you are suddenly a member of the community again.

Some of these newcomers realised that there was a niche in the market for new and exciting food, so they opened restaurants. The British diet was transformed from a dull menu of boiled vegetables and roast meat to a fantastic mix of international delicacies!

A nice cup of tea!

Tea is more than just a drink to the British – it is a way of life. Many people drink it first with breakfast, then mid-morning, with lunch, at tea-time (around 5 o'clock), with dinner, and finally just before bed. As a nation, they get through 185 million cups per day! No less than 77 per cent of British people are regular tea drinkers; they drink more than twice as much tea as coffee.

Most people use tea bags these days, but serious tea lovers still go through an almost Japanese-style ceremony: warm the pot, add tealeaves and boiling water, cover the pot with a cosy to keep it hot, leave to brew for five minutes and then pour into delicate china cups with saucers. The selection of tea is very personal: Darjeeling, Breakfast Tea, Assam, Earl Grey, Lapsang Souchong and many others.

Tea has worked its way into the language, too. At work people have tea breaks, even if they drink coffee or cola. Many British people call the main evening meal tea, even if they drink beer with it (it is also known as dinner or supper). When there is a lot of trouble about something very unimportant,

- **Do you think that cooking is an important part of life, or a waste of time?**
- **How do feel about the arrival of multinational restaurants like McDonald's?**

it is called a storm in a tea cup. When someone is upset or depressed, people say they need tea and sympathy. In fact, tea is the universal treatment for all sorts of problems and emergencies. As novelist Anthony Burgess (author of *A Clockwork Orange*) wrote: "The best thing to do, when you've got a dead body, and it's your husband's, on the kitchen floor and you don't know what to do about it, is to make yourself a good strong cup of tea."

The pub

The Red Lion, The King's Head, The Lamb and Flag … there are pubs (or public houses) everywhere in Britain. They come in a wide range of styles – noisy ones with sport on giant TV screens or rock music, where young people go to meet each other; and quiet ones with little tables in dark corners. These days many have a restaurant area and quite good food, but others still have nothing more than crisps and nuts. Some are just inhabited by regulars – drinkers who come in every day and who all know each other, making the place a kind of private club; others have only tourists and passers-by. Some pubs are pretty and charming; others are ugly and stink of old beer and cigarette smoke.

There are a number of peculiarities about the British pub which a visitor needs to know.

- The opening hours are 11am to 11pm. Do not try persuading the landlord to serve you after the final bell, as the police might shut down the pub!
- In some pubs you can get a cup of coffee, but it is not common; you are usually better off looking for a café.
- There are no waiters. You have to go up to the bar, get your drinks and pay for them straightaway.
- There are strict age limits, although they are more difficult to enforce: to drink alcohol, you have to be 18, but you can go in and have soft drinks such as cola or orange juice at 14.

In big cities the traditional pub has a new rival – the wine bar. This is a very different sort of place, much quieter and much more sophisticated, with far less beer, no sport on TV and no smel. Maybe this is the future for British drinkers, but the old-fashioned pub will take a very long time to die.

Indian

The British use the general term Indian although many, if not most, of the restaurants are actually Pakistani; others are Bangladeshi or Sri Lankan. The general term curry is used to describe a wide range of different dishes; what they have in common are strong colours, smells and flavours. Spices and herbs are the essence of Indian cooking: garlic, chillies, coriander, ginger, cumin and many others. In fact, Indian food is totally different from traditional British food – and yet it has become massively popular. In Britain there are more Indian restaurants than any other type. They are not only in the big cities – you will find one in almost every small town. Curry is now officially the country's most popular restaurant dish, having overtaken the traditional fish 'n' chips! More than two million British people go out for an Indian meal each week. Add to that the millions of ready-made Indian meals which are bought in supermarkets and taken home to the microwave – and all the Indian-style meals that the British now cook themselves, with varying degrees of success!

- **Do you think food is a significant part of a national culture, like music or literature?**
- **Could you easily give up your own eating habits if you went to live abroad?**

Italian

Italian food, or at least pizza and pasta, is an international phenomenon. As in many countries, children in Britain grow up eating spaghetti, and take away pizza is one of the top fast foods. But there is another reason why Italian restaurants have a special place in the history of food in Britain. There has been an Italian community there for more than 100 years, and Italian coffee bars and restaurants in the 1950s and 1960s gave the British their first introduction to foreign food. Once their natural conservatism had been broken down by a cappuccino and a plate of lasagne, Londoners were ready to experiment. Soon the whole country was enjoying the food of Italy.

Greek

There are a lot of Greeks in Britain, but actually not many come from Greece. Most are from the island of Cyprus, which used to be British. Their most typical dish, the kebab (meat and salad in an envelope of hot pitta bread), is perfect for eating in the street: that is why there are so many Greek and Turkish take away restaurants. But the Greeks are also famous for creating an atmosphere in their restaurants, with bouzouki music and traditional dancing, sometimes on the tables.

Greek food has really caught on in Britain. In every supermarket you will find hummus, taramasalata, Greek yoghurt and pitta bread.

Chinese

Chinese restaurant menus often have more than 100 different dishes on them. There are several reasons for this. Chinese history goes back a long way, and ancestors and traditions are important; so the old ways – and the old recipes – are not forgotten. Also, China is a very big country, with distinct regions such as Beijing, Szechuan and Guangzhou, each having its own cuisine. But most important is the Chinese way of eating: they like lots of different, small dishes at a meal rather than one or two big ones. Meat, fish, chicken and vegetables are often stir-fried in a wok: cooked quickly without much oil. The results are fresh and delicious, and should be eaten immediately. (Take away Chinese food is often very disappointing – it loses that all-important freshness.)

- **What foreign food is popular in your country?**
- **Have you tried any of the types of restaurant described on these pages?**

An interview with ... Jeremy Lee

Jeremy Lee, head chef at the Blue Print Café in London, learnt his trade the old-fashioned way in his native Scotland. He watched other chefs and says he practised until he became good enough to be in great demand – as a chef at one of London's most fashionable restaurants, as a cookery writer for newspapers such as The Guardian, *and as a TV cook.*

Why do foreigners make fun of British food so much?

Well, they probably make less fun now than they have done, but I think beforehand, it was a very crude, basic form of food that was far too fond of the vagaries of fashion, i.e. so long as it was fashionable and looked all right, they didn't really care what it tasted like and it was pretty stodgy, disgusting stuff on the whole. But it's become a lot more sophisticated – taste and the ingredients are so much better now that it's far easier to make good food. There is a vague attempt to keep it simple.

Fresh food needs and requires so little done to it if the ingredients are good, so there is a big move towards that but it's in fits and starts. Our great glorious dishes from the past – after two world wars and rationing here – people have just forgotten how to eat. Our priorities here are a mortgage for a home, a car, school fees, everything. Food is actually one of the things you spend less and less and less on per year, believe it or not.

So what you're really saying is that people aren't more interested in cooking and food nowadays?

Oh, they are, hugely interested. Almost to the level of obsession, I think. They can't get enough of it. There are now so many books; TV is huge. If a TV show is a hit, then it's global. It's a massive, massive success. The books just fly off the shelves and people are very, very interested.

Also, people travel more. Their palates are much wiser; they're a lot more canny than they used to be.

So are the British cooking more and are they cooking better?

Not in the cities. In the cities they eat out more. They may do the odd big Sunday lunch or something, but on the whole, there has never been anything like this before, ever. Restaurants just open almost on a daily basis – it's amazing. But I think out in the country, life goes on as normal. There's so much information now. They'll see something on TV or read it in the newspaper or magazine and they'll go: "Oh that sounds great, I'll try that." It's a maverick taste bud, the British one; it is very fiercely independent and it likes strong gutsy flavours. That's why probably, more Indian food is consumed in this country than anywhere else outside India.

Do the recent changes have anything to do with fusion cooking? What is fusion cooking?

There will always be this fashion thing in food. Always, always, always. Fifteen, twenty years ago there was this thing called *nouvelle cuisine*, which was a beautifully worked-out, crafted way of cooking, which lightened food, reduced the size of portions. Whatever dish you were serving up spoke for itself – in its quality rather than just being piled high with sauces and creams and butter and flour. Fusion is the heir apparent to that. Restaurants and chefs are getting amazing reviews, are hugely successful: the media are just going crazy about it. People can't get into these restaurants for months and months ahead of time. It just captures the imagination: people get very excited about it. But the problem with fusion food is, it's a very personal thing. You actually look at

• **What do you think of British food? How does your country's food compare to food elsewhere?**
• **What makes cooking enjoyable, or not?**

the people who've done it brilliantly and they're just naturals. You can't teach someone how to mix Scandinavian, Japanese and Indian food and put it on a plate and make it work. Because it's actually disgusting, horrible and has no relevance whatsoever. If you want to put red peppers with soy sauce, well, by all means, do. There's nothing stopping you. And if you like that kind of food then eat it happily, but it's almost like: "Oh, we're so bored with these dishes, let's try something else." And it's change for the sake of change rather than with any kind of savvy and knowledge of what we're actually doing.

There is a new phenomenon in Britain of the celebrity chef, who cooks on television and who writes books on food. Is cookery becoming a fashion?

I think it always has been. If you go back to ancient Rome and beyond, houses would bankrupt themselves, nobles would bankrupt themselves to outdo each other in the banqueting and feasting they'd put on for their friends. And that's gone right the way throughout history.

There have always been very famous chefs. Historically, they were always patronised by royalty, the very wealthy, nobility, the Church. So, dinner at Cardinal Richelieu's – you'd love an invitation, you knew it would be fabulous because Alexis Savoy would be cooking or one of these fabulous names. What is recent now is the huge magazine, book.

If you're a famous chef, you will get a TV deal, a book deal, a magazine column, a newspaper column – I mean it's unbelievable, the packages that come with it now – and it will propel you into superstardom and potentially a millionaire.

It is very easy to get into the doldrums, the grind, the unglamorous side of restaurants, which is the greater part, unfortunately. One night you can be the most celebrated person, awarded all sorts of things; you're still in the next morning peeling potatoes and carrots.

Would you say that London is one of the food capitals of the world?

It's trying to become one and there's a lot going on – an awful lot going on, which is exciting. But compared to Paris or San Francisco or Los Angeles or New York, no. It's got a very glamorous façade to it and there's some great food to be had in London, that's for sure; and it's got a fantastic – possibly one of the best – ethnic collection of restaurants and foods in Europe for sure. There's a definite wanting to get there but the actuality now is it's crazily expensive in this town to eat well.

• **Is cookery big business in your country?**
• **How is food important to you?**

Holidays

The classic British summer holiday used to be at the British seaside. But it had some fairly obvious drawbacks. Much of the coast is rocky rather than sandy. The water is so cold that bathers scream as they get in: according to the geography books, the Gulf Stream from Mexico warms the sea in this part of the world, but the British are sceptical – perhaps it does warm the sea, but not enough for most humans. Then there is the Great British Weather: one year there can be four weeks of hot sun in August, and the next it can be wet and windy almost every day. All this means that people do not spend a great deal of time swimming and lying on the beach.

A British family holiday, 1960s style.

Alternatives were developed. One of these was a whole culture of seaside entertainment centred around the funfair, with cafés and fish and chip shops, rides such as dodgem cars and ferris wheels, and a little light gambling on fruit machines. In the 19th century, dozens of seaside towns around the country built piers: pretty, ornate structures projecting out into the sea, like bridges leading nowhere, so that holidaymakers could promenade and enjoy the healthy sea breezes.

British tourists finding home comforts on the Spanish island of Ibiza.

Another alternative, for the more studious types, was to explore the coast for things of biological and geological interest. Many children developed their first interest in science while watching the wildlife in rock pools or picking up fossils beneath the cliffs.

In the 1960s, British people started to realise that they could escape their own unreliable summers by going south. Travel has become ever cheaper since then, and today half of the nation's holidays are taken abroad. In spite of that, the British are still quite nervous about dealing with foreigners, so the great majority choose package holidays. This means that the flight, the hotel and food are all paid for in advance and arranged by the travel company. The tourist does not have to worry about negotiating with taxi drivers and waiters who do not speak English. The favourite package destination has always been Spain, and every summer thousands of charter planes take off from airports around the country heading for Alicante, Ibiza and Palma de Majorca. British holidaymakers have suffered from a rather negative image because they demand British food, beer, music and TV programmes; they want to create little bits of Britain in the sun. But that image is slowly changing as more and more Britons travel further afield and try to make some sort of contact with the local culture.

- How important is the weather to you when you go on holiday?
- Do you ever meet British tourists? What do you think of them?

Turning work into play

Houses in Britain are seen as an investment. Property prices have risen steeply in the last 20 years and continue to rise, so people buy houses in the hope of making money. Home ownership is high, at about 70 per cent. One result of this is that people are happy to work on their houses: the work benefits themselves, not a landlord. DIY (do-it-yourself) has become massively popular, with 60 per cent of all men and 30 per cent of all women "doing it themselves". There used to be a certain amount of prejudice against it. The comic poet, Hilaire Belloc, wrote 70 years ago:
"Lord Finchley tried to mend the electric light Himself. It struck him dead, and serve him right! It is the business of the wealthy man To give employment to the artisan."

These days, not so many house owners are wealthy, so they try to avoid calling in the carpenter, plumber or electrician. But the DIY craze is not based entirely on economics. It has become a hobby which gives many people pleasure and a sense of achievement. In government statistics, DIY is listed as a leisure activity. Every TV channel has its own DIY programme, and giant DIY superstores, selling tools and materials, have sprouted up all over the country.

Together with the love of house decoration goes a passion for gardens. They buy gardening books and watch gardening programmes on TV. There are gardening sections in the newspapers.

Neighbours are quietly competitive about their gardens.

Of course, not all the British share this enthusiasm. Gardens are slow, long-term things, and even in this country most young people are not interested. However, some time in his or her 30s the average Briton starts learning plant names and buying seeds! About half of the people in Britain do some gardening, and they spend over £3 billion in garden centres every year.

As with DIY, gardening is work which people do in their leisure time. Some ambiguity remains – is it work or is it fun? Gardeners often talk about their hobby in the language of guilt, which would seem more appropriate for work, "Oh dear, I'm afraid I haven't had time to mow the lawn or prune those roses".

There are also conflicting attitudes to another national pastime – shopping. For some it is a boring task only to be done when it is absolutely unavoidable; for others it is an addictive pleasure. It is obviously more fun if you have a lot of money, and the rich have always enjoyed it in places like London's Bond Street, Knightsbridge or Piccadilly. But recently the habit has caught on among the rest of the population. Big American-style shopping malls have appeared, sometimes in town centres but very often out on a motorway and accessible only by car. The gigantic Bluewater in Kent, for example, looks almost like a theme park. It has branches of superstores, dozens of smaller shops, and, most importantly, parking for 13,000 cars. The idea, clearly, is not that the shopper drops in for a carton of milk

Why call in a house-painter? Do it yourself!

- **Which seems more sensible to you; doing jobs yourself or calling in an expert?**
- **Do you regard shopping as a pleasure or a necessity?**

Bluewater, Kent. American-style shopping malls have become popular throughout Britain.

and some cat food on the way home: this is designed for families to have a day out, wandering around, looking, dreaming and spending.

Unhealthy pleasures

It is pointless to pretend that all leisure activities are just good clean fun. The British are no more sensible than other nationalities when it comes to self-destructive activities like drinking and taking drugs. In fact, they have something of a reputation for drunkenness even though statistics show that alcohol consumption is not especially high. There is a possible explanation for this: in many countries, people drink quite a lot of wine with meals, whereas British drinkers often go to the pub and dedicate themselves to getting drunk. At 11 p.m., the pubs shut and drinkers are forced out into the streets, so drunkenness is a very public phenomenon. In spite of the 18-year age limit in pubs, there is more teenage drinking in Britain than in other European countries.

Unlike drunkenness, drug use is (for obvious reasons) a more private phenomenon. There may be a trace of marijuana in the air as you walk past a group of people in a park, and clubbers at raves are quite open about taking Ecstacy. But you would be unlikely to come across syringes lying on the ground, and it is very rare indeed to see someone actually taking hard drugs. Attempts to legalise marijuana have never got anywhere near succeeding, and all recreational drugs except alcohol, tobacco and solvents remain illegal. The police will let someone off with a caution if they have a few grams of cannabis, but otherwise enforcement of the law is quite strict. Since 1998, a national anti-drugs co-ordinator, known as the Drugs Czar, has been appointed to take charge of the whole issue.

Accurate statistics are hard to obtain in this field, but it is clear that drug use is widespread in Britain. About a half of all those in their early 20s have tried a drug at some time in their lives, and about 20 per cent of them use drugs regularly. Surprisingly, higher social classes experiment with drugs more than lower classes, but regular use and addiction is more common among the poor. Injected heroin, in particular, is associated with deprived housing estates in big cities like London, Liverpool and Glasgow. Cocaine, on the other hand, is the fashionable drug for rich young business people. Cannabis remains by far the commonest drug across different classes and age groups.

It may be surprising to find gambling in this section on unhealthy pleasures: it is very much a matter of opinion whether it is a serious vice or just harmless fun. Social reformers and the church have usually condemned gambling for two reasons: it is addictive, and men have often wasted their money

Pubs are a part of youth culture.

- **Do you agree with the 18-year age limit for drinkers in British pubs?**
- **Is drug abuse in your country very different from that in Britain?**

The winning ticket? Millions like this woman live in hope.

on it while neglecting their families. An element of guilt certainly remains: betting shops in the high street always have their windows covered so that the customers are out of public sight. Playing cards and similar games for money is illegal in public places, and casinos are few and far between. Most British gambling has traditionally been on horses and football pools (where players send in a form with a list of predictions for the weekend's matches).

Attitudes changed dramatically, however, with the arrival of the National Lottery in 1994. This seems like guilt-free gambling because 28 per cent of the money goes to good causes. You have to choose a set of six numbers between one and 50. If all six numbers are correct, you win several million pounds. The lottery is played twice weekly and a ticket costs £1. The chances of winning are millions to one, but it has been fantastically successful, with up to 70 per cent of all households in the country buying tickets. Along with cigarettes, alcohol, junk food and television, it has become another little addiction for millions of people in Britain.

Eccentricity

Visitors to Britain are often surprised by the titles of the magazines on newsagents' shelves.
Some of them appear to be extremely specialised.
There are lots on new technology, such as

Which Scanner? or *Digital Photo Effects*. But there are also some very obscure traditional ones: *Steam Railway World, Bus and Coach Preservation, Stamp and Coin Market*, and *Combat Aircraft*. This is the strange world of the British hobby.

The most celebrated, and generally considered to be the most pointless hobby, is trainspotting. Actually, it has largely died out today, but was very popular in the days of beautiful old steam trains. The idea of trainspotting was to list the identification numbers of the trains you saw, and ... well, that was it, really. Train spotters would often wear anoraks, and the anorak has now become the symbol of all fanatical hobbyists.

Some visitors are also surprised by an almost universal British custom: going for a walk. This sometimes means healthy exercise in the open country, with lots of natural life to study on the way. Urban walkers will seek out any little bit of park, broad pavement or canal bank. Actually, this may explain the huge popularity of dogs: if family or friends are unwilling to join them, British people are embarrassed about going for a walk alone, and the dog gives them the perfect excuse!

Some British men never lose interest in their toys.

- **Do you think gambling is unhealthy? Do you gamble?**
- **What kind of hobbies are popular in your country? What are your hobbies?**

Sporting inventions

It is rather extraordinary how many of today's international games originated in Britain – football, rugby, tennis, boxing, rowing and horse racing among them. Of course, the Romans had boxing matches between gladiators in their circuses, horse racing was popular with the Greeks and Arabs long before the British got hold of the idea: and people have been playing football in one form or another for thousands of years, all over the world. But the contribution of the British was to take these games or sports and formalise them in various ways.

Football is a good example. The Maoris, the Japanese and the medieval Europeans all played forms of the game. A sort of football was very popular in England in the Middle Ages, especially as a contest between neighbouring villages. But at that time, there were very few rules. As it was played in English schools, the game became progressively more standardised and rule-governed, and by the middle of the 19th century it had become very much the game that we know today; the first actual set of rules was written by Cambridge University.

A similar story can be repeated about a range of other sports. Why did this happen in Britain before other countries? There are a number of possible explanations. Following the Norman invasion of 1066, there was little resistance and Britain was comparatively peaceful, and has largely remained so ever since. As a result, people have had the time and peace of mind to develop sports. The Normans sent armies off to fight the Saracens in the Crusades, who came back with very fast, light Arab horses, quite unlike their own big, heavy animals. From this lucky chance a passion for horse racing developed in England which has survived until this day.

The Grand National is a major event in the horse-racing calendar.

In the history of sport in general, horse racing was extremely important. From an early date, a major part of the pleasure of a day at the races was betting. Of course, when money is involved, things get serious. So racing was carefully regulated: the length of the race was standardised, and there were strict rules about the behaviour of riders. As soon as accurate watches became available, times were written down so that people could compare the performance of horses in different races. As other sports developed, these systems of regulation (and the attitudes of mind) were applied to them, too.

Factories in Britain's industrial revolution were based on highly organised work, hierarchies, teams and strict time keeping. The same discipline was applied to sport. So uniforms, referees and punishments were introduced to football and other games. Teachers thought that team games were good training for military or industrial careers; and they often quoted the Latin phrase *mens sana in corpore sano* (a healthy mind in a healthy body).

The beginnings of rugby at Rugby School in 1870

- **Have you ever thought about the history of sport? Is it interesting?**
- **How important are rules in sport? Why are judges so unpopular when they enforce the rules?**

Sport today

Every country has its own mix of favourite sports. What is the British mix? One might start by mentioning a few sports that are not very important. For obvious reasons, the British are not very good at skiing, as in most parts of the country there is only about one week of snow per year. Englishman Chris Boardman won an Olympic gold medal for cycling in 1992, but he is a great exception: Britain is not a major country for cycle racing. The essentially American sports – baseball, basketball and American football – have never really caught on.

School girls play something which seems a lot like basketball – until you look closer. Netball is different from basketball in many details; for example, the ball is lighter, the court is bigger, and netball has seven players in each team (not five). There is something very strange about netball: it is never played by boys. There is no biological reason for this; it is simply tradition. It is popular throughout the English-speaking world, and the Australians and New Zealanders usually win the competitions.

Lacrosse is another game that is common to English-speaking countries and Japan. The lacrosse stick is a sort of a hockey stick with a basket at the end.

On village greens all over England, summer Sundays mean cricket.

Both netball and lacrosse are definitely minority interests, but cricket is a major part of English summer life. You can watch it all day on TV (or, bizarrely, listen to it on the radio), and then get the highlights again in the evening. News programmes keep you up-to-date with the score. Men, when they meet, exchange a few words about the state of the game.

One reason that cricket becomes so much a part of life is that the games are so long. An ordinary game at a boys' school takes up a whole afternoon. But the big international games, known as test matches, are up to five days long! And that is not all; a number of test matches are played one after the other to make up a series.

Fair play

"Serious sport has nothing to do with fair play. It is bound up with hatred, jealousy, boastfulness, disregard of all rules and sadistic pleasure in witnessing violence: in other words it is war minus the shooting." *The Sporting Spirit*, George Orwell.

The idea of "fair play" in sport is a powerful part of the British self-image. But hooliganism is just one of the things which has undermined this real or imaginary tradition. In the old days of amateur sport it was perhaps possible to say: "Winning is not important; what matters is how you play the game." But when money comes into it, attitudes change: it is significant that horse racing, which has long been associated with betting, has always had a problem with cheating.

One of the most unfortunate results of this is the spread of drug use in sport. The British are not among the worst offenders, but neither are they 100 per cent clean. A number of athletes have failed drug tests. In one high profile case in 1996, the bobsledder Mark Tout was caught and then openly discussed his use of steroids. His honesty was most unusual, as there appears to be a conspiracy of silence on drug use in the sporting world. The shot-putter Matt Simpson won a gold medal at the Commonwealth Games in 1994 and then gave up the sport. He was anti-drugs, and said he could not continue to compete against all the athletes who took them. His advice to young athletes was simple but depressing: "Don't go into athletics at the highest level."

- **What are the top sports in your country? Which are your own favourites?**
- **Does it matter if sports people take drugs? What should be done about it?**

Tennis at Wimbledon

There are other great championships around the world, but tennis players still regard Wimbledon as the number one challenge. Yet it is a long time since Britain was the home of the top champions: the last British woman to win the women's singles was Virginia Wade in 1977 and the last British man to win the men's was Fred Perry in 1936!

German Boris Becker, aged 17 in 1985, was the youngest man to win the singles, and the youngest woman was English, Lottie Dod, aged 15 in 1887. Probably the greatest champion ever was Martina Navratilova, who won the women's singles nine times between 1978 and 1990.

The event goes on for two sunny (or sometimes wet) weeks in June and July, and is a big social occasion: people dress up smartly, and eat strawberries and cream with their champagne. Centre Court seats are very expensive, but you can get into the grounds, enjoy the atmosphere and see most matches for about £10.

Pete Sampras is one of the all-time great Wimbledon champions.

Football crazy

"Some people think football is a matter of life and death; I can assure them that it's much more important than that." Bill Shankly, Liverpool manager.

One important thing to remember about British football is that there is no such thing. There are no British leagues or divisions; there is no British team. This can be a cause of confusion even in Britain; you sometimes see a Union Jack (the flag of the UK) at England football matches, where of course only the English red and white flag is appropriate. For the Olympic Games there is a British team of athletes, but for football (and quite a few other sports) Britain is strictly divided into England, Scotland, Wales and Northern Ireland.

Another problem for nationalists is that the home teams have not done particularly well in recent years. England has not won the World Cup since 1966 (and the result of that final against West Germany was highly debatable). In 1998, England went out of the tournament rather embarrassingly when, in a game against old rivals Argentina, David Beckham kicked a player in anger; he was sent off and England failed to win with only ten men.

An English disease?

Fifty years ago, football hooliganism was almost unheard of. Crowds were very big indeed, and they could be noisy, excitable, even drunk. But violence was unusual. Then in the 1960s, things started to go wrong. There were pitch invasions, and serious fights between groups of fans during and after matches. In the 1970s, it became necessary to segregate rival fans: the seating was divided into two areas with barriers between them and separate entrances.

The terrible climax of an era of football violence came at the European Champions' Cup final in 1985 in the Heysel Stadium in Brussels. In front of 100 million TV viewers worldwide, Liverpool supporters charged fans of the Italian team Juventus, and put so much pressure on a barrier wall that it collapsed. Thirty-nine spectators, mostly Italian, died and 400 were injured. Even the hooligans themselves were shocked into a period of inactivity, and the other

• **Do you ever watch the tennis from Wimbledon? What makes a good spectator sport?**
• **Is football "more important than life or death"? How important is it to you?**

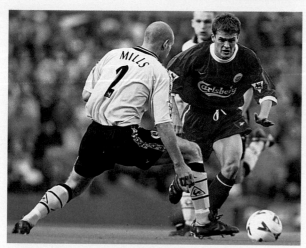

A Premiership game: Michael Owen of Liverpool and Danny Mills of Charlton Athletic.

Fans (they prefer to be called supporters) are fiercely loyal to their club. This loyalty is strong with London clubs such as Chelsea and Arsenal, but even stronger in the spiritual home of English soccer – the North. If you think about it, most of the great names are from northern England: Manchester, Liverpool, Newcastle, Leeds, Blackburn, Sheffield, Middlesbrough. These cities produced great football clubs 100 years ago, when they were thriving, young, industrial centres, and the working-class men had money to spend on tickets for the Saturday game (big sporting events often take place on Saturday, not Sunday). These days heavy industry has declined but, paradoxically, the role of the local football club is more important than ever.

Imagine that you live in Blackburn, Lancashire. Your town's economy is doing badly. People in London do not even know where Blackburn is. But your soccer team, Blackburn Rovers, are up there with the great names; they were actually Premier League champions in 1995. The great Alan Shearer used to play for the team – and when the club sold him to Newcastle, they got a world-record-breaking £15 million!

Nationalism is not really at the heart of football in Britain. Clubs and their fans are what count. Proof of this is the way that foreign players are welcomed in British clubs: Di Matteo, Vialli, Zola, Flo, Leboeuf, de Goey and Petrescu all played in one season for one club, Chelsea!

result was that UEFA banned English teams from playing in Europe.

In fact, people in Europe were keen to see English clubs again, and UEFA was soon quite willing to welcome them back. But the British government used the continuing ban as a way of forcing the football community to sort out the problems. It insisted on all-seater stadiums, rules against alcohol and other measures to make the game more attractive to families. There was trouble in Italy at the 1990 World Cup, when 300 English supporters were deported in military aircraft. But even so, the ban was lifted in July of that year.

The whole atmosphere has greatly improved, and ordinary supporters have begun to feel safe again. But occasionally the old problems rear their ugly head. In 1995, England's match against Ireland in Dublin was abandoned because of rioting by some England supporters. It was particularly sinister that the troublemakers were members of a fascist group called Combat 18, who wanted to protest against peace moves in Northern Ireland. Significantly, as you can see in the photo, they carried Union Jacks rather than English flags.

English hooligans attack an Irish fan.

• **Which are the top footballing nations today?**
• **How would you explain the phenomenon of soccer violence? Is there any in your country?**

🎧 📼 An interview with ... Robin Smythe

Robin Smythe, aged 22, is a player with the London Broncos Rugby Football Club. He was born and bred in the north of England where Rugby League is one of the most popular spectator sports. Smythe has played for England at junior level. As a professional player in a contact sport, he has to play to the highest standards.

How important is rugby in Britain today?

Rugby is very important in Britain today. Australia – it's the number one sport there. But, over here, obviously, football takes over and a few other sports. But up north, where I'm from, it's generally one of the number one sports to be played. It's played through all the schools from a very early age through to whenever you finish. There's a lot of amateur, which is players who don't make it and get paid. But where we are in London, it's very hard to get going, especially with all the football teams – so many being in the capital – so we have to look to our development side of it and make it important for the Rugby League to be developed down here.

Is rugby fighting a losing battle for popularity with football?

In some ways yes, in some ways no. Rugby League is getting more popular every year. The Rugby League are trying to expand it throughout the country. Now, the League is a lot tougher than it actually was. A couple of years ago, it was mainly just two teams that were ever winning anything and you knew who was going to win. But now, because it's more competitive, more even, they've brought in a salary cap, where you can only spend so much on players. You can't have all the big players at one club, and it makes it a lot harder, and now the competition is a lot tougher, and it makes it better for the spectators. With Sky TV, they have the rights to the Super League matches, so a lot more people see it on Sky, 'cause everyone now is getting Sky, whereas before it was very rarely seen on telly.

What is being done to promote rugby in Britain?

The Rugby League called it *On the Road*, where we started taking the game to Scotland, we went and played Bradford Bulls, who are from Yorkshire, in Scotland, Edinburgh. They take the big international games to Wembley and into Wales and they move them around the country. They've also got the TV; they've got a mid-week programme called *World of Rugby League*, which is on Sky again.

- **What are your national sports? Do you have a version of rugby?**
- **Does the media make some sports more popular than others?**

How did you first get interested in the sport?

I had a neighbour who used to coach my local amateur team. I was only 10, and I was brought up with a football background by my dad because my dad's from Liverpool. And then one day they were all playing in the street outside, so I was just playing, and because I was quick, they used to give me it and I used to run around – that's what a winger does, they just get the ball and run. And I went along and I realised that all my friends played rugby; I didn't know because I was always playing football. So it was a toss-up then between football and rugby. Because all my friends played rugby, I started playing Rugby League. It was just a good laugh at the beginning; I didn't realise it would take me to where I am today.

Where have you played so far?

I've played here for the last year. Previously, I played for four years at Wigan, which are, like, one of the biggest clubs in the world. They're like, if you talk about rugby over in this country, everyone knows Wigan. You go anywhere in the world people will know Wigan Rugby League because they went through a period of winning eight League Championships on the run and eight League Challenge Cups on the run.

Have you had any notable successes?

Yes, I've represented my country, played for England and I've captained my country – it's called Academy but it's like younger age, like youth team, I was Captain of them and that was a big honour for me. And I've also won a Championship; I've got a runners-up medal at Wembley, which we got this year. I've still got hopefully another ten years to play, so I just hope for a few more.

What is the outlook for a retired rugby player?

It depends on how well he did out of the game. Some players, even when they finish, whether they did well or not, like to stay in Rugby League – either development, coaching kids, coaching a youth team, just going into coaching.
But sometimes, you have the bad side, where some players come out of it more or less crippled – they've had that many bad injuries. That's where you've got to make sure you've got your insurance with your club and also your personal insurance so you can claim on them.

How much do you agree with the traditional image of rugby as a sport, which features muscle and honesty and heartiness?

To me, Rugby League is just a game. I don't care what anyone reckons. People always said rugby is a rough game – it's not a rough game; it's a tough game. All it is, is people getting the ball, trying to run through.
People might say that it's a thug's game, but I wouldn't play the game if it was a thug's game. Everyone says that Rugby League's tough – it's played by big men. I'm only small, only five-foot-seven. There are a few people like me, but you know, I wouldn't play the game if it was going to be too dirty.

Do you get a sense that young people consider you a role model?

In any sport, if a kid's watching you, you are a role model, 'cause if you play for his team – and you happen to be his favourite player, or one of his favourite players – when he's playing at home his daddy's going to say: "Ah, it's Rob Smythe" or any player.
It's not when you're on the pitch – when you're off the pitch you've got to be sensible and smart about what you're doing. You can't just go setting any kind of example. The example that I set to my kids is the same example that I'd set to anyone else's kids.

- Is sport "just a game"?
- Is it a good thing that sports stars are role models for children?

Key

abandon	(v)	97	give s.th. up
abolish	(v)	33	officially put an end to s.th.
absence	(n)	38	not being present
absorb	(v)	69	soak up s.th.
abuse	(v, n)	11; 59; 103	treat s.o./s.th. badly; using s.th. for a bad purpose; rude things said or written about s.o.
academic	(adj)	65	involving traditional school and university subjects rather than e.g. practical skills
accent	(n)	9	way of speaking which shows what area you come from or what social group you belong to
access (to)	(n)	22	being allowed and able to enter a place or use s.th.
accessible	(adj)	58	able to be reached, used etc.
acclaim	(v)	53	say publicly that s.th. is very good
accommodate	(v)	19	provide room for s.th./s.o.
accountable	(adj)	67	required to give reasons for what you do
accountant	(n)	87	s.o. whose job is to keep track of money spent and received by an organisation
accurate	(adj)	7	exact
achievement	(n)	9	difficult thing that s.o. has managed to do
act	(n)	22	law made by a **parliament**
activist	(n)	11	s.o. who works actively for a political organisation or purpose
actuality	(n)	117	how things are now
acute	(adj)	67	very bad, requiring immediate action
AD	(abbrev)	4	after the birth of Christ
adaptation	(n)	13	a change made in s.th. in order for it to fit a new situation or purpose
addicted (to)	(adj)	112	unable to give s.th. up
addiction	(n)	59	being unable to give s.th. up
additional	(adj)	37	more of s.th.
adequately	(adv)	71	well enough
administer	(v)	68	run (a system)
adoption	(n)	12	starting to use s.th.
affairs	(n)	42	your affairs are all the things you do and the matters which affect you
affluent	(adj)	67	wealthy
agenda	(n)	35	list of things to be done or discussed
aggressive	(adj)	84	tending to be violent or very competitive
agricultural	(adj)	16	of farming
agriculture	(n)	20	farming
airforce	(n)	47	the part of a country's armed forces which fights in the air
airline	(n)	52	company which runs passenger/freight aircraft
alien	(adj)	34	strange, foreign
allegiance	(n)	40	loyalty to s.o./s.th.
alliance	(n)	44	agreement between two or more countries to help each other, e.g. in a war
ally	(n)	48	a country's ally is another country which has agreed to help it, esp. in war
alter	(v)	15	make changes to s.th.
alternative	(adj)	91	not following traditional attitudes
amateur	(adj)	91	doing s.th. as a hobby, not as one's job
ambiguity	(n)	119	existence of more than one possible meaning
analysis	(n)	80	studying/explaining s.th. in detail
anathema (to)	(n)	52	s.th. which is completely against your way of thinking
ancestral	(adj)	11	of your ancestors (the people who lived in earlier times to whom you are related)
ancient	(adj)	19	very old
anodyne	(adj)	106	not adventurous or exciting
anonymity	(n)	17	not being known
anonymous	(adj)	17	(of a place) where people do not know each other
anorak	(n)	121	type of waterproof jacket with a hood
anti-	(prefix)	16	against
apparent	(adj)	18; 68	(reason etc.) easy to see; seeming clear
applicant	(n)	62	s.o. who applies for a place, e.g. to study or to work in an organisation
appoint	(v)	31	give s.o. a particular job
appreciation	(n)	88	showing that you think s.o. has done a good job
appropriate	(adj)	14	suitable
approve	(v)	43	say yes to s.th.
arable	(adj)	23	of the farming of plants not animals
arch	(n)	96	stone or brick structure with a curved top and straight sides, used to create a doorway, window or other space in a building
archaeological	(adj)	4	of archaeology: the study of how people lived through the examination of bones, tools etc.
architecture	(n)	18	the design or style of a building
aristocracy	(n)	8	the group of people of the highest social class (esp. in a country ruled by a king or queen)
armed forces	(np)	47	[pl] organisations a country can use to protect itself from attack, or to attack other countries, e.g. a navy or airforce
arms	(n)	46	[pl] objects used to injure or kill others, e.g. guns, knives or bombs
arrest	(v)	57	if the police arrest you, they accuse you of committing a crime and take you to a police station
arsenal	(n)	40	store of **weapons**
artificial	(adj)	15	made by humans, not natural
assert (one's self)	(v)	55	make sure your opinion is heard, rights are respected etc.
astrology	(n)	75	belief that the positions of the stars and planets in relation to each other have an effect on people
athlete	(n)	123	s.o. who takes part in athletics (sports such as running, long jump etc.)

atmosphere	(n)	18	feeling which a particular place gives you
authoritarian	(adj)	32	an authoritarian leader makes everyone do what he/she wants them to
autocratic	(adj)	30	making decisions without asking anyone else
autonomy	(n)	39	being able to take decisions for one's self
average	(n)	66	value you get by adding together numbers, then dividing by the number of numbers you added together (used to show what is the 'normal' amount of s.th.)
award	(v)	53	give (a prize etc.)
awareness (of)	(n)	28	knowing that s.th. exists
backwater	(n)	108	quiet place where nothing new or exciting happens
balance	(n)	41; 82	the amount or importance of one thing relative to another; situation in which different things are equal in importance, power etc.
bankrupt (one's self)	(v)	117	make yourself so poor that you cannot pay what you owe
banqueting	(n)	117	organising large, rich meals for large numbers of people, or taking part in such a meal
baptise	(v)	75	accept s.o. into the Christian church by sprinkling water on him/her or putting him/her briefly under water
barrier	(n)	7	s.th. which makes it impossible for s.th. to happen
basis	(n)	19; 39	starting point; method by which s.th. is organised
battle	(n)	17	fight between large groups of people
BC	(abbrev)	4	before the birth of Christ
beam (across)	(v)	88	send by electronic means, e.g. as radio waves
bed-and-breakfast	(n)	72	inexpensive accommodation where breakfast is included in the price of the room
beg the question	(vp)	43	make people want to ask a particular question
behead	(v)	30	cut s.o.'s head off
benefit	(n)	17; 33	advantage; money given by the government to people who need it, e.g. because they are unemployed or sick
benefit (from)	(v)	5	be helped or improved by s.th.
bet (on)	(v)	94	risk money on the result of s.th. (e.g. a football match or horse race)
bilingual	(adj)	11	speaking two languages
bizarre	(adj)	33	strange
blockade	(n)	48	action to stop goods and people from entering or leaving a place
boastfulness	(n)	123	claiming to be better in some way than you really are
boom	(v)	109	grow rapidly in size and success
borough	(n)	34	a part of a city
bouncer	(n)	111	s.o. whose job is to keep order in a club or pub
brewery	(n)	72	place where beer is made
bribe	(n)	56	money given to s.o. to persuade him/her to do s.th. (esp. s.th. dishonest)
brilliant	(adj)	91	very clever
Briton	(n)	6	person from Britain
broad	(adj)	20	wide
broadcasting	(n)	82	television and radio

brutal	(adj)	111	violent and cruel
budget	(n)	26	the amount of money provided for s.th.
bureaucracy	(n)	29	organisation which has (too) many rules and (too) many people controlling its activities
button-hole	(v)	37	[coll] stop s.o. and make him/her listen to you
buzz	(n)	18	feeling of excitement and energy
calculation	(n)	26	working out the value/amount of s.th.
campaign	(n)	11	series of actions planned and carried out by a group of people in order to make s.th. happen
cancer	(n)	70	disease in which the body's own cells start to grow out of control
candidate	(n)	38	s.o. who applies for a job or position
cannibalism	(n)	93	when an animal eats others of its own kind
canny	(adj)	116	[coll] clever in a practical way
cap	(n)	126	rule to stop s.th. (esp. price or salary) growing beyond a certain size
capacity	(n)	45	ability
capital	(n)	41	money, esp. which is available to be used for business purposes
capitalism	(n)	39	political system in which property, business and industry are owned by individuals, not by government or by the people as a whole
capture	(v)	48	take control of s.th., esp. in war
casino	(n)	121	place where people play cards etc. for money
casual	(adj)	64	informal
catch on	(vp)	12	become popular
cause	(n)	121	aim which people support
celebrate	(v)	14; 107	be glad about; show that an event (e.g. s.o.'s birthday) is important to you by doing s.th. enjoyable
celebrated	(adj)	56	famous
celebrity	(n)	80	famous person
census	(n)	11	an official study of facts concerning the population of a country, carried out by asking people questions
centralise	(v)	35	control all of s.th. from one place
ceremony	(n)	36; 77	special, formal behaviour; formal event, e.g. wedding or prize-giving
challenge	(v)	32; 92	question what s.o. has said or how he/she behaves; try to beat s.o.
champion	(n)	124	s.o. who is the best at a particular sport
championship	(n)	124	sporting contest to find a champion
character	(n)	16	person in a novel, play etc.
charcoal	(n)	20	black substance produced by burning wood
charity	(n)	60	organisation which raises money from the public and spends it on useful activities e.g. helping the poor
charm	(n)	19	being likeable
charter plane	(np)	118	passenger plane in which all the places have been booked by holiday travel companies for their customers
chef	(n)	112	cook who runs a restaurant kitchen
chemical	(n)	27	substance produced artificially or by a natural reaction or process
chic	(adj)	110	smart and fashionable
choral	(adj)	104	for a choir
chronically	(adv)	69	(of a problem, disease etc.) over a long period of time

circuit	(n)	16	path or route that forms a circle (i.e. ends where it begins)
circus	(n)	122	(in ancient Rome etc.) place where fights and races took place, with seats arranged in a circle
citizen	(n)	5	s.o. who has full rights as a member of a country
civil war	(np)	30	war between two groups in the same country
claim	(v)	49	if you claim s.th., you say it is yours
class system	(np)	7	system of dividing people in society into different groups depending on their jobs, how much money they have etc.
classic	(n)	10; 91	book which is well-known and considered very good; s.th. which is considered a very good or very typical example of its kind
classy	(adj)	102	[coll] smart and professional-seeming
claustrophobic	(adj)	23	making people feel that there is not enough space
clergy	(n)	78	a religion's priests as a group
climate	(n)	20	the weather patterns which are normal for a particular area
clinic	(n)	69	place where sick people are treated
clout	(n)	79	[coll] ability to control others and make things happen
clue	(n)	7	piece of information which helps to solve a problem
co-operation	(n)	32	working together
co-ordinate	(v)	29	organise several activities so that they fit together or run smoothly together
coach	(v)	127	train s.o. in a sporting event
coalition	(n)	29	two groups of people (esp. political parties) working together to achieve the same things
cockney	(adj)	9	from the working class of eastern London
code	(n)	81	rules of behaviour or for doing a particular thing
collapse	(v)	15	fall down
collection	(n)	109	the new clothes which a fashion designer has designed for the coming season
collective	(adj)	32	shared amongst a group
colony	(n)	4	area controlled by people from another country
column	(n)	97	tall stone post used to hold up part of a building
combat	(v)	6	fight against s.th.
comedian	(n)	19	s.o. whose job is to amuse people, tell jokes etc.
comedy	(n)	12	entertainment which tries to amuse people
comic	(adj)	93	of comedy
	(n)	91	s.o. whose job is to amuse people, tell jokes etc.
commercial	(adj)	8	concerned with buying and selling things
commitment	(n)	53	s.th. you have promised to do or must do
Commonwealth	(n)	44	group of countries, made up of the UK and most of the countries which it used to rule
communist	(adj)	38	of a political system in which the workers control business and industry
community	(n)	9	group of people who live in the same area
commute	(v)	86	travel daily from your home to your place of work and back again, esp. over a long distance
comparative	(adj)	70	based on a comparison
compatible	(adj)	55	if two things are compatible, they are both possible at the same time
compatriot	(n)	104	s.o. from the same country
complex	(adj)	11	complicated
compose	(v)	104	write music
composition	(n)	33	how s.th. is made up of various parts
comprehensive	(adj)	84	thorough, leaving nothing out
compromise	(v)	22	give up s.th. you want so that you can reach an agreement with s.o.
compulsory	(adj)	61	required by law or rules
concentrate (on)	(v)	27	give s.th. all your attention
concern	(n)	14; 94	worry; s.th. which s.o. has an interest in
condemn	(v)	75	say that s.o./s.th. is wicked or unacceptable
conduct	(n)	45	how s.th. is done
conduct business	(vp)	36	deal with the tasks which need attention
conductor	(n)	105	leader of an orchestra or band who directs the musicians
confirm	(v)	89	say that s.th. is true
confiscate	(v)	74	take s.th. away from s.o.
conflict	(n)	5	serious disagreement or fighting
confront	(v)	32	argue with s.o., esp. face to face
conquest	(n)	4	beating and taking control of s.o. or s.th.
conscription	(n)	47	system in which ordinary people have to join the **armed forces**
consensus	(n)	16	opinion accepted by most people in a group
consequence	(n)	85	result
consequently	(adv)	12	as a result
conservation	(n)	24	protecting s.th. (e.g. nature, old buildings)
conservative	(adj)	40	having traditional ideas and values
consider	(v)	5	believe (s.th./s.o. to be s.th.)
consideration (for)	(n)	63	if you act with consideration for s.th., you take it into account
consign (to)	(v)	40	send
consistent	(adj)	38	s.o. who is consistent always does/says similar things in the same situation
conspiracy	(n)	123	when two or more people make secret plans together
constituency	(n)	39	an area which chooses and then is looked after by a particular **Member of Parliament**
constituent	(adj)	42	forming a part of s.th.
constitution	(n)	30	a country's system of laws, containing an explanation of the things the people of the country are allowed to do and must do
construction	(n)	14; 51; 101	group of words used together; the building industry; s.th. which is built
consult	(v)	31	ask s.o. for advice
consume	(v)	116	eat
contagious	(adj)	12	(of disease etc.) able to be passed from one person to another
contemporary	(n)	99	s.o. who lived at the same time
context	(n)	5	situation in which s.th. exists/happens
contract	(n)	54	agreement between two or more people or organisations, e.g. to do work for an amount of money
contradictory	(adj)	105	saying two things which cannot both be true
contribution	(n)	19	s.th. given to help achieve a purpose
conundrum	(n)	7	s.th. which is difficult to understand, a puzzle
convenience food	(np)	112	food which is easy and quick to prepare, e.g. ready-made meals which are frozen or in tins
convert (to)	(v)	76	change to another belief or religion
convict	(v)	56	if you are convicted of a crime, it is decided in court that you did it
conviction	(n)	110	being convinced about s.th.

correlation (n) 6 connection between two facts
corruption (n) 56 dishonesty by people in power
cost-effectively (adv) 55 in a way that does not waste money
costume (n) 5 special clothes worn for a part in a film, at a party etc.
costume drama (np) 90 play set in the past, in which a lot of attention is given to historically correct clothes and other details
council (n) 34 a local government
councillor (n) 34 member of a **council**
counter-balance (v) 25 if you counter-balance s.th., you provide s.th. equal and opposite to it
cradle (n) 68 type of bed used for a baby
crane (n) 97 tall machine for lifting heavy objects
craze (for) (n) 107 widespread but short-lived enthusiasm for s.th.
creativity (n) 19 being able to invent and make new things
crest (n) 87 picture which symbolises a particular family or organisation
crippled (adj) 127 disabled
crisis (n) 27 situation in which s.o./s.th. is affected by very serious problems
critic (n) 16 s.o. whose job is to comment on the quality of works of art, literature etc.
criticise (v) 12 say what you think is wrong with s.th./s.o.
crop (n) 21 plant grown for food
crucial (adj) 41 very important
crude (adj) 116 not made carefully or skilfully
cruel (adj) 7 taking pleasure in causing pain
crumble (v) 108 fall to pieces
cuckoo (n) 15 type of bird which lays its eggs in another bird's nest
cuisine (n) 112 way of preparing food which is typical of an area or a country
cult (adj) 91 very popular, but only amongst a particular group of people
cultivate (v) 24 grow plants in (garden) or on (land)
culture (n) 10; 19 group of people with the same ideas and beliefs; the ideas and ways of doing things which exist among a particular group of people
current (adj) 32 of the present time
curriculum (n) 61 list of subjects to be taught in a school etc.
custom (n) 31 how things have usually been done in the past
customs officer (np) 30 person whose job involves controlling what people bring into the country
cut all ties (with) (vp) 16 stop having any contact with s.o./s.th.

daring (adj) 98 new and unusual in a way which might shock some people
deal (n) 84; 87 bargain; agreement between two or more people or organisations that each will do s.th. for the other(s)
debatable (adj) 124 questionable
debate (n) 34 discussion in which different opinions are put forward
decade (n) 16 period of ten years
decay (n) 17 being gradually destroyed (literally: dead bodies decay in the ground)
decline (n) 11 becoming less important/powerful etc.
decrease (v) 46 become fewer/less
dedicate (one's self to) (v) 120 concentrate totally on one thing
dedicated (adj) 104 concentrating only on one thing
defeat (v) 24 act of beating s.th. or s.o. or being beaten
defence (n) 40 protection against attack

defend (v) 40 protect
defendant (n) 58 (in court) person accused of the crime
defiance (n) 48 behaviour which shows that you are not prepared to do what s.o. wants
deforestation (n) 20 destroying areas of forest or woodland
delicacy (n) 112 unusual food which some people find delicious
delicate (adj) 95; 113 gentle, light; not strongly built
delight (n) 102 feeling of happiness and satisfaction
deliver the goods (vp) 43 [coll] to do what you said you would or what you were supposed to
demand (n) 50 amount of s.th. which is wanted or needed
democracy (n) 30 system of government in which leaders are chosen by the people in regular elections
demolish (v) 96 knock down (building etc.)
demonstration (n) 22 when people gather in a place to show that they are angry about s.th. or want s.th. to happen
denomination (n) 78 religious group which is part of a larger one
densely populated (adj. p) 17 containing many people in a small area
deny (v) 77 say that s.th. is not true
dependence (on) (n) 25 not being able to do without s.th.
(v) 50 make less (the amount of s.th. which is available)
deport (v) 125 force s.o. to leave a country
depressed (adj) 19; 114 not producing enough jobs and wealth; sad
deprivation (n) 67 not having what most people have
deprived (adj) 66 s.o. who does not have what most people have
deregulate (v) 54 remove rules which control s.th.
descendant (n) 10 your children, your children's children, etc.
desert (v) 81 leave s.o., esp. when he/she needs your help
desire (n) 56 wish
despair (n) 17 having no hope
despise (v) 9 consider s.o./s.th. to be worthless, stupid etc.
destructive (adj) 111 destroying s.th.
deter (from) (v) 47 persuade s.o. not to do s.th.
determine (v) 42 decide
devaluation (n) 54 making s.th. worth less
development (n) 29 how s.th. changes over time; group of buildings etc. which were planned and built together; act of building on land
device (n) 69 s.th. which has been invented for a particular purpose
devolution (n) 35 moving to a system in which power is shared between different parts of a country
dialect (n) 12 form of a language spoken in a particular area
dictatorial (adj) 32 behaving like a dictator (the leader of a **dictatorship**)
dictatorship (n) 32 country in which the leaders are not chosen by the people and have unlimited power
die out (vp) 12 stop existing as a species
diet (n) 70 what you eat
differ (from) (v) 11 be different
dignity (n) 71 being able to feel that you are important and valued as a person

dilemma	(n)	69	problem which involves a choice between two or more things (all desirable or all undesirable)
diminish	(v)	53	become less
dirty	(adj)	127	[coll] using unfair methods
disastrous	(adj)	21	very bad
discharge	(n)	26	any material that is let out into the air or water
discipline	(n)	61	behaving in a controlled way, obeying the rules
discriminate (against s.o.)	(v)	6	treat s.o. worse than others
discrimination	(n)	5	treating s.o. worse/better than others
dismay	(n)	13	strong feeling of disappointment or unhappiness
dismiss	(v)	9	think/say that s.th. is unimportant/doesn't exist
disparity	(n)	51	difference between two or more things
displacement	(n)	4	moving s.o. or s.th. from a place
dispose of	(vp)	26	get rid of s.th.
dispute	(n)	48	argument
disregard	(n)	123	not taking any notice of s.th.
dissolve	(v)	31	make s.th. (a meeting etc.) end
distinction	(n)	8	difference between two or more things
distinctive	(adj)	12	clearly different from all others
distinguish (between)	(v)	81	recognise that there is a difference between two or more things
distribution	(n)	92	getting a product to customers
disturbing	(adj)	6	worrying
diversity	(n)	6	being made up of many different things
divide	(n)	41	large gap, e.g. between the opinions of two people
division	(n)	39; 124	being split into different groups; group of teams of similar ability within a **league**
document	(n)	31	an official text
(the) doldrums	(n)	117	situation where nothing much happens (literally: area of sea where there is no wind)
dome	(n)	97	rounded roof in the shape of a ball cut in half
dominant	(adj)	10	tending to control others
dominate	(v)	35	have control over s.o./s.th.
donor	(n)	111	s.o. who gives s.th.
downside	(n)	50	disadvantage
drama	(n)	56	play for television, film or theatre
dramatic	(adj)	21	sudden and noticeable
dramatist	(n)	91	s.o. who writes serious plays
drawback	(n)	25	disadvantage
drift	(n)	4	slow movement without a particular direction or goal
drop-out rate	(np)	64	number of people who give up doing s.th. in a certain period of time
due	(adj)	63	suitable, necessary
dump	(v)	27	throw away
dynamic	(adj)	76	full of energy
(at) ease	(adj. p)	11	comfortable, without difficulties
eccentric	(n)	27	s.o. who does strange things/has strange ideas
ecology	(n)	27	the study of how animals, plants, humans and the rest of the natural world depend on and affect each other
economic	(adj)	8	of the **economy**; s.o.'s economic situation is how much money he/she makes and how he/she spends it

economist	(n)	30	s.o. who studies how money, business and industry are organised
economy	(n)	47	a country's economy is how money, business and industry are organised there
efficient		21	able to do s.th. well without wasting time or money
elect	(v)	37	choose, e.g. member of parliament, government by **voting**
election	(n)	27	act of choosing leaders, e.g. politicians or a government by **voting**
electorate	(n)	40	all the people who can **vote** in an **election**
élitist	(adj)	64	only open to people of very high ability or social class
embrace	(v)	50	accept enthusiastically
emerge	(v)	70; 107	become known; come into existence
emission	(n)	25	letting out (a gas or smoke) into the air
emotive	(adj)	68	causing emotion
empathise (with)	(v)	73	understand s.o. else's feelings
emphasis	(n)	66	s.th. which is concentrated on
empire	(n)	5	group of countries ruled by one country
enclose	(v)	20	put a wall, hedge or fence around (an area of land)
encourage	(v)	11	if you encourage s.th., or encourage people to do s.th., you try to persuade people to do it
endure	(v)	108	last a long time
enforce	(v)	11	make s.th. happen
engage (s.o.'s) attention	(vp)	13	make s.o. take notice
engineering	(n)	47	designing and building machines
ensure	(v)	11	make sure
enterprise	(n)	52	company
enthusiasm	(n)	48	liking for s.th. or being keen for s.th. to happen
environment	(n)	13; 24	surroundings; the natural world
environmental	(adj)	24	concerned with the natural world
environmentalist	(adj)	27	concerned with protecting the environment
epidemic	(n)	69	disease outbreak which quickly affects a large number of people
equal opportunities	(np)	6	giving all people the same chances whether they are male or female, black or white etc.
essence	(n)	57	most important part of s.th.
established	(adj)	112	which has existed for a long time and is unlikely to die out
establishment	(adj)	36; 42; 103	organisation; setting s.th. up; the people who have influence and power in a society
estate	(n)	22	large area of land owned by the same person or organisation
estimate	(v)	71	make a calculation which is not based on exact figures
ethnic	(adj)	5	concerning/expressing s.o.'s race and culture (esp. of a **minority** group)
Eurosceptic	(n)	41	s.o. who thinks that being a member of the European Union may be a bad thing
evidence	(n)	11	fact which shows s.th. to be true/untrue
exception	(n)	13	s.th. which does not follow the general rule
exchange	(v)	123	swap
exclusion	(n)	41	keeping s.o. out of s.th.
exclusively	(adv)	11	only, without any others
executive	(n)	31	the part of a government which carries out decisions and controls the country day to day

exhaust fumes	(np)	85	gases emitted by an engine
exotic	(adj)	23	unusual and foreign
expanse	(n)	20	large area
expansion	(n)	4	becoming larger in size or area
expel	(v)	4	push s.o./s.th. out of a place
expendable	(adj)	100	which can be used and thrown away
at the expense of	(prep. p)	55	if s.th. is done at the expense of s.th. else, it is done even though there will be negative effects on s.th. else
experimentation	(n)	95	trying out new ideas
exploit	(v)	50	make use of s.th.
export	(n)	47	goods sold to s.o. in another country and sent there
expose (to)	(v)	10	cause s.o./s.th. to have contact with s.th.
extract	(v)	51	take s.th. out of s.th.
extraordinary	(adj)	22	very unusual and surprising
extreme	(adj)	38	farthest from the centre or from what is normal
extremist	(n)	77	s.o. who has beliefs and/or uses methods which are not acceptable to most people
fabulous	(adj)	101	wonderful
façade	(n)	117	appearance, esp. when false (literally: front of a building)
factor	(n)	12	anything which affects or helps to cause a situation
fade	(v)	52	grow less strong, bright etc.
failure	(n)	18	being unsuccessful
faith	(n)	75	religious belief
familiar	(adj)	21	well known
famine	(n)	71	when large numbers of people are unable to get enough to eat
fanatical	(adj)	102	liking or believing in s.th. more than is reasonable
far-flung	(adj)	14	a long way away
fascinating	(adj)	19	very interesting
favour	(v)	40	treat s.o. better than others
be in favour (of)	(vp)	44	think that s.th. is a good idea
featureless	(adj)	50	all the same, without anything special about it
fee-paying	(adj)	9	(of schools) for which parents have to pay to send their children there
ferry	(n)	86	ship or boat which carries passengers back and forth between two or more places
ferry	(v)	88	carry back and forth
fertiliser	(n)	21	food for plants
fertility	(n)	69	ability to produce children
festival	(n)	75	occasion on which s.th. is celebrated publicly
finance	(n)	34	money, esp. the money needed to pay for s.th.
finance	(v)	53	provide the necessary money for s.th.
fine	(n)	58	money paid as a punishment
firearm	(n)	57	gun
first-past-the-post system	(np)	32	system of government in which the person who gets most votes wins
flat out	(adj. p)	88	[coll] very busy, without time to stop
flat-broke	(adj)	73	[coll] owning no money at all
flee (from)	(v)	5	run away (from s.th. dangerous or frightening)
flexible	(adj)	54	able to change to fit new situations
flight	(n)	5	running away (from s.th. dangerous or frightening)
flourish	(v)	104	become successful and widespread
flower	(v)	10	develop to a high level
flu	(n)	69	common disease which causes dizziness, high temperature, sore throat, sneezing etc.
focused	(adj)	65	concentrating on what you want to achieve
folk-music	(n)	107	the traditional music of a region or country
folklore	(n)	9	traditional stories which have been made up to explain s.th.
food chain	(np)	21	series of (plants and) animals, the connection between them being that each one is food for the next one up the chain
force	(v)	11	make s.o. do s.th.
formalise	(v)	122	make rules to control how s.th. is done
fortune	(n)	18; 84	(good) luck; large amount of money
fossil	(n)	118	shape of a long-dead animal or plant preserved in rock
found	(v)	19	start or create (an organisation etc.)
fragile	(adj)	109	easily damaged or broken
fragment	(n)	4	part broken off s.th.
frail	(adj)	37	weak, easily hurt
framework	(n)	42	overall system into which s.th. fits
fringe	(n)	24	the outside edge of s.th., not the main part
on all fronts	(adv.p)	102	everywhere where a particular thing exists or is active
frustration	(n)	39	feeling of anger caused by not being able to do s.th.
fully-fledged	(adj)	109	fully developed
function	(n)	33	what s.o./s.th. is supposed to do
fund(s)	(n)	18	money available for a particular purpose
fundamental	(adj)	33	basic and important
funding	(n)	53	money provided for a particular purpose
funeral	(n)	75	ceremony which is held when s.o. has died
fusion	(n)	116	when two things come together to become one new thing
gay	(adj)	19	homosexual (esp. of men)
gender	(n)	6	sex (i.e. being male or female)
general election	(n)	36	an **election** in which a new government is chosen
general practitioner (GP)	(np)	68	doctor who works in the community rather than in a hospital, and does not specialise in a particular area
generate	(v)	84	create or cause s.th.
genetically modified (GM)	(adj. p)	27	produced by changing the basic structure (DNA) of a living thing
genitals	(n)	111	external sexual organs
genius	(n)	99	very great ability in a particular area
geology	(n)	20	the study of what the Earth is made of and how it changes over time
Germanic	(adj)	4	of the peoples who became the modern Germans, Scandinavians, Dutch and English
get going	(vp)	126	start to be successful
gigantic	(adj)	20	very large
give way (to)	(vp)	10	move out of s.o.'s way
gladiator	(n)	122	(in ancient Rome etc.) s.o. whose job was to fight and kill others, as a form of entertainment
glamorous	(adj)	83	special and exciting
glance (at)	(v)	80	take a quick look at
global	(adj)	14	found in or affecting the whole world
globalisation	(n)	15	the increase in communication between organisations and people all over the world, leading to fewer differences between countries and cultures

glorious	(adj)	116	wonderful
govern	(v)	15	control
gradually	(adv)	15	slowly, bit by bit
grass-roots level	(np)	27	the ordinary people who are the main part of an organisation
grave	(n)	68	hole in the ground in which a dead person is buried
greenhouse effect	(np)	25	warming of the Earth caused by gases produced by human activities
gregarious	(adj)	37	preferring to be with others
(the) grind	(n)	117	hard and boring work
Gross Domestic Product (GDP)	(np)	47	total value of everything produced by a country, except income from abroad
guarantee	(v)	26	promise that s.th. will happen/be given etc.
guerrilla	(n)	35	fighter who is not part of an official army
guilt	(n)	58	being responsible for a crime or other bad act
guilty	(adj)	45	feeling that you have done wrong
gulf	(n)	80	wide gap
gym	(n)	62	building or room in which physical exercise takes place
habitat	(n)	16	surroundings in which an animal or plant lives
hail	(v)	109	greet s.o. enthusiastically
half-timbered	(adj)	23	a style of building which uses frames of wood filled with other materials
handout	(n)	73	money which is given free to s.o.
hand-up	(n)	73	s.th. which helps s.o. to get out of a difficult situation
harass	(v)	81	disturb, annoy or frighten s.o. repeatedly
hardware	(n)	92	equipment required to do s.th.
hatred	(n)	81	very strong dislike
have in common	(vp)	5	share (e.g. interests, hair colour etc.)
haven	(n)	5	place where people are safe from danger
head of state	(np)	31	leader of a country
heavy-handed	(adj)	82	clumsy, unnecessarily severe
heir (to)	(n)	78	s.o. who will take over s.th. after the death of the person who has it at present
hereditary	(adj)	33	passed from one generation to the next, e.g. from father to son
hero	(n)	21	male person who is admired for being good, brave etc.; main (esp. good) male character in a book or film
hierarchy	(n)	40	system in which people are organised into different levels of power and importance
high-profile	(adj)	27	attracting the attention of many people
high-tech	(adj)	19	using the latest, best machines
higher education	(np)	6	education at a university or college
historic	(adj)	17	of long-term importance
historical	(adj)	7	which happened or existed in the past
holistic	(adj)	68	looking at the whole of s.th. rather than just a particular problem
homoerotic	(adj)	93	concerning sexual feelings between people of the same sex
hooliganism	(n)	123	noisy, violent behaviour
horoscope	(n)	80	prediction of s.o.'s future based on his/her star sign
horrific	(adj)	73	shockingly bad
hostile	(adj)	5	having and showing a strong dislike (of s.o./s.th.)
hostility	(n)	5	strong and openly shown dislike (of s.o./s.th.)

House of Lords	(np)	30	the less powerful of the two Chambers of the British parliament
huge	(adj)	10	very large
humorous	(adj)	8	amusing
humour	(n)	7	ability to find things amusing
hygiene	(n)	111	keeping things clean in order to avoid health problems
hymn	(n)	75	religious song in the Christian religion
identify	(v)	6	describe or find out who s.o. is or what s.th. is
identity	(n)	10	sense of who you are and how you are different from others
ideology	(n)	38	set of political beliefs
idiom	(n)	12	group of words which has a different meaning from what you would expect if you knew only the meanings of the individual words
illiterate	(adj)	60	unable to read and write
illogical	(adj)	111	not resulting from reasonable thinking
image	(n)	7	how s.o./s.th. is seen by others
immigrant	(n)	5	s.o. who has come to live in a foreign country
immigration	(n)	5	coming to live in a foreign country
impact	(n)	29	(strong) effect
impact (on)	(v)	28	affect (esp. in a strong way)
impaired	(adj)	79	not working perfectly
impartial	(adj)	36	not taking sides
imperialism	(n)	77	system of government in which a powerful country controls other countries
implant	(n)	69	s.th. which is put inside the body in an operation
implication	(n)	87	s.th. which is suggested but not proven
import	(v)	27	buy s.th. abroad and bring it into the country
impose (on)	(v)	10	to make s.o. accept s.th. (e.g. an idea, a language)
impressionism	(n)	99	style of painting etc. which tries to give a general idea of the subject through light and shadow, rather than drawing every detail
improvise	(v)	93	invent s.th. as you go along, rather than planning it in advance
incentive	(n)	35	reason to want to do s.th.
incite	(v)	81	cause (bad feelings etc.)
incompetent	(adj)	56	not able to do o.'s job properly
incomprehensible	(adj)	95	impossible to understand
inconsistent	(adj)	10	changing for no good reason
incorporate (into)	(v)	34	make s.th. a part of s.th. else
indecision	(n)	44	not being able to decide
independent	(adj)	31	not controlled by s.o. or s.th. else
indicator	(n)	8	s.th. which acts as a sign
indifference	(n)	11	not being interested
indigenous	(adj)	5	belonging naturally to a country
individuality	(n)	44	having your own personality, not just being part of a group
inevitable	(adj)	43	unavoidable
infection	(n)	111	catching a disease
inferiority complex	(np)	112	believing (without good reason) that you are not as good as others
inflation	(n)	53	rise in prices
influence	(n)	10; 47	the way s.th. affects s.th. else; the ability to persuade others to do what you want

information technology	(n)	15	using computers and other electronic methods to store and provide information
inhabit	(v)	16	live in a place
initially	(adv)	18	at first
innovation	(n)	100	attempting new things
insecurity	(n)	109	not being safe
insensitivity	(n)	22	not thinking about other people's feelings or needs
insight (into)	(n)	95	understanding of s.th.
insoluble	(adj)	25	not able to be solved
inspiration	(n)	97	source of ideas
inspire	(v)	99	provide the idea or motivation for s.th.
institution	(n)	6	official organisation
insult	(v)	76	say s.th. rude or hurtful about s.o./s.th.
insurance	(n)	51	system in which people make small regular payments to an organisation which will pay them a large sum if s.th. bad happens to them
integrate	(v)	5	become a part of s.th.
integration	(n)	6	making s.o. a part of s.th.
intellectual	(adj)	60	of the human mind and its ability to think and form ideas
intensive	(adj)	21	putting a lot of effort into a small area
interaction	(n)	7	how people/things affect each other and behave towards each other
intercession	(n)	74	trying to persuade a powerful person not to punish a weaker person
interfere (with)	(v)	31	stop s.th. from working properly or s.o. from doing as he/she wants
interpret	(v)	70	decide what s.th. means
intervene (in)	(v)	34	step in and change how s.th. is done
interventionism	(n)	52	(esp. of government) belief that government should directly influence the **economy**, e.g. by spending money to help industries to survive
intimidating	(adj)	59	frightening because of being very big, powerful etc.
intonation	(n)	12	how your voice rises and falls as you speak
invade	(v)	4	take an army into an area against the wishes of the people who live there
invest (in)	(v)	29	provide money for s.th. you believe will be useful to yourself or others
investigate	(v)	57	look at s.th. closely in order to find out the reasons for it, who did it etc.
investment	(n)	17	providing money for s.th., usually in order to make more money
invincible	(adj)	52	unbeatable
irritate	(v)	89	become or make sore
isolation	(n)	85	being alone
issue	(n)	6	problem which people discuss
item	(n)	80	(in newspapers) piece of writing, story
jargon	(n)	59	expressions which only experts understand
jealousy	(n)	123	feeling of anger caused by s.o. else having s.th. you want
joint venture	(np)	87	business run by two or more companies together
judge	(n)	31	s.o. who decides how the law should be understood and used in individual cases
judicial	(adj)	58	concerning judges and courts
judiciary	(n)	31	the part of a government which decides whether laws have been broken

junior	(adj)	126	not adult
junk food	(np)	121	unhealthy but popular food
justice	(n)	56; 94	applying the law; fairness in the way people are treated
key	(adj)	29	very important
Kiwi	(n)	72	[coll] New Zealander
laboratory	(n)	88	room or building where film is developed into photos
labour	(n)	20; 44	work, esp. physical work; people who work
labour market	(np)	5	the people looking for work and the employers looking for workers
landfill site	(np)	26	place where rubbish is put in a hole in the ground and covered with earth
landlord	(n)	20; 114	man who owns land and rents it to others; man who runs a pub
at large	(phrase)	66	in general
Latin	(n)	10	the language of the Romans
league	(n)	19	group of teams which play against each other to see which is best
legal	(adj)	22; 31	allowed by law; of the law
legislate (on)	(v)	13	make laws (about s.th.)
legislation	(n)	33	laws
legislature	(n)	31	the part of a government which makes and changes laws
lesbian	(n)	75	homosexual woman
liberalism	(n)	41	belief that people and organisations should have as much freedom as possible
licence	(n)	57	piece of paper which states officially that you are allowed to do or own s.th.
limit	(v)	17	to stop s.th. becoming bigger than a certain size
linguistic	(adj)	8	of language
literacy	(n)	66	being able to read and write
literary	(adj)	16	of literature
local	(n)	88	[coll] pub which s.o. goes to most often
loch	(n)	23	in Scotland: lake, or arm of the sea which cuts deep into the land
lone-parent family	(np)	66	family in which there is only one parent
lord	(n)	7	man of the highest class in British society
low-prestige	(adj)	12	not considered to be of high value
lyric	(n)	95	the words of a song
magic	(n)	76	ability to do things which **science** shows are impossible
mainstream	(adj)	12	of the usual kind, accepted by most people
major	(adj)	5	important, on a large scale
majority	(n)	10	the greater number of people in a group
make it	(vp)	126	be successful
management	(n)	24; 53	how s.th. is controlled or dealt with; managers as a group
Mancunian	(n)	18	s.o. who comes from Manchester
manifest o.s.	(v)	111	become obvious
manifesto	(n)	33	list of promises which a political party produces before an **election**
manipulate	(v)	82	control or influence s.o./s.th., esp. in an unfair way

manufacturer	(n)	47	maker of goods
manufacturing	(n)	51	industry in which things are made in order to be sold
margin	(n)	10	edge of an area
market (for)	(n)	5	the people who are prepared to buy a certain thing
market researcher	(n)	8	s.o. who finds out what people buy and why
marketing	(n)	8	advertising and selling products
mass	(adj)	38	involving large numbers of people
massive	(adj)	17	very large
master	(n)	60	[old] male teacher
mature	(adj)	62	grown-up
maverick	(adj)	116	adventurous and unusual
maxim	(n)	38	saying which is believed to be a useful rule
maximum	(adj)	55	the most/largest possible
measure	(n)	25	step taken to try to solve a problem
measure	(v)	55	find out the exact size, amount or weight of s.th.
mechanisation	(n)	21	using machines to do work which used to be done by hand
media	(n)	12	the various ways of sending information to a large number of people: TV, radio, newspapers etc.
medieval	(adj)	20	from the time between AD 476 and AD 1500
Member of Parliament (MP)	(np)	31	politician who is **elected** to **parliament**
mental	(adj)	73	of the mind
merge (with)	(v)	10	(of two or more things) become one/make into one
meritocracy	(n)	9	system which gives power to the people with the most ability
microscope	(n)	67	instrument for looking at very small things
migration	(n)	4	moving from one area to another
military	(adj)	44	of the **armed forces**
millennium	(n)	20	period of a thousand years
mine	(n)	51	place where s.th. useful or valuable (e.g. coal or gold) is dug from the ground
minimum	(adj)	15	of the smallest size/amount
minister	(n)	31; 79	head of a government department; s.o. whose job is to look after people's religious needs
ministry	(n)	79	service as a **minister** of religion
minor	(adj)	38	small or unimportant
minority	(n)	11	small number of people in a much larger group
misbehave	(v)	63	behave badly
misfortune	(n)	17	bad luck
mish-mash	(n)	14	[coll] mixture of very different things
monarch	(n)	30	ruling king or queen of a country
monetary union	(np)	54	when a number of countries start to have the same currency
monitor	(v)	64	watch s.o. to see how well he/she does
monolingual	(adj)	10	speaking only one language
monologue	(n)	95	long speech by one person
monopoly (on)	(n)	83	complete control of an area of business by one company
monotheist	(n)	77	s.o. who believes in only one god
moral support	(np)	48	encouragement, rather than practical help
mortgage	(n)	116	money borrowed to buy a house
motivate (one's self)	(v)	73	find the determination to do s.th.
motivation	(n)	13; 60	being determined to do s.th.; reason for doing s.th.
motto	(n)	88	sentence or phrase which is used as a guide to s.o.'s behaviour
movement	(n)	28	group of people in art, politics etc. who have similar ideas
multi-culturalism	(n)	78	being made up of several different **cultures**
multi-racial	(adj)	7	made up of many **races**
Muslim	(n)	74	s.o. whose religion is Islam
myth	(n)	14	well-known but untrue story
National Health Service (NHS)	(np)	5	the system of health care in the UK, paid for by taxes
nationalised	(adj)	40	run by the government, not by private companies
nationalist	(adj)	11	believing that your country should be independent
nationalistic	(adj)	44	believing that your country is better than others
native	(adj)	72	(place) you were born in
native speaker	(np)	10	s.o. who speaks a particular language as his/her first language
navy	(n)	20	the part of a country's **armed forces** which fights at sea
neglect	(n)	11	not looking after s.th.
negotiator	(n)	92	s.o. whose job is to make agreements with other individuals or organisations
neighbouring	(adj)	17	next to s.th. previously mentioned
network	(n)	26	when several people, towns or organisations are all connected to each other, they form a network
niche	(n)	83	gap
noble	(adj)	79	good and unselfish
noble	(n)	8	member of the highest class in a country which has a king or queen
nostalgic	(adj)	75	seeing the past in a positive way compared to the present
note of caution	(np)	8	warning to be careful
notion	(n)	15	unclear idea
notorious	(adj)	56	famous for a bad reason
nuclear	(adj)	25	of atoms; nuclear energy is the energy produced by splitting atoms
oblige	(v)	45	if you oblige s.o. to do s.th., you leave him/her with no choice but to do it
obscure	(adj)	93	known or understood by few people
observe	(v)	77	keep to a rule etc.
observer	(n)	45	s.o. who watches s.th. carefully (but does not take part)
obsessed (with)	(v)	7	able only to think only about one thing
obstruct	(v)	22	block
obtain	(v)	40	get
occult	(n)	76	**ceremonies** and beliefs involving beings and powers which **science** does not accept
occur	(v)	39	happen
oddity	(n)	85	strange or unusual thing
offender	(n)	59	s.o. who has broken a rule/law
official	(adj)	8	of an organisation or person in authority
oil platform	(np)	27	metal structure which floats on the sea or stands on the sea bed and is used to drill for oil
operate	(v)	36	run (an organisation etc.)

opportunity	(n)	5	chance to do s.th.
oppose	(v)	25	try to stop s.th. from happening
opposition	(n)	5	trying to stop s.th. from happening
optical	(adj)	100	concerning the eye
optimism	(n)	68	believing that good things will happen
organ	(n)	75; 78	musical instrument which has pipes of different lengths, often used in a church; organisation which has a particular purpose as part of a larger organisation
organic	(adj)	27	using only natural methods in farming or gardening
origin	(n)	5	where s.o./s.th. comes from
original	(adj)	22; 90	which existed in the beginning; not based on anything which existed previously
originate (from)	(v)	38	come from
orthodoxy	(n)	50	opinions accepted and approved by the people in authority
outfit	(n)	110	set of clothes
outlaw	(v)	55	make s.th. against the law
outlook	(n)	127	possibilities for the future
output	(n)	51	how much of s.th. is produced
outright	(adj)	29	completely
outstrip	(v)	69	become larger, faster etc. than s.th. else
overawe	(v)	36	impress s.o. so much that he/she feels afraid
overcome	(v)	43	if you overcome a difficulty, you find a way to beat it
overtake	(v)	17	catch up with and pass s.o./s.th.
overthrow	(v)	49	remove from power
pace	(n)	89	speed
palate	(n)	116	sense of taste (literally: roof of the mouth)
panic	(n)	39	very strong fear, which makes you act without thinking carefully
paradox	(n)	74	two facts which appear to contradict each other
parliament	(n)	30	group of people within a country who make and change its laws; length of time between two **general elections**
participate (in)	(v)	29	take part in s.th.
partisan	(adj)	106	strongly in favour of one thing rather than another, without clear reasons
pass	(v)	24	officially accept (a law)
passion	(n)	22; 119	strong feelings; powerful feeling of love
passionate	(adj)	11	feeling strong emotions
patriotic	(adj)	30	loving one's country
patronise	(v)	117	be a customer of s.o./s.th.
pay off	(vp)	66	bring worthwhile results
peak	(n)	20	top of a hill or mountain
peasant	(n)	20	person of low social class who does farm work
penalty	(n)	58	punishment
pension	(n)	40	regular income which a person lives on when he/she no longer works
percentage	(n)	59	fraction, expressed out of 100
performance	(n)	93; 122	entertaining an audience e.g. by acting; how well s.o. does s.th.
periphery	(n)	54	outside edge (in contrast to the centre)
permanent	(adj)	33	not ending
persecution	(n)	5	treating s.o. badly and unfairly, e.g. because he/she belongs to a particular group
persistent	(adj)	56	a persistent problem is one which keeps recurring
personnel	(n)	47	the people who work for an organisation
perspective	(n)	55	way of looking at s.th.
perverse	(adj)	26	deliberately doing/saying things which are not sensible
pest	(n)	22	animal which eats useful plants or animals
pesticide	(n)	21	substance for killing insects
pharmaceutical	(adj)	53	concerning medicines
phenomenon	(n)	15	s.th. that happens, esp. s.th. interesting or strange
philosophy	(n)	10; 52	the study of the relationship between human thought and reality; system of ideas and beliefs
physical	(adj)	4	which can be seen, touched, smelt, tasted and/or heard
piercing	(n)	110	making holes in your body in order to decorate it with rings etc.
playwright	(n)	91	s.o. who writes plays
poetic	(adj)	12; 95	reminding you of or suitable for poetry; of poetry
pointless	(adj)	120	having no reason
polar	(adj)	20	of the North or South Pole
police	(v)	15	make sure that rules are not broken
policy	(n)	11	what an organisation has decided to do about s.th.
political exile	(np)	5	s.o. who has to leave a country because of his/her political beliefs
politicise	(v)	40	make s.o. become involved in politics
poll tax	(np)	40	(in the UK in the 1980s) local tax which every adult had to pay
pornographic	(adj)	80	designed to cause sexual excitement
pornography	(n)	82	material (text, photos etc.) designed to create sexual excitement
port	(n)	5	town on the coast or on a river, where ships can load and unload passengers and goods
portrait	(n)	74	picture of s.o.
posh	(adj)	40	[coll] typical of the upper classes
poverty	(n)	17	being poor
power generation	(np)	24	electricity production
power station	(np)	25	building and machinery used for electricity production
practice	(n)	21	how a certain thing is done
pragmatism	(n)	13	dealing with problems in a practical way, rather than according to fixed ideas or rules
prayer	(n)	74	s.th. said to a god, e.g. in thanks or asking for help
precious	(adj)	23; 30	too concerned with prettiness; valuable
predict	(v)	16	say that s.th. will happen in the future
predominantly	(adv)	45	mostly
prejudice	(n)	11	being unfairly for or against s.o./s.th.
prescriptive	(adj)	15	telling people what to do
preserve	(v)	10	protect s.th. and stop it from being destroyed
pressure	(n)	45	an attempt to make s.o. do s.th.
pressure group	(np)	28	group of people which tries to persuade a government or organisation to do s.th.
prestigious	(adj)	64	admired by many people
prevailing	(adj)	25	which exists most of the time
prevent (from)	(v)	27	stop s.th. from happening
pride	(n)	18	believing that s.th. you have or have done is particularly good
pride (one's self on s.th.)	(v)	74	think that you have a particular good quality

priest	(n)	74	s.o. who looks after people's religious needs
Prime Minister	(np)	31	the leader of the British government, and the leaders of the governments of some other countries
primitive	(adj)	13	of a very simple kind
principal	(adj)	25	main
priority	(n)	64	s.th. which is more important/urgent than other things
privacy	(n)	81	being free from public attention
private	(adj)	9; 17; 60	not open to everyone; of/by companies or individuals, not the government; acting as individuals
privatise	(v)	26	sell an industry which was controlled by the government
privilege	(n)	36	s.th. special which you are allowed to do although most people are not
procedure	(n)	37	usual way of doing s.th.
process	(n)	4	several events which happen one after another
processed food	(adj)	112	food which has been treated in some way before being sold
productive	(adj)	27	able to produce
productivity	(n)	53	how much s.o. produces in a particular length of time
professional	(adj)	37	relating to your job
professor	(n)	9	highest level of teacher in a university department
profile	(n)	45	how s.th./s.o. is seen by others, esp. how important they think it is
profit	(n)	53	amount of money which you gain when you sell s.th. for more than it cost you to make, do or buy it
profitable	(adj)	49	making money for the person/organisation that owns it
programme	(n)	29	series of events which are planned together
progress	(n)	9	moving forward/becoming better over a period of time
promenade	(v)	118	walk for pleasure, esp. in town
promote	(v)	126	try to make s.th. popular
propagate	(v)	79	spread s.th. more widely
proportional representation	(np)	32	system of government in which there is a direct connection between the number of people who **vote** for a party and the number of members the party is allowed to have in **parliament**
proposal	(n)	29	s.th. which is suggested
proscribe	(v)	43	forbid
prospect (for)	(n)	79	chance of s.th. happening
prosperity	(n)	18	being wealthy
prosperous	(adj)	51	wealthy
prostitution	(n)	17	having sex with s.o. for payment
protest	(v)	22	complain about s.th.
provision	(n)	34; 89	arrangement included in an agreement; preparations for s.th. which might happen
psychology	(n)	43; 62	way of thinking; the study of the mind
public figure	(np)	7	famous person
public school	(n)	40	school which charges fees
public service broadcasting	(np)	82	TV and radio provided by the **state**
publicity	(n)	41	mention of s.th. in newspapers, on TV etc.
publishing	(n)	53	industry which produces books, newspapers, magazines etc.
punter	(n)	121	[coll] s.o. who **bets**

Puritan	(n)	91	member of a 16th–17th century religious group which believed in living a very simple life according to strict rules
purity	(n)	14	being clean, not mixed with anything else
put (one's) money where (one's) mouth is	(vp)	43	[coll] follow your words by putting them into practice
put up	(v)	72	allow s.o. to stay in your home
qualification	(n)	6; 66	examination you have passed; fact about you which means that you have a right to s.th.
quasi-	(prefix)	87	almost
quota	(n)	50	set quantity of s.th. which must be produced, bought etc.
quotation	(n)	74	repetition of s.o. else's words
race	(n)	4	very large group of people belonging to the same physical type
racism	(n)	5	unfair treatment of s.o. because of his/her race
racist	(adj)	5	treating people unfairly because of their race
radical	(adj)	33	involving very large changes
radically	(adv)	22	very much
radioactive	(adj)	25	giving out a harmful type of energy
raise	(v)	35	if you raise a tax, you collect the money
at random	(adv. p)	58	by chance
rape	(n)	59	forcing s.o. to have sex
rave	(n)	120	very large party with loud music and dancing, held (often without official permission) in a large building or in the open air
raw material	(np)	50	s.th. which is in its natural form and can be used to make s.th. else
reaction (to)	(n)	42	what you do, say or feel about s.th.
rebel (against)	(v)	76	start to fight against s.th. you previously accepted or which most people accept
rebellious	(adj)	32	refusing to behave how people in authority (e.g. bosses, parents etc.) want you to behave
be in receipt of s.th.	(vp)	66	receive s.th.
recommend	(v)	19	say that s.th. is worth visiting, having, doing etc.
reconcile	(v)	35	if you reconcile two aims, you find a way in which both can be achieved
record	(n)	24	how well or badly s.o. has done in the past
recover	(v)	18	become healthy again (after illness etc.)
recreational	(adj)	120	used for fun
recruit	(v)	5	find people and persuade them to work for you
rectify	(v)	6	put s.th. right
recycle	(v)	26	make s.th. new out of s.th. which has been used
reduce	(v)	27	make less/fewer
referee	(n)	122	(in football, rugby, boxing etc.) s.o. whose job is to make sure that the players keep to the rules
reference	(n)	73	letter recommending s.o. to s.o. else, e.g. for a job or house
referendum	(n)	43	when the people of a country are invited to decide about a particular question

reform	(v)	33	change the way a system works
refugee	(n)	5	s.o. who has to leave his/her own country because of war or other serious problems
regard (as)	(v)	36	see s.th./s.o. as s.th.
regeneration	(n)	87	causing or experiencing new growth
regime	(n)	5	undemocratic or cruel government
regional	(adj)	9	from a particular part of a country
regulate	(v)	15	control
relic	(n)	8	s.th. left over from an earlier time
relief	(n)	71	s.th. which makes a problem less serious
relieve	(v)	67	make a problem less bad
reluctant	(adj)	54	not keen
remarkable	(adj)	9	surprising
remnant	(n)	23	a part left over from s.th. larger which no longer exists
renewable	(adj)	25	which does not become used up
renowned	(adj)	112	famous
repressive	(adj)	94	allowing little freedom
republican	(adj)	30	of government based on the idea that all people are equal, having an **elected** leader instead of a king or queen
reputation	(n)	7	what people in general think of s.o./s.th.
research and development	(np)	19	discovering new knowledge and methods, then using them to create new products
resemble	(v)	9	look/seem similar to s.o./s.th.
resent	(v)	48	be angry about s.th.
resentment	(n)	5	anger
resist	(v)	96	fight against s.th.
resistance (to)	(n)	57	trying to stop s.th.
resolution	(n)	25	s.th. which s.o. decides to do
resource	(n)	17	s.th. which s.o. has and can use
responsibility	(n)	32	if you have responsibility for s.th., you are the one who has to make decisions about it and take the blame if it goes wrong
restless	(adj)	96	unwilling to behave in a quiet, peaceful way
restriction	(n)	55	if there are restrictions to s.th., it doesn't apply (or is not allowed) in all cases
retire	(v)	70	leave your job and stop working
reveal	(v)	26	make known
revenue	(n)	53	money which an organisation receives from its activities
revere	(v)	77	have great respect for s.o.
reverse	(v)	34	make s.th. go in the opposite direction
review	(n)	116	opinion of a restaurant, play, novel etc. in the media
revise	(v)	33	examine s.th. (esp. a text) and make changes to it
revive	(v)	35	bring back to health, strength or life
revolution	(n)	9	complete change in a system, e.g. of government
rhyme (with)	(v)	12	(of two or more words) to end with the same group of sounds
ridiculous	(adj)	57	silly, completely wrong for the situation
right-of-way	(n)	22	route (e.g. road or path) which everyone has the right to travel on
rigid	(adj)	60	unable to change
riot	(n)	17	situation in which angry people destroy property, attack the police etc.
ritual	(n)	75	fixed series of actions which are carried out for their **symbolic** importance, not for any practical reason
rival	(n)	53	s.o. who is trying to get s.th. which you also want
robe	(n)	59	long, loose clothes worn on certain formal occasions

robust	(adj)	36	strong, not easily damaged
role	(n)	13	what s.o. is supposed to do, how he/she is supposed to behave
role model	(np)	127	s.o. whom you admire and try to copy
Romance	(adj)	10	of the languages which came from Latin
romance (with)	(n)	10	love affair
Romantics	(n)	16	a group of writers and artists in the 18th and 19th centuries who were interested in emotions, nature etc.
root	(n)	10	original part of s.th.
roughly	(adv)	73	about
row	(v)	62	move a boat using oars (long pieces of wood, flat at one end)
rude awakening	(np)	72	s.th. unpleasant which happens to you and makes you see how things really are
rules of engagement	(np)	82	rules agreed on for a fight
(on the) run	(adv. p)	127	one after another
runner-up	(n)	127	person or team which comes second in a competition
rural	(adj)	16	of the countryside
rush hour	(np)	84	time when there is most traffic on the roads (weekday mornings and evenings)
sack	(v)	32	remove s.o. from a job
sadistic	(adj)	123	taking pleasure in s.o. else's pain
satellite	(n)	88	object which circles around a planet in space
satellite dish	(np)	23	bowl-shaped object for receiving signals from a **satellite**
satire	(n)	8	play or novel which shows society's problems through making people or organisations look silly
saviour	(n)	109	s.o. who saves s.th. or s.o.
scale	(n)	8; 97	system of measurement; size
scandal	(n)	27	bad event or situation which a lot of people find out about
sceptical	(adj)	118	doubtful about the truth of s.th.
scholar	(n)	60	s.o. who studies an **academic** subject
science	(n)	10	study of the world and how things work
scientist	(n)	13	s.o. who studies science
scorn	(n)	7	considering s.o./s.th. to be stupid/useless
Scouse	(adj)	19	[coll] from Liverpool
scrap	(v)	68	get rid of s.th.
screen	(v)	70	check s.o. for a disease or other problem
screenplay	(n)	92	story for a film
scrutiny	(n)	37	looking closely at s.th.
sea change	(np)	42	important, long-lasting change
second-class	(adj)	13	not considered as good as others
secondary	(adj)	46; 50	not main or most important; coming second in a series
sect	(n)	74	religious group, esp. one which has separated from a larger religion
sectarian	(adj)	35	concerning or caused by the differences between religious groups
sector	(n)	50	part of s.th., or small group within a larger group
secure	(adj)	49	safe
segregate	(v)	124	separate one group of people from another
select	(v)	58	choose (from a group)
selective	(adj)	64	choosing the best/most suitable
self-satisfied	(adj)	13	pleased with one's achievements and not feeling the need to do any more
sensation	(n)	89	feeling

sentence	(n)	58	(in court) punishment
serial	(n)	90	film which is shown in parts over several days or weeks
series	(n)	20; 90	number of things following one after another; number of programmes at regular intervals concerning the same characters, subjects etc.
servant	(n)	97	s.o. whose job is to work in s.o. else's house, doing the cleaning, cooking etc.
service	(n)	17	s.th. which is done by one person (or an organisation) for another
service	(v)	47	check a machine and make any repairs which are needed to keep it running efficiently
set the tone	(vp)	8	behave in a way which others then copy
settle	(v)	4	go to an area and live there
settle in	(vp)	5	become used to living in a place
settlement	(n)	5	coming to live in a new place
sexism	(n)	13	treating people differently because of their sex
sexuality	(n)	93	sexual feelings and relationships
shortage (of)	(n)	69	not having enough of s.th.
significant	(adj)	7	important, meaningful
sinister	(adj)	125	worrying, because it makes you think that s.th. evil or dangerous is happening
slave	(n)	18	person who is owned by s.o. else and has no rights or freedom
sleep rough	(vp)	73	sleep in the open air
slogan	(n)	6	phrase or short sentence used to express a particular belief
slum	(n)	16	part of a city where houses are in a very bad condition
smog	(n)	24	mixture of smoke and fog
smug	(adj)	13	pleased with one's self
snail	(n)	87	legless and boneless animal which has a shell and moves very slowly
snobbish	(adj)	7	considering o.s. better than others
soap (opera)	(n)	12	continuing television play about the daily lives of a group of characters; different from a **serial** in that it doesn't have one main story, and so doesn't have a definite beginning and end
social	(adj)	7	of people and how they live together in groups
social services	(np)	34	services provided by government to help people who have problems
socialism	(n)	40	political system which believes that wealth should be shared equally and that important industries should be run by the government
solar	(adj)	98	of the sun
solvent	(n)	26	substance which dissolves other substances, used in glue
sophisticated	(adj)	13	of a complicated and clever kind
source	(n)	25	where s.th. comes from
sovereignty	(n)	43	a country's right to make its own decisions
spark off	(vp)	17	cause s.th. (esp. accidentally)
species	(n)	7	kind of animal or plant, e.g. rabbit and fox are two species
spectrum	(n)	38	wide range of things (literally: the range of colours which the eye can see)
speculation	(n)	53	buying things in the hope of selling them again at a higher price
sphere of influence	(np)	49	a country's sphere of influence is the other countries which it can affect
spiritual	(adj)	79	concerning religious thoughts and beliefs, not practical matters
spirituality	(n)	77	being concerned with religious thoughts and beliefs, not practical matters
sponsor	(v)	40	help s.o. to do s.th. by giving money or other help
sprout up	(vp)	119	appear suddenly in large numbers (like plants in the spring)
stab	(v)	56	stick s.th. sharp into s.o. or s.th.
stadium	(n)	29	special building in which sporting contests are held
staff	(n)	5	the people who work for an organisation
stage	(n)	91	the theatre (literally: platform on which actors perform in a theatre)
staggering	(adj)	18	very surprising
take a stand (against)	(vp)	15	try very hard to stop s.th.
standard	(adj)	12	usual, normal
standard	(n)	14	how well s.th. is done; a level that people accept as being good enough
standardise	(v)	10	make s.th. obey fixed rules
state	(n)	34; 58	country; the official organisations which run a country
static	(adj)	60	not moving
statistics	(n)	6	information expressed in numbers
status	(n)	13	how important s.th. is, or is seen to be
status quo	(np)	40	the way things are, in contrast to the way things could be if changes were made
stereotype	(n)	7	fixed idea of what s.o./s.th. is like
stock	(n)	50	amount of s.th. available
stocks and shares	(n)	8	parts of a company's value which can be bought and sold
stodgy	(adj)	116	(of food) solid and heavy
store	(v)	13	keep in a place for use in the future
take by storm	(vp)	100	to suddenly become very successful in a place or among a group
straightforward	(adj)	6	easy to understand
strained	(adj)	48	tense and difficult (situation etc.)
strait	(n)	48	narrow arm of sea which joins two larger areas of sea
strategically vital	(adj. p)	49	very important to control, because it gives you a big advantage over others e.g. in war or business
strengthen	(v)	14	make stronger
strike	(v)	33	stop working, in order to make your employer do what you want
striking	(adj)	51	very noticeable
structural	(adj)	42	concerning how s.th. is put together
studio	(n)	82	building or room in which a film or television programme is shot
studious	(adj)	118	interested in studying and reading
subject (to)	(adj)	43	required to obey s.o./s.th.
subject (to)	(v)	66	make s.o. experience s.th. unpleasant
subjugate	(v)	4	make a group of people do what you want
submarine	(n)	47	ship which is able to travel underwater
subscription	(n)	83	regular payment in order to be allowed to use or receive s.th.
subsidy	(n)	26	money provided (e.g. by the government) to pay for part of the cost of s.th.
subtle	(adj)	110	not obvious
(in) succession	(adv.p)	80	one after another
successive	(adj)	20	one after another
suffer (from)	(v)	11	if you suffer from s.th., then s.th. bad happens to you
suffragette	(n)	55	one of a group of women in early 20th-century Britain who fought for women to be allowed to **vote**

superficial	(adj)	82	unimportant, only touching the surface
supervision	(n)	63	watching s.o. while he/she does s.th. to make sure it is done properly
supplement	(v)	71	add to s.th. in order to improve it
supply	(n)	49	amount of s.th. which is available
support	(n)	27; 48	agreement with a person, opinion etc.; help
support	(v)	40; 66; 70	agree with s.o./s.th.; help s.o.; enable s.o. to carry on living, by providing money, food etc.
suppress	(v)	11	stop s.th. from happening/existing
surgeon	(n)	87	doctor who carries out operations on patients
surgery	(n)	68; 69	doctor's workplace; act of operating on s.o.
surreal	(adj)	91	like a dream, i.e. with impossible things happening in a realistic way
survey	(n)	6	an examination of a situation which involves asking a large number of people the same questions
survive	(v)	10	remain living, not die
suspend	(v)	6	make s.o. leave (an organisation) for a time
symbiotic	(adj)	91	depending on each other for particular advantages
symbolic	(adj)	31	not of practical use, but used as a sign of s.th.
syringe	(n)	120	instrument for injecting a drug or medicine into the blood
tackle	(v)	57	try to solve (a problem etc.)
tadpole	(n)	15	the young of frogs
take office	(vp)	36	begin in a new position (in government etc.)
talent	(n)	54	special ability
tariff	(n)	50	tax which is collected on goods coming into a country
taxation	(n)	68	taking money from people through taxes
technical	(adj)	10	used for a specialised purpose
technology	(n)	29	practical use of **science** in building new machines etc.
telecommunications	(n)	51	long-distance communication, e.g. by telephone
temperate	(adj)	20	having neither very hot summers nor very cold winters
temple	(n)	77	building which has a religious function
temporarily	(adv)	10	only for a certain time, not for ever
tendency	(n)	17	s.th. which s.o. often does
term	(n)	9	word
terminal	(n)	29	building in an airport where passengers go to get on a plane
terrestrial	(adj)	82	(of TV) not sent by cable or **satellite**
terrified (of)	(adj)	32	very scared
territory	(n)	88	area of land owned by a country, esp. in a different part of the world
terror	(n)	35	using violence to make a government do what you want
terrorise	(v)	57	make s.o. very scared
textile	(n)	52	cloth, material
theatrical	(adj)	32	exaggerated, as in a play
theme	(n)	47	important idea which s.o. returns to frequently
theme park	(np)	120	park with rides and other entertainment based on one particular subject
theory	(n)	16	set of ideas which tries to explain s.th.

threat	(n)	13	s.th. which is likely to harm s.o. or cause problems for him/her
threaten	(v)	44	be likely to harm s.o./s.th.
thrilling	(adj)	37	very exciting
thrive	(v)	17	do well
throne	(n)	78	position as king or queen (literally: seat on which a king or queen sits)
throw (s.th.) down the drain	(vp)	29	waste s.th.
thug	(n)	127	violent person
tiny	(adj)	23	very small
tolerance	(n)	57	being prepared to put up with s.th.
topic	(n)	7	subject (for discussion etc.)
toss-up (between)	(n)	127	[coll] two possibilities, each of which is as likely as the other
touching	(adj)	93	which affects people emotionally
tournament	(n)	124	competition in which a number of teams or players compete with each other over a series of games
toxic	(adj)	24	poisonous
trade	(n)	18; 116	buying and selling; job, esp. one which requires skill with your hands
trade union	(np)	39	organisation set up by workers to protect their interests and communicate with their employers
tradition	(n)	36	way of doing things or belief which has existed for a long time
traditional	(adj)	16	which has existed for a long time without change
traffic congestion	(np)	25	having too many vehicles on the roads, so that traffic jams result
tragedy	(n)	81; 90	very sad event or situation; type of play which is serious and sad
tragic	(adj)	21	very sad (event etc.)
transform	(v)	18	change s.th. completely
transition	(n)	44	change (e.g. from being one thing to being s.th. else)
treaty	(n)	34	an agreement between two or more countries
	(n)	56	process of finding out in court whether a person has committed a crime
tribe	(n)	109	group of people who all do things in the same way, dress similarly etc.
tricky	(adj)	79	difficult, full of problems
triumph (over)	(v)	8	beat
tropical	(adj)	20	between the tropic of Cancer and the tropic of Capricorn
troublesome	(adj)	45	causing difficulties
try	(v)	31	decide in a **court** whether s.o. has committed a crime
try (one's) hand (at)	(vp)	89	try s.th. to see whether you can do it
tuition fee	(np)	42	money paid by students for being taught
turban	(n)	77	head-dress made of a cloth wound round the head
tyranny	(n)	57	unfair, cruel and complete control of a society by an individual or small group of people
ultimate	(adj)	86	final and complete
umpire	(n)	36	s.o. who controls a competition and makes sure that both sides keep to the rules
unarmed	(adj)	56	not carrying a gun or other dangerous object

unconditional	(adj)	48	with no **restrictions** or **exceptions**
unconscious	(adj)	13	unaware
under-represented	(adj)	6	having too few people in a particular group or organisation
underachieve	(v)	67	not achieve as much as you should
undermine	(v)	44	gradually damage s.th.
undertake	(v)	71	(try to) do s.th.
unify	(v)	9	make into one group
union	(n)	30	joining together (e.g. of two countries)
Union flag	(np)	45	the flag of the UK
Union Jack	(np)	6	the flag of the UK
unique	(adj)	39	the only one of its kind
unite (with)	(v)	35	make two or more things into one
unity	(n)	97	fitting together to form one complete thing
universal	(adj)	60	of/for everyone
unprecedented	(adj)	108	not achieved before
unrest	(n)	57	violence or **demonstrations** as a result of people being angry or dissatisfied
uproar	(n)	79	angry and noisy disagreement
urban	(adj)	16	of cities
usage	(n)	15	the way a word or phrase is used
utility	(n)	52	organisation which provides s.th. (e.g. gas or electricity) which everyone needs
vacancy	(n)	73	job which has not been filled
vaccination	(n)	69	method of stopping s.o. from catching a disease, by injecting him/her with a very mild form of the disease
vacuum	(n)	42	completely empty space
vagaries	(n)	116	[pl] unexpected changes
vague	(adj)	11	not definite or exact
vandalism	(n)	58	damaging property deliberately and for no purpose
vanguard	(n)	102	the first part of a new development (literally: the part of an army which attacks first)
variant	(n)	103	one of a number of different forms of the same thing
variation	(n)	12	one of a number of different forms of the same thing
variety	(n)	12	type, kind; existing in many different forms
versus	(prep)	32	against (s.o. in a competition)
veto	(v)	46	in an official meeting: stop s.th. happening, esp. when others have agreed to it
viable	(adj)	51	capable of succeeding
vice	(n)	95	bad quality in s.o.'s personality
vice versa	(adv)	63	[Latin] the opposite way around (to what has been said)
vicious circle	(np)	17	situation in which two or more things make each other worse, so that the situation as a whole keeps getting worse
victim	(n)	18	s.o. to whom s.th. bad happens
victory	(n)	8	success in sport, war or some other kind of competition
vigorous	(adj)	107	lively and strong
villain	(n)	21	person who does harm to others or breaks the law; main bad character in a book or film
virtual	(adj)	87	existing only on computers
virtue	(n)	38	good quality in s.o.'s personality
virtuoso	(n)	107	s.o. who plays a particular instrument exceptionally well
vision	(n)	79; 99	ability to imagine and plan the future; unusual experience in which you see things which others cannot see

visual	(adj)	83	which can be seen
vitality	(n)	103	energy, liveliness
vocational	(adj)	65	related to a particular job
voluntary	(adj)	24; 28	a voluntary organisation is one that uses unpaid workers; voluntary work is work you are not paid for but do willingly
volunteer	(n)	29	s.o. who chooses to work without being paid
vote (for)	(v)	27	in an **election**: say which person or organisation you want to choose
waste	(n)	26	useless material left over from making s.th., rubbish
watchdog	(n)	82	organisation whose job is to make sure that rules are not broken
watershed	(n)	82	s.th. which divides two things
weapon	(n)	40	an object used to injure or kill others, e.g. a gun, knife or bomb
weed	(n)	21	plant which is unwanted and usually grows rapidly
weighty	(adj)	80	important, serious
welfare	(n)	53	help (esp. from the government) for people who have problems with health, money etc.
well represented	(adj. p)	12	having many members in a particular group
widespread	(adj)	17	existing in many areas
wig	(n)	59	false hair which you wear on your head
wilderness	(n)	23	wild area
wildlife	(n)	21	wild animals
will	(n)	11	ability to make decisions and carry them out
witch	(n)	76	woman who is believed to be able to perform **magic**
withdraw (from)	(v)	35	leave an area
wither away	(vp)	45	gradually become smaller/weaker and finally disappear
witness	(n)	56	s.o. who sees a crime taking place
witty	(adj)	93	clever and amusing
workforce	(n)	21	total number of people who work or are available to work
workshop	(n)	66	session in which people learn by doing s.th. or discussing it in a practical way
worship	(n)	74	giving thanks or showing respect to a god
xenophobic	(adj)	102	hating and fearing foreigners
yield	(n)	21	how much food can be produced on an area of land
youth	(n)	99; 103	young person; being young
zone	(n)	51	area which is different from others in some way